THE
BETRAYAL

ALSO BY ROBERT MAZUR

The Infiltrator

THE
BETRAYAL

THE **TRUE STORY** OF MY BRUSH WITH DEATH IN THE WORLD OF **NARCOS** AND LAUNDERERS

ROBERT MAZUR

ICON

Published in the UK in 2022
by Icon Books Ltd, Omnibus Business Centre,
39–41 North Road, London N7 9DP
email: info@iconbooks.com
www.iconbooks.com

First published in the USA in 2022
by Little A, New York

Sold in the UK, Europe and Asia
by Faber & Faber Ltd, Bloomsbury House,
74–77 Great Russell Street,
London WC1B 3DA or their agents

Distributed in the UK, Europe and Asia
by Grantham Book Services, Trent Road, Grantham NG31 7XQ

Distributed in Australia and New Zealand
by Allen & Unwin Pty Ltd,
PO Box 8500, 83 Alexander Street, Crows Nest, NSW 2065

Distributed in South Africa
by Jonathan Ball, Office B4, The District,
41 Sir Lowry Road, Woodstock 7925

Distributed in India by Penguin Books India,
7th Floor, Infinity Tower – C, DLF Cyber City,
Gurgaon 122002, Haryana

ISBN: 978-178578-839-0

Cover design by Jarrod Taylor

Unless otherwise noted, all interior photos are courtesy of the author.

Printed and bound in Great Britain
by Clays Ltd, Elcograf S.p.A.

In solemn remembrance of the more than twenty-two thousand US law enforcement officers who made the supreme sacrifice in the line of duty and are honored on the marble walls of the National Law Enforcement Officers Memorial in Washington, DC

SOURCE MATERIALS

The events referenced in this book occurred. The names of several of the characters have been changed to protect their identities. While I was writing this book, many of the individuals referenced consented to interviews, and in some cases, recorded interviews. Through numerous Freedom of Information Act requests and other legal processes, I obtained copies of undercover meeting transcripts, recordings, and reports related to this story. The majority of the conversations quoted are verbatim, but in instances where the transcript dialogue rambled or I had no transcript, I took literary license and re-created conversations from my recollection, references in reports, the recollection of individuals I interviewed, and my experience as an expert in money laundering and drug trafficking.

DRAMATIS PERSONAE

The following are primary characters in *The Betrayal*.
A full glossary of all names appears after the epilogue.

Emir Abreu: US Customs special agent who was Robert Mazur's partner in the US Customs undercover operation known as Operation C-Chase

Dominic: Italian American informant who worked undercover with DEA special agent Robert Mazur

Juaquin "Quino" Gonzalez: DEA Task Force officer assigned to work undercover with DEA special agent Robert Mazur

Jorge Krupnik: Former close associate of General Manuel Noriega and prominent businessman in Panama, involved in drug-money laundering

Rinaldo Laguna: Panamanian attorney who introduced money launderers to Robert Mazur while Mazur posed undercover as Robert Baldasare

Luis Fernando Latorre: Cali cartel money broker, launderer, and drug trafficker

Elvin "Al" Melendez: DEA Task Force officer who worked undercover with Robert Mazur

Steven Richards: DEA confidential source who worked at Avid Investment Group, Robert Mazur's undercover business operated in Sarasota, Florida

Pedro Rodriguez-Castro: Bogotá-based money launderer and drug trafficker working with the Cali cartel, partner of Luis Latorre

Gilberto Rodriguez-Orejuela: Coleader of the Cali drug cartel with his brother, Miguel

Miguel Rodriguez-Orejuela: Coleader of the Cali drug cartel with his brother, Gilberto

Antonio Ruiz: Undercover identity used by DEA Task Force officer Juaquin "Quino" Gonzalez while working undercover with DEA special agent Robert Mazur

Jorge Sanz Jr.: Money launderer working with the Cali drug cartel. Son of Jorge Sanz Sr.

Jorge Sanz Sr.: Freighter captain trafficking in cocaine and laundering money on behalf of the Cali drug cartel

Gilbert Straub: High-ranking associate of Robert Vesco and US fugitive who fled to Panama and provided money-laundering services

Edith Uribe: Money launderer and drug trafficker operating in New York City and Tampa

Harry Uribe: Money launderer based in Tampa

Mario Uribe: Drug trafficker based in Tampa

Jaime Vargas: Primary DEA-controlled source from Bogotá who worked undercover with DEA special agent Robert Mazur in Operation Pro-Mo

Julio Hilaro Vicuna: Money launderer for the Cali drug cartel operating houses of exchange in Houston, Texas

PREFACE

A BRUSH WITH DEATH

Panama City, Panama
September 24, 1993

A cool shower rolled in from the surrounding mountains, dousing Panama's scorched streets. Through a mist of steam, Robert Baldasare and one of his bodyguards approached their offices at Chartered Management Group. Baldasare's mission was to meet with Luis Latorre, a friend and launderer for the leaders of the Cali cartel. Baldasare had won Latorre's trust nearly two years before, at a meeting in a Doral Beach Hotel penthouse when both men took the chance of revealing their secret lives. Through a dizzying maze of import/export transactions funneled through the hands of dozens of dirty bankers, Latorre managed a team of launderers that made the return of the cartel's drug fortune into Colombia appear to be the innocent repatriation of export revenue from hundreds of front companies.

Years of Baldasare's enchanting the Mafias of Colombia and Panama had convinced them he was one of them, a serpentine professional feeding off the profits of the drug world. In Panama City, he shared offices and trust with Gilbert Straub, a notorious US fugitive who, with his close friend Robert Vesco, had stolen hundreds of millions from unsuspecting Americans. Straub may have fled the United States for Panama, but he took with him his relationships with Mafia royalty, drug dealers, bagmen for politicians, and even Russian KGB officers.

Baldasare ran a trade finance company with offices in Florida and Panama, a perfect cover for moving the filthy money of his Colombian clients, and the members of an army of Panama's "professionals" were tripping over one another to help Baldasare enhance the veils of secrecy that sheltered his movement of cocaine fortunes.

As Baldasare waited in his pretentious office suite, the twin engines of a Cessna 421C Golden Eagle whined toward Punta Paitilla airport in downtown Panama City. As it passed over the tiny offshore islands topped with lush green vegetation, dozens of freighters popped up on the horizon, waiting to cross the isthmus. Latorre took a deep drag from his Marlboro, wincing past the controls as he steered the plane over the surrounding jungle mountains toward the city's skyscrapers. Turbulence from the nearby thunderstorm scattered a line of Latorre's cigarette ash to the cockpit floor. He gripped the yoke tightly, grimacing from the pain in his swollen joints, brought on by the lupus that ravaged his body. If it weren't for special meds, available to him only in Colombia, lupus would destroy him.

The runway was nestled near the heart of the city. Latorre nudged the wheels down for a perfect landing. As the Cessna approached the hangar, Latorre was relieved. "There're Raul and Santiago; let's shut her down." He shouted orders at a guard stationed near the plane. "Refuel her. We're headed back to Bogotá in two hours, not a minute later."

Latorre and his copilot joined two locals waiting in an SUV. A cache of assault weapons was strewn behind the back seat. The stocks of the machine guns chattered against one another as the SUV hit a bevy of potholes. Latorre noticed that one of the AK-47s was equipped with a 75-round drum magazine capable of cutting a few men in half in seconds. The bluing on the Mac-10 Ingram 9mm submachine guns was chipped from heavy use. Their fold-out metal bar stocks, two-stage suppressors, and 32-round magazines made them perfect compact, low-noise killing machines.

Latorre rode in silence and shot an icy stare out the window. His team exchanged quick looks of wonder as the SUV rumbled through the streets. The driver couldn't help but glance every few seconds in his rearview mirror, wondering when Latorre would unfreeze. They parked a block from Baldasare's office. The driver couldn't wait any longer. "Luis, Luis . . . we're here."

Latorre's head slowly turned to the driver. In a cold monotone, with a calm that said he had done this before, he spoke. "Gentlemen, I have pictures for all three of you. This is Baldasare. His office is on the sixth floor, suite 6B. If I'm not back here thirty-five minutes after I enter the building, you need to storm the office and get me the hell out of there. If I'm late, it's because he betrayed us. If you have to come to get me, make sure you take out Baldasare and anyone else in that office. We need to be in the air before anyone finds the bodies."

Latorre exited the air-conditioned SUV into a bolt of Panama's steam. As he approached the building, his calm melted away, and his steely eyes darted around in lonely looks of caution. As he approached suite 6B, he took a deep breath and reluctantly turned the knob with the care of a bomb-disposal expert, his fear of the worst driving him to paranoia. He forced a smile at the receptionist and announced his purpose.

The secretary opened Baldasare's office door. "Mr. Latorre is here to see you."

Baldasare smiled. "Show him in."

Latorre looked pale as a ghost. His eyes burned through every detail of Baldasare's bodyguard, who doubled as a manager of cash pickups for the cartel in the States, nervously cataloging the bodyguard's ponytail and flashy gold jewelry. Unlike the upper-echelon players like Latorre, the bodyguard wasn't wearing a suit or tie—a clear breach of cartel protocol. Baldasare could feel Latorre's unease but couldn't let on. That would only push Latorre's caution button harder.

"Luis, welcome to Panama. Let me introduce you to Alberto, my man who does everything that Antonio Ruiz used to handle for me." Baldasare was distracted by Latorre's nonverbal cues of tension. He was white-knuckling his mobile phone; his eyes flashed in a new direction every few seconds; and his breathing was quick and heavy. As he leaned back in his chair, small beads of sweat appeared on his forehead, despite the roaring air-conditioning, and his foot twitched uncontrollably. Baldasare tried to calm him. "Luis, how about some water, or maybe a Bloody Mary to start the day?"

Latorre didn't return Baldasare's smile as he offered a quick no and glanced at his watch.

"Luis, I have three million dollars in the US that I need converted to Colombian pesos. Can you put it through your system and deliver it to my client in Colombia? I need a good rate."

"Bob, before we can do business again, there's something I need to know." Latorre's eyes drove like an arrow into Baldasare's head. The silence was deafening. "I need to know if I can trust you with my life, because if there are any more mistakes with our business, I won't be given another chance to explain. As you know, there were mistakes in the past, the cause of which was never settled. I won't be given another pass."

Baldasare matched Latorre's focus. "I assure you, Luis, there will be no mistakes on my end. I know what that would bring my way. But if you have any doubts, I suggest we simply remain friends and not take the risk of resuming business."

As though the ice in his veins had melted, Latorre's expression slowly grew into a big smile. He laughed and declared, "Okay, let's do it. *Todo está bien* [Everything is good]." But as their conversation wore on, Latorre kept glancing at his watch. Now, something else was wrong.

Baldasare could feel it. "Luis, I'm hosting a dinner-cabaret in Sarasota for about fifty important friends. I'd like you to join us so you can meet some people on my team. I'll cover all your expenses."

"Thank you," he said, taking the glossy brochure, which shook slightly in his clammy hands. "Let me see if I can work it into my schedule. I've been very busy."

On the street below, the killers, clutching their death machines, sat like statues, avoiding movement so as not to draw attention behind the SUV's heavily tinted windows. The driver whispered, "When we get close to the door of the office, put your ski masks on, and we'll break in. Here, look at Baldasare's picture one last time. I'll take him out. You take out anyone else in the room with Luis. Let's go."

As they jumped from the SUV, their guayabera shirts stuck to their backs with sweat. While the Sicarios hustled and entered the lobby, a couple in quiet, close discussion looked up, sensing that these were more than just well-armed security guards, which were common in Panama at the time. They scattered quickly, and the assassins moved to the elevator. As the elevator doors parted, they nearly charged into Latorre on his way out. He looked past them and whispered, "Let's go. It's off."

They hurried back to the SUV. The sicarios tossed their weapons behind the back seat and jumped in. A second later, the vehicle screeched away from the office complex and sped toward Punta Paitilla airport. Baldasare didn't know it yet, but if the meeting with Latorre had lasted a few minutes longer, those men would have stormed his office and blown his head off.

As they approached the plane, Latorre revealed his deepest secret. "That motherfucker Baldasare is a fucking DEA agent. I know it, but I can't say why. The next time we meet him will be his last day on Earth."

Latorre was right. Robert Baldasare was actually me, Robert Mazur, an undercover DEA agent. But how did he know? To figure it out, I needed to retrace my every step over the past five years. In that span, I had ended my last undercover assignment as Pablo Escobar's money launderer, Robert Musella, and been reincarnated as Robert Baldasare, a man who earned the right to become a launderer for Escobar's nemesis, the Cali cartel.

And it all began with a snifter of cognac.

1

A NEW LIFE

June–October 1991

My first day on the new job, I was early, dressed in my best suit and tie. It screamed rookie, but it wasn't like this was an entirely new world for me. I'd already spent twenty years as a fed in two other agencies, but this was my first day as a special agent with the Drug Enforcement Administration (DEA). I thought my reputation would precede me and I'd get the red-carpet treatment—no way. I was a beginner in the eyes of my DEA peers.

"Who are you?" I was asked from behind the bulletproof glass at the reception area.

"I'm Bob Mazur. I'm reporting for duty."

"Have a seat." Eventually the receptionist returned. "Oh, okay. You're the guy from Customs. You're a little earlier than most of our staff. Things don't generally get moving here until sometime after nine thirty a.m. When the boss is in, we'll let you know." That hour passed slower than any before in my life.

This wasn't what I expected, and I was anxious. Anxious to leave behind what had become a grueling episode in my life at Customs. I had completed a marathon of two years undercover as Bob Musella, working as a launderer for the Medellín cartel. Then I spent the last two years preparing for and testifying in trials around the world, where my every move was protected by SWAT teams looking for the hitmen witnesses swore were dispatched to whack me before I could reveal the secrets I'd learned about some of Pablo Escobar's most important men.

It was true; I had pissed off the brass at Customs, but that was because I blew the whistle about an inexplicable effort by the front office to derail the operation. I was outraged that they pulled resources and personnel that dead-ended the development of cases against some very powerful people.

Once the DEA office started to fill, I was introduced to the agents. Things were abuzz. A major case was about to go down.

"So, when do I get my credentials, equipment, and weapons?"

The answer: "When you complete your four months of training at Quantico. Until that day, you're nothing. If you flunk out, you'll be terminated."

"Really? So, in the meantime, do I pull duty at the copy machine, or run out for coffee?"

Mike Powers, the boss of the entire office, was a legend in the agency and a veteran of the Marines and CIA. Well known for his bravery, ability, and relentless desire to make a difference, Powers was a no-nonsense guy with an obsession to make sure his team had everything necessary to make big cases. He'd earned the respect of every real leader in the agency. Those incapable of effectively leading had one of two choices—either get out of his way, or be prepared to get run over. For Mike Powers, failure was not an option.

Thankfully, he made me feel at home. "Listen, Mazur, we have a major operation going down tonight, and I'm going to make an exception." He threw me a .357 Magnum. "Be at the briefing at one p.m. Listen, we offered you a slot here because we want you to do another long-term UC Op [undercover operation]. Don't fuck up at the Academy, and you'll get your chance to do something bigger and better than what you did at Customs."

At the briefing, it was clear that this was serious. A DEA undercover agent had orchestrated a 350-kilogram delivery of cocaine. There would be half a dozen dopers at the meet, so in step with DEA protocol, we would have them outnumbered by no less than four to one. I was the new face on the block. The DEA agents and local law enforcement teams had done this drill several times a month. But here I was, no credentials, no body armor, and no raid jacket to identify me as one of the good guys. All I had was a handgun. Worse yet, not everyone was at the briefing, so raid-team members who missed the meeting might not recognize my face as a "good guy."

When we got to the takedown site, I was coupled with a rookie Tampa cop, and our turn on the eyeball (watching from our car for the takedown sign by the undercover agent) was the difference between life and death for the undercover agent who signaled for the bust to begin. We called it out to the entire team. Within seconds, dozens of cop cars and a constellation of red and blue flashing lights came to a screeching halt at every critical point of escape. It took only a second for the screams. "Police, get on the fucking ground or I'll fucking kill you. Down, get down. Get the fuck down or you're dead."

As the dopers' cars were searched, an arsenal was laid out on the ground. They had come to kill. Another agent and I took down the buyer, a yuppie whose restaurant and mortgage business had seen bad times. This drug buy was his hope for survival.

We forced him facedown in the gravel parking lot, cuffed him, and threw him in the back seat of our car. I could see his heart pounding under his Grateful Dead T-shirt. Sweat poured from his body, and his face was covered with dirt, cuts, and blood from our struggle to get him under control. Then, the smell and sound were unmistakable: he pissed himself, shaking as though he had been hit by a Taser. His eyes were the size of saucers, and he couldn't speak. He was in shock.

At that unforgettable moment, I learned the DEA version of the Miranda warning. Instead of "You have the right to remain silent," one of my new colleagues spouted, "I have two or three words of wisdom for you. You're going to get a lawyer who will soak you and tell you not to talk, 'cause he wants your money. Or, you can work with us, starting now, and we'll help you. It's your decision, pal. We can be your friends, or we can make your life more miserable than you could ever imagine. Without our help, you'll become a love doll in every prison you call home for the next twenty years."

It took him about five seconds to think it over. "I'm with you. I'll do everything I can for you if you'll do the same for me."

My partner answered, "Listen, the only guarantee I'm giving you is that if you don't go all the way for us, you're fucked."

I was the only cop with a pen and paper, my anal-retentive way of approaching policing. I read the yuppie his rights and wrote down every word of his confession. He had no way of turning back.

As things were wrapping up, I met Juaquin "Quino"(key-no) Gonzalez, the young undercover agent who, with the help of an informant in Colombia, had put this operation together. Quino was a DEA Task Force officer, a detective on loan to us from the Tampa Police Department. At thirty-one, he was already seen as a superstar by DEA leadership. Although he was Puerto Rican, dopers often mistook him for Colombian. He had a stable of Colombian informants from Medellín, all members of the Uribe family, who educated him about the drug world. His lead mentor was Mario Uribe, a guy with arrests for handing out near-fatal beatings, kidnapping, possession of a concealed weapon, and attempted murder. Uribe and his siblings had a sound knowledge of the drug world, and some considered them to be the biggest dealers in the Tampa Bay area.

Quino had the right look: tall, thin, dark hair, olive skin, upscale Rado watch, clothes that fit the part, and a vocabulary that included key words and accents unique to a *Paisa*, someone from the region of Antioquia, Colombia. Some saw his air of superiority as the defense mechanism of a guy who was in over his head, but I didn't see it that way. Quino was one of very few Hispanics in a city police department that had a history, at that time, of not being inclusive. I got the sense that he felt slighted, unrecognized for his accomplishments. As he walked through the carnage of the takedown, it seemed he was enjoying a victory lap—a rooster in a yard of hens he controlled. A lot of those with badges thought Quino was at the head of his class, but there were whispers to the contrary. It confused me.

A week later, at 5:00 a.m. on a sweltering Florida morning, it was time to join my new colleagues on another raid. By now, I was able to scrounge up a raid jacket, so at least the players could outwardly see which team I was on. This time we hit a nasty group that ran a crack-cocaine factory in Bradenton, Florida. After we got control of the house and the half dozen monsters that ran the operation with no respect for the lives of others, a search uncovered the special tools of their trade—a twin-barrel high-powered Gatling machine gun that could fire a thousand rounds per minute, Mac-10 submachine guns outfitted with silencers, sawed-off shotguns, an AK-47 machine gun, and a sniper rifle.

Later the same day, the seized crack, cash, and weapons were displayed for the media. A naive young reporter made the mistake of asking me a dumb question: "How do you know these weapons were intended for street violence?" He pointed to a silencer. "What's this?"

I couldn't resist. "Oh, the silencer is for deer hunting, so other deer won't get scared when the first one goes down." I'm not sure my sarcasm registered with him. He never blinked.

Like all wannabe DEA agents who were hired but hadn't graduated from the Academy, I wouldn't be paid for overtime. I got straight salary for eight-hour days that usually lasted twelve hours, but that didn't matter to me. I was now on the front lines of a war that was assaulting America in more ways than one, doing what I wanted to do for the rest of my career. There was no place I would rather be.

In between raids, I started building a new false identity, one I could use to pose as a money launderer for the leaders of Colombia's Cali cartel, the targets of our future UC Op. Before I could start, I needed to build this mythical but verifiable businessman and his businesses. I had a few very close and trusted friends who worked in the financial markets, one of whom had a mortgage business and an insurance company that had been active in prior years but were now dormant. They would be perfect to buy, on paper, and revive. They had history.

Two other sources were senior officers at international banks. They could create the paperwork and vouch for me as having worked as their personal financial adviser for years. I'd also need my trusted friend Bill King, former prosecutor and now attorney in a major law firm, to have one of his colleagues pose as my attorney and draw up the appropriate documents for these acquisitions.

When all else failed, I knew headquarters personnel could open doors with the State Department and other agencies to get me a passport, driver's license, Social Security card, and other ID. My instincts shied away from using headquarters, but given the warp speed at which I was asked to put this facade together, with some documents I had no choice.

Then there were my contacts in local financial institutions who would open personal and business accounts, lines of credit, and credit cards.

Before I could turn to my sources for help, I needed a name. Who would I be? It was time for another walk in a Staten Island cemetery, full of grave sites of Italian Americans. I'd done this several times over the years and knew exactly what I was looking for. There it was: Robert

Baldasare. Born nine months before I was, he passed away as a young child. I had my starting point.

With only a few weeks before I had to report to the Academy at Quantico, and knowing it always takes the government twice as long as it should to do anything, I filled out all the paperwork to get an undercover passport, driver's license, and Social Security card. I needed these documents in place when I returned, so I could finish building the myth of Robert Baldasare.

Before I left, I checked in with Emir Abreu, my old partner at Customs. He and I had traveled the world together during Operation C-Chase, our prior journey undercover. Abreu could be described in two words: honorable and talented. Unlike too many other undercover agents, he had the ability to push his ego aside for the good of the team. When I played the "Mr. Big" role of Robert Musella, Abreu was the wind beneath my wings, an unwavering ally who ran street operations for our organization. Robert Musella would never have made it to first base without Abreu's support. You can count on one hand the federal undercover agents with his integrity and abilities. He was the barometer that kept me out of trouble. "How you doing, brother?"

"I'm good, Bob. They've got me back undercover. I'm running a money-service business in Tampa, operating in the Colombian community. We're targeting a jewelry store run by a family we're convinced are big-time dopers, the Uribe clan. The Uribes are bad news, especially the middle brother, Mario."

In his undercover persona, Abreu was getting himself established and earning credibility in the Latin community. He was moving money for some Cali traffickers out of New York and Miami, but he had kind words about what he felt his UC Op was missing. "Bob, I wish you hadn't pulled the plug here at Customs. We could have done another one of these together. How is life at DEA?"

"Better than walking around at Customs with a bull's-eye on my back. They would never have let me go back under. You saw it. When our operation ended, they gave me every lackey job in the office, including getting the boss's car washed and ferrying it from the airport to her house. It was only a matter of time before they would have transferred me to Pembina [North Dakota]. I leave for Quantico next week. It was a long time ago that I was in army boot camp, but they tell me this will be similar. Once I get back, I'm slated to go under. I'm supposed to have offices in Florida and Panama. Let's stay in touch, brother."

Before I headed to the Academy, it was time to say goodbye to Evelyn and the kids—again. No matter how many times we'd done that, throughout my career, it never got easy. Scott was now seventeen. He had to take on the role of the man of the house. He had a driver's license, so he could share the load of helping Andrea, now fourteen, get to and from gymnastics practice and meets. They were both competing on a national level, so there was a lot of travel. Ev was still devoted to first graders as a teacher and mentor.

As I held her, Ev whispered her goodbye. "Bob, I know this is what you want to do. I've always tried not to step in the way of the career path you've chosen. We've faced every challenge together since high school. I know how badly you want to do this. It's not my first choice, but like Richard Marx's 'Right Here Waiting,' that's where I'll be."

On the flight from Tampa to DC, I could see Ev in my mind's eye and hear the start of Marx's song. "Oceans apart, day after day, and I slowly go insane." The lyrics speak to Ev's sacrifice. It hadn't been long since it looked like my career decisions might end our marriage, but we were now stronger than ever. This is the path traveled by many spouses of law enforcement officers, but I don't think anyone has endured that journey with more grace, love, and thoughtfulness than Ev. If not for her, I would be a very lonely man today. She not only kept us together, but she did it while raising two beautiful children and achieving recognition as an outstanding educator.

The bumpy landing at Reagan International jarred me back to reality. It was time to take the forty-minute cab ride to the DEA Academy at the Quantico Marine Corps Base. As I struggled with my bags toward the main building, a DEA class rhythmically trotted by in formation, chanting. They were dressed in black fatigues. No smiles or chatter, just discipline, a flashback to Fort Leonard Wood, site of my basic training in the US Army.

But the scene inside the building confused me. There seemed to be two worlds coexisting under one roof. Although DEA trainees projected military discipline, even as they walked the halls, other young men and women were dressed in baby-blue collared pullover shirts with beige khaki pants. Most wore their collars pulled up, a look that was popular among preppies. To say they were casual, compared to the DEA recruits, is an understatement. I soon learned that the DEA and FBI Academies shared the same buildings. The "Febies," as we called them, carried themselves like they were frats on a college campus, while the DEA recruits were all military.

My class coordinator, Van Quarles, was hard as nails, but he cared a hell of a lot about each and every one of his "basic agent trainees." We had no right to do anything other than what we were told to do, when we were told to do it. That message was delivered by our class coordinators, who often yelled at us, nose to nose. Eventually, we understood that the training approach of the DEA staff was serious for a very good reason. It was their goal to open each trainee's eyes and mind to the fact that when we left the Academy, we would be members of a team, a team that often faced death. They wanted survival to become our sixth sense, so we could go home to our families at the end of an operation. Everything was structured to help us realize that we had to fight to live and to help our fellow agents survive. We were now part of a special force, dedicated and prepared to do whatever was necessary to make sure no one was left behind.

As in all DEA basic training classes, we were asked to elect a trainee to be our class representative, a liaison between class members and our coordinator and counselors. My fellow trainees chose me, an honor I took as seriously as a father speaking for his children. Although I just wanted to be one of them, they were closer to my son's age than mine, some nearly twenty years younger than I was.

Living quarters were bare bones: two of us to a small room, each bathroom shared by four trainees. We were up by 5:30 a.m. every day, and most mornings our training started by 7:15 a.m. Our daily morning uniform consisted of combat boots, black fatigue pants, a medium-gray collared pullover with black "DEA" lettering over the left breast, and a black ball cap with gray "DEA" letters on the front. Needless to say, no one pulled their collar up. If they had, they would have been doing extra push-ups all day. We had to run everywhere we went, and the DEA class counselors patterned themselves after drill sergeants as they led us in cadence.

The first half of each day usually found us either in the gym or on the firing range. Daily workouts generally involved one thousand sit-ups, five hundred push-ups, a 6.2-mile run, and ninety minutes of hand-to-hand combat. Push-ups were often dished out at the rate of twenty-five every five minutes in the gym, although the last set had to continue until we collapsed. In the first five weeks, we fired ten thousand rounds at the outdoor range, usually in ninety-degree heat. Academics started every day at 1:00 p.m. and often went until about 8:00 p.m., sometimes later.

And then there were the occasional "special events." My favorite was "bull in the ring." The class was divided into two equal groups on opposite sides of the gym. We donned boxing gloves and headgear; then we each had a turn surrounded by twenty-two or so of our class-mates, who came separately at the trainee in the middle trying to kick his or her ass for twenty seconds as the trainee tried to fight back, until the entire class had pummeled the student in the middle for a total of about seven minutes. I had a slight advantage. My dad had been a boxer in the US Navy and had taught me how to throw a dart of a jab and a good left hook after I came home complaining that the infamous grammar-school bully was beating me up day after day. I never forgot his lessons. "Bull in the ring" taught us to find strength to fight harder than we had ever thought we could. No one quit.

On weekends, the most popular pastime was the movie house on the base. It was generally packed with twenty-year-old Marines, along with us and the Febies in their baby-blue shirts. The other major non-work event was meals in the cafeteria. The food sucked, but I never ate so much in my life. Despite that, by the time I left Quantico, I'd lost fifteen pounds and probably added that much in muscle mass.

Six weeks into training, I received a call from Nancy Worthington, who identified herself as the deputy assistant secretary of enforcement at the Department of the Treasury. She wanted a few hours of my time to question me about my role in the US Customs investigation that had led to the prosecution of senior officials at the Bank of Credit & Commerce International (BCCI).

"Ms. Worthington, have you read my resignation letter? I think that spells everything out. I'm here at the DEA Academy, trying to move on."

She wasn't impressed. According to her, this had to be a face-to-face interview, and although she had read my resignation letter, the issues she wanted to discuss went beyond it. I wrote a memo detailing my call with Worthington and gave it to both the assistant special agent in charge of the Academy, Tony Wilson, and the head of our Tampa office, Mike Powers. Each of them said I could invite her to the Academy, and they would pull me out of class to answer her questions. Wilson offered advice. "Just don't do anything to embarrass our agency. As long as you carried yourself honorably at Customs, everything will be fine."

Before Worthington and her group visited me, I got another call. This time it was Michael Isikoff, a renowned investigative reporter with the *Washington Post*. "Mr. Mazur, I've read the resignation letter you wrote to the commissioner of Customs, and I've been following the BCCI affair since your undercover operation broke in 1988. Customs says you're just a disgruntled employee. I'd like to hear your side."

I politely referred him to the DEA public affairs officer and told him I couldn't speak without approval from the Department of Justice. This was getting serious. What was brewing?

Then came the call from Ev. "Bob, I don't want to create pressure for you, but I don't want you hearing this from anyone else. I'm looking at a big article in the *New York Times* by a reporter named Dean Baquet. I looked him up, and he's big-time, a Pulitzer Prize winner. The headline is 'Bureaucratic Snags Blocked BCCI Inquiry in 1988.' When this guy references you, he wrote, 'The debate within the bureaucracy became so rancorous that Robert Mazur, the Customs Service agent, quit.' He wrote that you're in training at Quantico, and he apparently has your letter of resignation, because he quoted it: 'The Tampa case could have had far greater results if there had been more resources placed on the case.' Bob, are we going to be all right?"

"Don't worry, Ev. We have the truth on our side, and I have enough friends back at Customs who will refuse to lie for the front office. I just want to get this all behind us and start this new career. I'm fine as long as I have you."

All of a sudden it seemed like members of Congress were coming out of the woodwork, asking to speak with me. Chuck Schumer of the House Judiciary Committee asked for time, followed by the House Banking Committee, then Senator John Kerry's Senate Subcommittee on Terrorism, Narcotics, and International Operations, then the Senate Subcommittee on Government Affairs and Investigations, then the Senate Judiciary Committee headed by Senator Orrin Hatch, then the Senate Banking Committee, and finally Special Counsel for Assistant Attorney General Robert Mueller.

Although this had nothing to do with DEA, the attention wasn't helping my new career. This wasn't a time when I could afford to be seen as anything other than a team player, regardless of the issues. Beyond that, I needed to demonstrate to DEA that I knew my place, a newbie trying to earn his stripes.

Eventually, I got a call from a couple of staffers on one of the Senate committees. "Listen, Bob. There's a plan at the Treasury to discredit you because of your resignation letter. You accused your bosses of intentionally taking the case down prematurely, and then withdrawing resources from one of the country's most important investigations in decades, all for political reasons. They're pissed. They are going to try to turn the tables on you. They're going to claim that you failed to ask for resources that they were ready, willing, and able to provide. They're going to claim that you were unstable as a result of your undercover work, and that because you were a loose cannon, they had no choice but to take the case down when they did."

"That's horseshit," I replied. "I wrote a dozen memos begging for more resources and spelling out the consequences of their repeatedly taking personnel off the case. What they probably don't realize is that, thanks to my anal-retentive compulsion, I have copies of all of those memos in a safe place. When I'm interviewed by the dozens of sub-committee members who have asked to speak with me, I'll be happy to give them copies. Plus, at the end of the operation, I was debriefed by a psychologist engaged by Customs, and I have a copy of his report. He gave me a clean bill of health."

During my last few weeks at the Academy, I spent more time in conference rooms, answering questions posed by Congressional staffers and Treasury officials, than I did in class. In the end, the truth prevailed. I eventually testified before the Senate Subcommittee on Terrorism, Narcotics, and International Operations. The chairman, Senator John Kerry, publicly proclaimed, "Customs management placed at potential risk a critically important investigation and possibly the lives of the agents involved, for the purpose of obtaining favorable publicity . . . [Mazur's] willingness to press on in the face of threats to his life gave the US government the evidence necessary to begin the prosecution of BCCI and highly placed Colombian drug lords, and money launderers . . . I wish to express my personal admiration for Robert Mazur, who not only took the lead undercover role, but fought valiantly against the bureaucratic difficulties which he found were undermining his ability to make the kind of case against BCCI he wanted to make, and wish him good luck in further endeavors."

When it came time for our graduation ceremony, as the class representative, I was given the privilege of addressing my fellow trainees, their family members, and DEA staff, including the head of the agency. As I looked out at the beaming faces of my colleagues, I wanted to underscore the importance of what we'd endured together over the prior four months.

"It's not an easy life we have chosen," I said. "There will be substantial sacrifices we will have to endure together in the future. There will be many missed birthday parties, many lonely nights away from home, many long phone calls in the middle of the night to the people we love most, many cups of coffee while on twenty-four-hour surveillances, and many potential threats to our lives. But despite these sacrifices, we will prevail, because we have each other"—I paused, looking over the families and then directly at Ev—"and your relentless support."

It was time to go home to Tampa and finish building the new undercover operation, but what I came home to was nothing like what I had expected. Instead, my close friend Emir Abreu had been arrested.

2

FIREWORKS

October 1991–January 1992

As he strutted into the Club Colombia de Tampa, a mecca for many
of the movers and shakers in Tampa's Hispanic community, Francisco
Suarez was on the hunt. He knew this was one of the Uribe brothers' favorite hangouts. The Uribes were major players in Tampa's drug
world, and Suarez wanted to work himself close to them. He knew he
could deliver what the Uribes needed, a business that could clean their
dirty money. When Mario Uribe saw Suarez head for the men's room,
Mario followed. Of all the Uribe brothers, Mario had the most power.
He had doubts about Suarez, and a plan to test him. As Suarez stood at
a urinal, Mario washed his hands and laid a line of white powder. When
Suarez came to the sinks, Mario threw his curve.

"Hey, Mr. Suarez, this one's on me."

Suarez smiled and shook his head. "No, I ain't doing this shit here."

With a wary glare, Mario let Suarez know he'd failed. "You know what, you really have some big balls for coming to this party at the club. I know who you are."

Mario had finally taken notice of him, but was it for good or bad? He would soon learn.

The caravan of marked Tampa police cars pulled into the strip mall and filled the parking spots in front of Envios Servicios Monetarios, the small money-service business that served the Hispanic community. The locals knew Envios provided a reliable service, sending money to foreign countries, especially Colombia, at a reasonable cost. Special people in Tampa's underworld also knew that it was a good place to have dirty money laundered. The owner, Francisco Suarez, was a player, a guy at home on the dark side. His Spanish was far better than his English, and he was stoic—nothing shook him. He had massive wrists, a thick neck, and a matching physique. His eyes looked through people, and he reeked of *Don't fuck with me*.

Suarez wasn't in the store when the four uniformed cops arrived. As the officers entered, they revealed their purpose to Suarez's assistant. "We need to speak with Francisco Suarez."

"I'm sorry, sir, but he's not here today. He's in New York until tomorrow."

The lead cop shook his head in frustration, his face flushed and neck veins pulsing. "Which of these is his office?"

Suarez's assistant slowly raised his hand and offered a meek gesture in the direction of the large corner room. The sergeant turned to the other officers and gave the order: "Toss it." As they scrambled to Suarez's office, the sergeant offered the humble assistant some advice. "I think it would be smart for you to stay here with me, my friend. They need to make sure Mr. Suarez isn't hiding under his desk."

The sound of drawers opening and closing rang out for a few minutes, during which the sergeant fixed a constant cold smile toward Suarez's assistant. These cops had clearly fallen asleep during their

Academy class on lawful searches and seizures. Regardless, after a few minutes, they emerged from the office empty-handed. The sergeant stared at Suarez's man. "Tell Mr. Suarez we're sorry we missed him, but we'll be back."

The next day, as Suarez sat in his office working the phones, his door flew open. The cops had returned. "Mr. Suarez, we're investigating a burglary, and your business card was found at the crime scene, an apartment on West Kansas Avenue in Tampa."

Suarez furrowed his brow in disbelief. "I don't even know where that is. I haven't robbed anyone."

Incredulous, the officer delivered a second barrel of accusation. "What makes matters worse, I ran your name in our system, and it looks like there is a warrant outstanding for a Francisco Suarez in Miami. Mr. Suarez, I need you to face the wall and put your hands behind your back."

In seconds, Suarez was wearing a new set of bracelets and was being escorted from his office. Since both cops were gringos, he felt safe giving his assistant a quick instruction in Spanish. *"Llame a la oficina y hágales saber lo que pasó, pero dígales que me dejen correr con esto."* ("Call the office and let them know what happened, but tell them to let me run with this.")

Before he knew it, Suarez was in the back seat of the marked car. He leaned forward, struggling to get comfortable with his hands cuffed behind his back. No one spoke in the car, but increasingly intense stares were exchanged in the rearview mirror.

The marked unit pulled up to the side gates at Tampa Police Department headquarters, and Suarez was delivered to the staff at the intake desk. After being searched and having his personal items stored, he was led to an empty eight-by-eight-foot room with a cold tile floor and no windows. His only contact with the outside world came when the tiny metal-hinged sliver near the top of the door occasionally unlocked and a set of eyes peered at him.

Suarez paced alone in the room for an hour. Despite the order he had given his assistant, he was denied the chance to handle this dilemma by himself. Inexperienced managers from his office, thinking they were about to rescue him, caused his demise.

A supervisor from the Florida Department of Law Enforcement (FDLE), dispatched by Customs brass, was only following orders when he showed up at the Tampa Police Department. "Listen, Sarge, I'm with FDLE. I've been authorized by Customs to vouch for him. There's no paper on this Suarez in Miami or anywhere else. We'd know if there was, because he's a snitch that works for us and Customs. Envios is our and Customs' operation. You need to keep that to yourself. If that gets out, he could be a dead man."

The arresting officer deceived the FDLE supervisor. "Listen. We were just going to release him because his prints don't match the Francisco Suarez tied to the Miami warrant. You can go to the lockup and get him out now. I'll let them know you're coming for him."

That was a lie. No one had even bothered to roll Suarez's prints. Something other than honest policing was driving this.

As soon as the FDLE liberator pulled away with Suarez in his car, he explained. "Listen. We didn't let them know you're an agent, Emir, we told them that you're a snitch running that business for us. We weren't going to burn you. They promised us they'd keep that under wraps, so everything is cool. We got you covered."

Abreu's eyes nearly bulged out of his face. Because he was more of a gentleman than I could ever be, he bit his tongue and screamed in his mind, rather than out loud. *My front office is filled with fucking idiots! They're so far from the street that they've lost all common sense. Why the hell did they do this? Why didn't they just let me work my way out of this, or at least simply tell them I was a target of their work?* Abreu knew his rescuer should have only said he was a badass, that they were about to tap his phones, and they needed him on the street committing crimes. No doubt, word of his working for Customs and FDLE would now spread like wildfire. They might as well start packing the furniture in Envios. He was fried, his cover blown. After venting within, Abreu punched the door of the car so hard, his knuckles bled. He leaned back in his seat, laid his head back, and put his palms over his eyes. In a whisper to himself, he faced reality. "All that fucking work down the drain." Then he finally offered the supervisor one loud word as he snapped his head up and yelled at the top of his lungs, "Shit!"

At 3:30 a.m., the phone on the sergeant's bedroom nightstand shook him from a deep sleep. He spoke, but his mind wasn't yet in full gear. "Yeah . . . who's calling?"

"I'm sorry to call you so late, but I just got here in Miami, and I'm tight for time. I've got a meet in an hour to put a deal together. What did you get on that Suarez guy in Tampa?"

"Oh, between us, it turns out he's a snitch for Customs, and he's running that business for them and FDLE. Some kind of a sting."

"Really? Are you sure? That doesn't make sense."

"I got this straight from an FDLE supervisor. What I'm telling you is one hundred percent on the money."

"Okay. I owe you. Bye."

The next day, the black BMW M1 pulled up to Uribe Jewelers, the high-end jewelry store nestled a mile down the road from Envios Servicios Monetarios. Salsa music blared from his car as Harry Uribe finished listening to his favorite song, the one he always asked his brother Mario to play at Mario's bottle club, a popular haunt in Tampa's Latin community. Unlike Mario, Harry was low-key. He was educated and had developed stunning skills as a designer of jewelry. He was Mario without a hot head or the balls to pull off a five-hundred-kilo deal. He was a thinker, better at the finesse of laundering than the muscle.

Each morning, Harry went through the same drill: shutting off the alarms, opening the safe, putting the inventory back in the cases. This was a family business. His uncle, a jeweler for four decades whose back had arched from a lifetime of bending over his work, showed up fifteen minutes later and started his day in the rear workshop. As usual, Mario arrived late.

Until he spoke, you might underestimate Mario Uribe. He was five feet six and had a slight build, but his wiry physique was all muscle, and the bend in the bridge of his nose was earned on the street. His short, jet-black hair and brown eyes complemented his olive skin and the small brown mole on his left cheek. When he opened his mouth, his gravelly voice was cocky, totally unafraid. Most often, he had a Walther PPK tucked in the small of his back, and he wouldn't hesitate to use it. He wore the best silk shirts and always sported either his Rolex or the latest high-end Rado watch.

As Mario entered the store that morning, the phone rang. Harry took the call. "Hey, Mario, it's for you."

"Mario here. What you got?"

"It's Frankie. It's confirmed, and a damn good thing we did this. Envios is a Customs operation. He's working for them. Stay the fuck away from Suarez." The line went dead.

The day after Abreu was rescued from the holding cell, he told his bosses, "Fuck it, it's over. We're wasting our time. The Uribes have a pipeline into the Tampa PD. I'm done."

Because cops put their lives on the line for each other and naturally feel indebted as family, it is against their instinct to fathom that their own kind can commit crimes, even when logic tells them otherwise. That's what Abreu faced when his vengeance boiled against the murky evil that outed him to the Uribe family. In return for his accusations against the officers, he got little support. The minds of his bosses were fogged by this phenomenon. "Listen, Emir," they said. "You'd better watch what you're saying. Those guys are cops, you know. You can't prove shit. They've earned the benefit of the doubt."

Abreu was replaced at Envios by another undercover Customs agent, but the operation that had previously shown great promise under Abreu's leadership never recovered.

Not long after Abreu was burned, Ev and I celebrated New Year's Eve with friends. As the night drew closer to the big moment, I could tell something wasn't right. She wore concern all over her face.

"Bob, you know I've never stood in the way of you following your dreams, but I'm worried that the only thing that may change in this new job is the color of your badge. At some stage, you need to come home. To be honest, I'm not as prepared for this as you are."

"Listen, Ev. They're giving me a chance of a lifetime to go back into that world. It's the only way I can get people to see the elephant in the room."

"Elephant, what elephant?"

"There's a big fat reason why governments never see ninety-nine percent of the underworld's fortunes. It's not an accident, and it's not because Mafias trick people into laundering their money. The elephant is the routine business of hundreds, probably thousands, of private bankers in the world's biggest international banks washing trillions for Mafias, so they can control countries and the lives of ninety-five percent of the people on this planet. That's their business model—it's what they do. This is my last chance to open the eyes of the world to that reality. I promise, when this one's over, I'll be home for good. I came to DEA only because they offered me this chance. It's the opportunity to finish what I started when the last operation was taken down early for all the wrong reasons."

"I hope the kids and I are still here when you decide to come home. The elephant in the room that you don't seem to see is us."

As partygoers started the countdown, I held Ev in my arms and made my promise. As I spoke, I had to lean closer into her ear because the volume of the countdown increased with every number. "I have a plan, Ev. It won't take me more than two years to get this done. I'm as confident that I can make this happen as I am that the Times Square Ball will descend in the next few seconds." Two years wasn't what she wanted to hear, and tears silently ran down her cheeks, hinting at her concern that this last trip into the underworld might have a very bad ending.

As the ball fell and the New Year lit up, I kissed Ev and felt the same love we had enjoyed when we first met. Fireworks of all colors exploded over the Manhattan skyline, but as it turned out, that fire wasn't nearly as intense as the explosion and flames about to consume the walls of my new office.

At 2:00 a.m., while everyone else was celebrating the New Year, a single obscure silhouette crept up to the front entrance of the Tampa DEA office and entered with a key. Once in the lobby, fingerprints shielded by a surgical glove punched in the security code. The intruder never turned on the lights, walking directly to the back entrance. After opening the rear door and retrieving a plastic gallon milk jug filled with gasoline, whoever it was moved toward the office's evidence vault, a large secure room where dozens of kilograms of cocaine and other drugs were routinely stored. After hours, when the door to the vault was locked, there was only one access point to put anything in the vault, a big mail chute in the hallway that shared a common wall with the vault.

In the darkness of the hall, the chute opened. A long-stemmed funnel was wedged in the chute, followed by the gurgling of the gasoline down the mouth of the funnel toward a particular corner of the vault where seven kilos of cocaine were stacked. As the fumes filled the vault and began to seep out the chute door, the arsonist flicked a cigarette lighter and held it under a fire starter to create a reliable ignitor. Within a few seconds of the flaming fire starter's sliding down the chute, a high-pitched tone began to emanate from the vault, followed almost immediately by a huge explosion. The blast knocked the intruder against the opposite wall of the hallway. Stunned, the arsonist staggered toward the rear entrance, dragging along the milk container and funnel. By now, the flames were ravaging everything inside the vault.

After cracking the door open to ensure no one was in sight, the wobbly intruder slithered in a crouched position toward his car. With ringing eardrums, the arsonist fumbled to get a key in the ignition. Seconds later, the parking lot was empty. The arsonist had escaped.

What this person didn't realize was that the vault was actually an interior room with concrete walls that encased rebar from floor to ceiling. The floor was solid concrete, and the ceiling was made of a very hard material that would prevent access from above. The only source of fresh air in the vault came from a small vent. As the fire raged, it consumed all of the oxygen in the room, causing the walls to bow inward and the fire to smother. Although the flames slowly subsided, the entire office was filled with black ash, and much of the evidence in the vault was either destroyed or heavily damaged.

Thirty-two hours later, as a clerk came to the office to catch up on paperwork, the attempt to burn down the building was first discovered. After unlocking the front door, she noticed the alarm was off. But rather than finding a colleague hard at work, she saw everything covered in a thick layer of black ash. She worked her way around the office, gasping from the black dust and the smell. The wall by the chute was heavily charred. Seconds later, calls went out to the agent in charge, the Tampa PD, and agents of the Bureau of Alcohol, Tobacco & Firearms (ATF).

On Sunday afternoon, my DEA supervisor called. "Bob, we have an all-hands meeting on Monday morning at eight a.m. We'll explain at the meeting, but someone firebombed our office, and all signs suggest it was an inside job. As you know, the evidence vault was locked down just before New Year's Eve because Internal Affairs decided to do an unscheduled audit. We think there's a connection. See you Monday."

I explained it to Ev. "Bob, what kind of an organization have you gotten yourself into? You're going to put your life on the line for these people when you know you have someone so sick within your team that they would firebomb your own office? This is crazy."

"Ev, there's no turning back. This has nothing to do with me. There was a guy in the office who got fired last month because he supposedly stole two thousand dollars in drug money seized from a doper. Maybe this is his way of paying back, or maybe he was involved in a lot more than just that two thousand dollars. No matter what, I have to do the best I can with what I've got."

Over the next week, DEA Internal Affairs and the other investigating agencies were all over the problem. Although much of the cocaine in the vault had been destroyed, a portion hadn't. An analysis of the residue confirmed that some of the white powder that remained was actually baking soda. The logical assumption was that someone had stolen coke and swapped it out with sham. Then paper trails suggested that there were four kilos of cocaine missing. All of the questions led to the 350-kilo seizure of cocaine orchestrated by the office superstar, Juaquin "Quino" Gonzalez. That dope came from the first DEA raid I had participated in before heading to Quantico.

Quino and his co-case agent were questioned and then polygraphed. They both scored "inconclusive" in their first tests, but subsequent tests confirmed that they were telling the truth. They had nothing to do with the fire. That led to only one logical course of action. Everyone else in the office had to be polygraphed.

The night before my polygraph, as I tossed in bed, I saw it clearly. My supervisor did it. I could hear him howling in glee as he drove off. Then I woke up in a pool of sweat. This dream had absolutely no connection to fact, but ironically it led to suspicions that the arsonist might be me.

Later that morning, I reported to the hotel room where the polygrapher had his equipment set up. It was just him and me. The first step of this process involved my signing a form consenting to be polygraphed—as though I had a choice. After some small talk about what would soon happen, he went through the pretest interview, asking the same questions from every direction possible. Then I was wired up to the machine. I had difficulty getting settled because the air-conditioning in the room couldn't have been set any higher than sixty-five degrees. As things unfolded, everything seemed to be going fine, until the last fateful question. "Mr. Mazur, is there anything about the fire that you haven't disclosed?"

My dream popped in my mind, but I said, "No." Why shouldn't I? It was only a nightmare. The needles on the machine went ballistic.

I sensed the Internal Affairs polygrapher was about to leap for his weapon and take me away. He had that "gotcha" look on his face. "Mr. Mazur, your reputation is outstanding, but I have to tell you. There is absolutely no doubt in my mind that you are lying."

I swallowed deeply as I sat in stunned silence. "Okay, okay, I swear this is the truth. I had a dream last night that my supervisor firebombed our office, but it was only a dream. When you asked me if there was anything I hadn't told you, that nightmare popped into my head, but I didn't think I should mention it. That's it. I swear that's it; there's nothing more."

The polygrapher looked at me like I was a child. "Okay, I'll give you one more chance. We'll hook you up again and see what we get."

He questioned me for another thirty minutes and then hooked me back up to the machine. Then he offered the results. "Bob, it looks to me that you are now telling the truth, but I have to drill into this. Why do you think you dreamed that your supervisor is the arsonist?"

Undoubtedly the look on my face matched my words. I gave my speech as I ripped the bands that held the machine's wires to me. "Are you fucking kidding me? Listen, I know I haven't been on the job here at DEA for a full year, so I can probably get fired without cause, but I'm not playing your silly-ass games. You know, and I know, that I didn't have shit to do with this fire, and I have no information about who did. As far as I'm concerned, this is over. I'm out of here."

He looked at me with amazement. He didn't speak a word as I grabbed my coat and walked out the door. He just stared. I never saw him again.

After this day, I needed to focus on what brought me to DEA. The slightest flaw in what I was about to do could get me kidnapped, tortured, or worse. I had to finish building Robert Baldasare, his companies, and, most importantly, the informants who would keep me alive. High on that list was my old Mafia connection, Dominic. It was time to make sure he was willing to play for high stakes, even if that meant his dying to keep me alive.

3

BUILDING THE FRONT

January–March 1992

Law enforcement agencies love to attach a code name to major investigations, and this one would be no different. Our goal was to go after the professional money launderers who serviced the Cali cartel and other major criminal organizations operating in Panama. What better gimmick than to borrow the first few letters from the description of our targets, <u>Pro</u>fessional <u>Mo</u>ney Launderers, and to label our undertaking "Operation Pro-Mo"?

Six months before we came up with the "Pro-Mo" name, I'd been notified I would eventually be the primary undercover agent in this long-term sting. During those six months, I enlisted every resource I had to fast-track the creation of my cover, Robert Baldasare, an Italian American businessman, originally from New York, who controlled an investment company and a mortgage brokerage business.

After acquiring all of Baldasare's essential identifying documents, I had informants create Baldasare's employment and personal histories, and I used sources in banks to establish accounts, credit cards, loans, and credit histories. But now I needed to take each of those building blocks of the cover and meticulously cement them together to establish a well-documented background.

The first line of oversight for an undercover operation is a case agent, an officer responsible for coordinating the investigation with other offices throughout the US and around the world. The case agent shouldn't be an undercover agent who would be out of pocket for extended periods of time. The case agent needs to be the equivalent of a sports team's head coach, coordinating with management, communicating with other coaches handling separate aspects of the game in different cities, and overseeing the players (agents).

Operation Pro-Mo was blessed when our boss decided to assign Jeff Brunner as its case agent. Brunner was one of the most talented agents in the Tampa office. He had graduated at the top of his Basic Agent class at Quantico, a very prestigious accomplishment. Out of about forty-five trainees in his class, he led in academics, on the range, and in the gym. His 2 percent body fat gave him a massive head start over his classmates. He was all muscle, all brain, and tactically focused. A total natural.

If you weren't ranked number one in your class, DEA Headquarters decided the city in which you'd work after graduation, normally on the other side of the country from where you wanted to live. Achieving top status in your class gave you the privilege of picking your office location. Having been a highly decorated detective in the St. Petersburg Police Department's Narcotics Squad before joining DEA, Brunner picked the adjacent town of Tampa. He already had several years on the job and a knack for developing and managing big cases. By the time Operation Pro-Mo was being built, Brunner had earned a national reputation as an outstanding agent within DEA and the entire Tampa Bay area law enforcement community. Most importantly for me, we got along well and respected one another. Within weeks of meeting Brunner, I realized I could trust him. I always felt I could tell him exactly what was on my mind. He didn't judge, just tried to find a way to make things right for everyone. He was a highly-talented peacemaker.

It would take Brunner and me several more months to put the finishing touches on Pro-Mo before launch. He needed to analyze a stable of Colombia-based informants to identify the best candidate to be Baldasare's man on the ground in Bogotá, promoting Baldasare's money-laundering prowess.

Eventually, when I went under, it would be Brunner's responsibility to assess and provide for what we thought was reasonable backup, referred to in law enforcement as a cover team. He knew that if an agent does a short-term undercover role, like picking up money from a courier, there clearly needs to be a cover team to ensure safety. But when I was in my long-term role, meeting targets day after day for long periods of time, a cover team could be more of a liability than an asset. Bad guys are smart. They'll pick up on repeated surveillance. Thankfully, Brunner and I made an arrangement. If he and another agent accompanied me to a different city or country, we would travel separately. I would let him know my itinerary in advance. If it changed, I had a mobile phone, and using code, I could let him know the change in plans. As long as I wasn't receiving a delivery of cash, there would generally be no surveillance in the vicinity of my meets. If I didn't come back or check in by the time I was scheduled to return, he and others should try calling me. If that didn't work, they needed to start looking for me, because nothing good would have caused me not to return. That approach didn't sit well with some senior managers, but then again, Brunner's peacemaking dictated that he was willing to put his ass on the line and sometimes tell people what they wanted to hear, rather than what we needed to do to stay alive.

Since my cover involved the ownership and management of an investment company and mortgage business, I needed to bring those dormant companies back to life. On paper, Baldasare purchased them. I also took file cabinets full of both companies' old transactions so I could have those placed in our undercover offices. I transferred the jurisdiction of the companies to Delaware and had them registered in Florida as foreign for-profit companies. When it comes to secrecy, Delaware's lack of transparency matches that of the British Virgin Islands (BVI) and Panama. If you're in the US-based money-laundering business, Delaware is a must.

I studied for and passed the state exam to get my (Baldasare's) mortgage broker's license from the Department of Banking and Finance in Florida, and obtained a mortgage lender's license for one of my companies, Avid Mortgage Services. I acquired all of the requisite city and state licenses and began to fund the company accounts with a million in government funds. We engaged a CPA firm that prepared and certified audited financial statements and independent auditors' reports for the companies. Then it was time to file our corporate returns with the federal and state governments.

A month or so later, Robert Baldasare's Dun & Bradstreet report told it all. Avid Mortgage Services, Inc., had entered into multinational agreements to act as the administrator of funds provided by institutions for short-term commercial needs. The company primarily extended short-term trade financing to foreign-based export companies, especially in South America. This was a perfect cover for the movement of funds between the US and South America. According to Dun & Bradstreet, Avid Mortgage Services had over $5.6 million in assets. The company began business activity seven years earlier. Baldasare was formerly employed by Chase Manhattan Bank and Montgomery Scott & Company in New York, Bank of the Commonwealth in Detroit, and Banque de Commerce et de Placements in New York. Former officers in those institutions would verify Baldasare's prior employment.

Baldasare's co-officers included a well-respected PhD graduate from Princeton University who was formerly employed as a professor of economics. He had extensive experience as an investment adviser in Panama. Another officer was an underwriter with a decade of experience in the Middle East and earlier employment as the chairman and CEO of banks in Switzerland, Lebanon, and Luxembourg.

Everything about Baldasare, his companies, his employment history, and his business associations was in place. It was all verifiable. And it was all a lie. That lie was more important to my safety than carrying a weapon, which I never did while working undercover. I put my faith and my life in the hands of my cover persona. If my cover was flawed or compromised, I'd be killed, even if I carried a weapon. I couldn't carry a gun to meetings in foreign countries anyway, and that was where I needed to go to attack the cartel's command and control. Carrying a gun would have screamed "cop."

Baldasare's credibility had to come from more than paper. High-quality sources—or as others call them, informants—needed to breathe life into the Baldasare story. I needed a bit of an insurance policy that would cause real crooks to think twice about double-crossing or trying to hurt me. I needed underworld street cred that caused the people we were going after to say, "I don't want to fuck with him." My best insurance policy was my old friend Dominic, a guy who earned his stripes working for Mafia types in New York and Florida. Dom's help in my last undercover gig, "Operation C-Chase," was invaluable. My concern this time around was that, unlike Operation C-Chase, our targets wouldn't strictly come from Colombian Mafias. It was very likely that I would be crossing paths with Italian American crime figures with roots in Panama. If any of them had Dom's loyalty, I needed to be certain how he would handle that. I had to have a heart-to-heart with him to satisfy myself that he was all in.

I knew Dominic had been a bone-crushing enforcer. He collected unpaid debts for Tampa-area traffickers, but sources often hold back details about their darkest secrets. He was cocky and fearless. His thick, hard body had developed long before his stint in the Marines. He had everything Hollywood was looking for when casting an Italian American mobster. His lush black hair was always well oiled and combed straight back, exposing the olive skin of his receding hairline. His eyes were piercing slits under his broad dark eyebrows and heavy brow, and his voice almost growled with a thick Brooklyn accent. To say that he had a unique vocabulary was to put it mildly. He had an amazing knack for using variations of the f-word as a noun, verb, adjective, adverb, and more.

We got together at an Italian joint that Dominic bankrolled. He had a habit of being a "silent partner" in restaurants and clubs.

"Dom, I'm going to be doing another operation, except with this one, I'll be spending a lot of my time in Panama. There are going to be situations when players from Colombia, Panama, and the States will visit me in Florida. When they do, I'm wondering if you might help me, the way you did in the last operation. But there's a twist to this one. There's a chance some of these people will be connected to one of the five families in New York. Before I ask for your help, I need to be one hundred percent certain that I'm not going to put you in a position where you have second thoughts or mixed loyalties."

"Bobby, those days are over for me. When I decided to come to your side ten years ago, I came all the way. You know I used to be a bodyguard for Carl Coppola in the Gambino family. When you helped get me into the Witness Protection Program and I agreed to testify, that was the end of my involvement in that world. I have no secrets; I told it all in the trials."

Dominic's story was vintage Mafia. I remember convincing him to tell all and trying to hide my shock as he revealed his reality. He was with Coppola when the hit was planned on Danny Forgione. Forgione was found at the steering wheel of his car, parked at a lounge, with six shots that blew open his head and chest. Dominic was with Coppola when plans were made to whack Dominic's partner, Joey Cam. Cam was found in a field by a group of schoolkids, his head shattered by four slugs. Coppola trusted Dominic so much that he gave Dom a bomb to plant in the car of one of Coppola's enemies. There wasn't much Coppola didn't entrust to him, including his pot and his coke businesses.

"You don't need to worry about me, Bobby. I've got your back. I have no more secrets, other than my friendship with you." Like me, Dominic grew up around mobsters in New York. He saw how they operated. It made no sense to Dominic that Mafia leaders hung out at social clubs on Mulberry Street, in Bensonhurst, and in Ozone Park, where they played cards all day. They got guys like Dominic to earn, and then the earners had to give their card-playing bosses a big chunk of what they made. He didn't want to be owned.

Dominic wasn't a made member of a crime family, so he knocked around doing some jobs for different families, as well as some work on his own. If he needed muscle on one of his gigs, he'd use his own. If he needed someone to scare the shit out of a punk to collect a drug debt, he'd pay his uncle, an old Italian baker, to dress up, sit in a car, and not say much. He'd tell his victim to meet him in Shore Park, near the base of the Verrazzano-Narrows Bridge. He'd tell the deadbeat that the guy in the car was the boss, and the boss was out of patience. He'd let it be known that if the guy didn't pay in the next two hours, the boss had told him he had to throw the punk off the middle of the bridge. He'd walk the kid over to the car so his uncle could roll the window down, give the kid a death stare, and say, "You're fuckin' dead if you don't pay now." When Dominic collected, he'd pay his uncle one thousand dollars for his help. That was a hell of a lot less than what the bosses in the social clubs would have expected.

"Bobby, I give you my word. I will be one hundred percent honest with you, and I will cover your back. Besides, we're goombahs [close friends] from Staten Island."

Dominic delivered a huge belly laugh. I had no doubt that he meant to keep his promise, but now I had to find someone equally trustworthy to be my eyes, ears, and mouth in Colombia. We needed a reliable source to sell me to the people at the top of the Cali cartel. Jeff Brunner and I interviewed several candidates for this role, and we found a winner.

Jaime Vargas, a DEA source, became my salesman in Colombia. The tiny Bogotá native had experience in banking, insurance, trade, and the drug side of things, but he didn't know much about laundering. He was related to traffickers, an important factor to get his foot in doors. He had a knack for putting people at ease. He was well read and a quick learner, had the smooth tenor voice of a radio announcer, and loved to sing. When this amazing guy decided to share his favorite aria, "*La donna è mobile*" from *Rigoletto*, you could easily mistake his voice for Luciano Pavarotti's.

Building success with informants requires certainty about their motives. Everything has to be on the table—no unknowns. Some motives, like revenge against your targets, are a formula for disaster. Jaime's were pure: patriotism and money. He felt an obligation to help DEA reduce the violence and corruption in Colombia, and he wanted to be fairly compensated for putting his life on the line. He knew that what he was doing, if it backfired, would cost him not only his life but the lives of all of his family members. Knowing that, I felt a tremendous obligation to do everything I could to keep him and his family from being cut into little pieces and burned to ash, or dissolved in a vat of acid. That would be their fate if I failed him.

I spent several daily sessions with Jaime, teaching him everything I'd learned about laundering throughout my law enforcement career, especially the tricks I'd picked up from the PhDs of dirty money whom I'd dealt with during my undercover stint in the Medellín cartel. In no time at all, Jaime talked the talk. Now, together, we needed to walk the walk.

If Robert Baldasare was to be convincing, he needed a third dimension. Having cred in the US and Colombia was necessary, but having those credentials in another key narco-haven country would offer me three-dimensional believability. That was the unique factor that Steven Richards and his sister, Marlene, brought to the table. They were academics who had spent years in Panama collecting information about the movers and shakers in the *Star Wars* bar of crime under the iron fist of Manuel Noriega. Although Noriega had been swooped up by US forces just two years before, the nest of crime in Panama that had been built over many decades was too deep to follow its machete-waving leader to a US prison. Richards and his sister knew many of the major players in Panama's underworld. They volunteered to become Baldasare's ambassadors to the horde of lawyers, bankers, financial service providers, and other crooks that controlled Panama. The marriage of the Richards siblings to Operation Pro-Mo was orchestrated by DEA Headquarters. They were an odd choice to some, but that made them all the more convincing as people with no ties to law enforcement. Steven Richards was a short, portly gringo who looked and spoke like an Ivy League professor. His sister could have easily been mistaken for her brother in a long wig. They were bookends. Neither of them came across like they had an ounce of macho law enforcement DNA, a favorable trait in my book.

The US offices of Avid Mortgage Services and Avid Investment Group were established in the Belle Haven office complex, a beautifully restored three-story Mediterranean Revival–style office complex in Sarasota, built in 1926, the same year that construction of the famous Ca' d'Zan mansion of John and Mable Ringling was completed in the same town. My offices in Sarasota were plush, occupying seventeen hundred square feet of the second floor. The offices were staffed every day by Steven and Marlene Richards, and when I wasn't in Panama, I was most often with them at the Avid office suites. In Sarasota, I lived across a small harbor from the offices in a marina suite in Condo on the Bay, a colony of luxury homes set on eight acres that faced Sarasota Bay. A forty-four-foot Hatteras Cruiser was docked in my backyard. By

March 1992, as the final pieces of the front were pulled together, I called my good friend Emir Abreu to find out the going street rate to exchange Colombian pesos for US dollars. That was an important number to know in competing for narco-dollars.

"Bob, today it is 605 to 1. Are you getting ready to crank up your new operation at DEA?"

"Yeah, I've been building this machine for about nine months. It's time. I wish I were working this with you, but I know the bosses at Customs would never let you. I'll be working with this new super-star at DEA, Juaquin 'Quino' Gonzalez. He's assigned to us from the Tampa PD."

Abreu's silence blared a warning, but after five or so seconds, he spoke. "Brother, you need to be careful. There are some things I want to share with you, but let me talk to my people here at Customs to get the green light. If you don't play your cards right, you're going to get fucking killed. I'll call you back tomorrow."

The next day, he called.

"Sorry, Bob. My boss says that our agent in charge, Bonnie Tischler, doesn't want me near you, your partner, or your operation. They say if I go around them, I'm looking at thirty days with no pay, and that's just for starters. When you resigned, wrote your letter, and testified before Congress about all the crap she and her bosses in Washington did, they saw that as a declaration of war. They didn't like being pegged for illegal leaks to the press and playing politics with our work. Please believe me when I say I want to help, but I can't. If I do, they'll hang me by my balls. To be honest, between us, when I told them why I thought you were in danger, they said, 'Fuck Mazur, he's at DEA now. That's his problem.' I wish I could speak with you about this, because I'm worried. If my hunch is right, you could get whacked."

I was stunned. Emir Abreu didn't bullshit, at least not about anything serious. Nothing offered more reliable evidence to me than Abreu's gut feelings. I went to one of my bosses.

"Like me, you know and trust Emir. He and I share a special, insep-arable bond. When I told him that Quino was going to be my part-ner in this new operation, he said he knows some things, and Quino's working with me concerned him. I'm not sure what that means. I know Emir had a run-in with a couple of uniformed guys in Quino's depart-ment, but beyond that, I haven't got a clue. We've got a lot of Spanish-speaking agents who could handle this undercover assignment. What do you think about using someone from another department?"

"Listen, Bob. Quino is up for 'Officer of the Year' for the entire city. Whether a few uniformed guys in his department did something stupid or not, that's no reflection on him. I hired him, and I trust him one hundred percent. Let me put it to you this way. You have one of two options. You can either do this operation with Quino as your partner, or there'll be no operation. What's your choice?"

"Okay. You're right. I'm sorry. I've been around Quino enough to know he has that something extra that will be a big asset to this operation. He is a natural. You won't hear anything about this again from me."

A week or so later, Quino and his fiancée were at our home. I felt it would go a long way if we, as partners, got together with our loved ones, to show our mutual trust. After all, we would definitely be putting our lives on the line for one another. One false step by either of us could be the other's demise.

During cocktails after dinner, I explained to Quino and his fiancée the potential consequences of this assignment. Ev and I shared how we had to live underground for years after the last operation because of the threats against my life. It turned everything upside down for us, and our kids. Quino and his fiancée understood. She fidgeted in her chair, sighed repeatedly, and wore concern as I explained details about the half-million-dollar contract on my life.

After they left, Ev had a lot of questions. "Bob, why was it so important to have them here tonight? We still live under assumed names, and the contract on your life was issued only three years ago. Was this really necessary?"

"Trust me, Ev. I need to keep this kid as close to me as possible, to make sure I feel what he's feeling and thinking. Emir thinks there's something not right about Quino, but his premise is all guesses. Bringing him here makes Quino think I've decided to trust him totally. That's just my survival instinct kicking in. I need to make sure I know what makes his clock tick, and I have to keep him fully invested in the success of the operation. If Emir's right, then my grandfather's advice— to keep my friends close and my enemies closer—will pay off."

"Okay, Bob. I just thought it was unnecessary. Very few people in law enforcement know where we live. I worry about the kids, and I worry about . . ."

I gently put my hand on Ev's cheek. "Babe, I know what I'm doing. I would never do anything to put you or the kids in harm's way. I promise. Please trust me." I hugged Ev tightly, and we were ear to ear, so she couldn't see my face as my eyes were closed and I prayed that I'd made the right move. Time would tell.

Meanwhile, Jaime Vargas was frantically trying to call the undercover cell phone that I'd turned off. He had news that would change the course of many lives.

4

A HOME RUN

Jaime's excitement transformed his typically mellow and purposeful speaking style into the cadence of a marathoner gasping for breath. "Bob, Bob, you asked me to try to connect with some big fish in the laundering world, and I've hooked a blue whale. These guys are major players. They're ready to fly to Miami to meet you tomorrow."

"Whoa, whoa, slow down. I'm not meeting anyone tomorrow." Using code we established at the start of our relationship, I reminded Jaime that we had to assume that all of our conversations were being monitored. The cartel paid off a lot of employees at the Colombian phone companies to monitor calls that flushed out feds and their snitches. When we spoke on the phone or in an unsecure setting, we always had to assume the other side was listening, so we had to talk as though we were who we claimed to be. We were launderers.

"What makes you think these guys are worth the risk of my doing business with them? Is there any possibility they could be friends of Los Feos [the Ugly Ones]?"

"The Ugly Ones" is a term that everyone in the Colombian underworld used to describe US federal agents.

"Jaime, you know I have responsibilities here to some very important people. If I get myself involved with the wrong kind of people down south, it could cost me a lot more than money. I want to make sure these guys have their shit together and aren't going to bring heat on me."

"Okay, okay, I'll let that be known, but here's what I've got."

Jaime rattled off the details. Through a mid-level dope dealer, he was introduced to Luis Fernando Latorre and Pedro Rodriguez-Castro, the owners of Definsa SA, a financial consulting business in Bogotá. They were part of a network that was laundering for leaders of the Cali cartel. Through a flock of dirty bankers, some corrupt executives with two oil companies, and Colombian Customs officials on the take, they had the paperwork and resources to launder a million dollars a week by accepting checks and wire transfers of US dollars that they disguised as legitimate repatriated revenue from the sale of Colombian exports. But they lacked a sufficient number of corrupt businessmen in the US capable of accepting trunk loads of cash from cartel couriers, getting that cash into business accounts, and then wiring those funds from the US to their accounts in Bogotá. They wanted to deal only with people like Robert Baldasare in the US, people who were involved in international trade. Avid Mortgage Services was right up their alley, since Avid offered short-term trade-related financing.

The people in the Cali cartel they serviced were selling huge amounts of cocaine in San Francisco, Europe, New York, and Miami. Jaime gave me phone numbers and addresses for Latorre, Rodriguez-Castro, and their business in Bogotá. Through DEA resources, it didn't take long for us to determine they were for real.

Although I hadn't previously participated in the laundering method used by Latorre and Rodriguez-Castro, I'd heard of it. It was commonly referred to as *reintegro* (reintegrate). The official name of the process is "*Reintegrar las divisas*" ("Reimbursement of Exchange"). Traffickers acquire companies that export, or appear to export, goods sold for US dollars, like fruits, precious stones, precious metals, or coffee beans exported to the States by major factory and plantation owners. When the exporter in Colombia ships two million dollars in coffee beans, Colombian Customs issues the exporter documents confirming what was exported and its value. When the foreign buyer sends payments in US dollars to the Colombia-based exporter, the exporter gives its banker the Customs documents confirming that US wire transfers of two million dollars are payment for legitimate exports. When the banker receives the funds, the dollars are converted to Colombian pesos and sent to an account designated by the exporter.

The Cali cartel's launderers corrupted bankers who helped them camouflage narco-proceeds as legitimately repatriated export revenue. If you've got a dirty banker and extra exportation documents, you can pull off this scheme. There are many ways to buy exportation documents on the black market. Some are sold to cartel launderers by legitimate export companies that don't intend to repatriate their sales revenue; some are forged by corrupt Customs officials; some are produced when exporters intentionally overvalue exports; and some are simply pulled from other customer files by dirty bankers. Most experienced bankers handling trade-based transactions are likely to see red flags in these fake export transfers. As an added level of protection, the cartel's banker gets a piece of the action. It was clear to me that Cali's laundrymen were smarter than those in the Medellín cartel. As I was told, the Colombian bankers in the pocket of the Cali cartel applied the CVY factor: *¿Cómo voy yo?*, meaning "How am I?" or "What do I get?"

Three weeks later, Quino and I met with Latorre and Rodriguez-Castro in a penthouse suite of the Doral Beach Hotel in Miami Beach.

During this and all of his undercover work on Operation Pro-Mo, Quino assumed the identity of Antonio Ruiz.

Latorre was a class act. Owner of a finance company, this college-educated civil engineer had Paso Fino horses and was an aficionado of equestrian racing. Despite his polished fingernails and tailored suits, he was also an experienced private pilot who could have excelled at delivering loads of cocaine to dusty runways. He was tall, thin, and despite his engaging humor, often dead serious.

Pedro Rodriguez-Castro was an economist who represented many multinational corporations in financial matters. Pudgy, fumbling, and awkward, he was a numbers cruncher, Latorre's technical guy. They'd met six years before and been partners ever since.

Latorre said he had extensive contacts in the banking community. I told him I was impressed, but before I was comfortable getting into details, I thought it best for Quino to share some private time with Latorre and Rodriguez-Castro while I took a break. This was my way of letting Latorre know that I didn't want to be in the room when the initial discussion about laundering went down. My purpose: send a passive message to Latorre that I was cautious. As soon as I left the room, Quino sold me to the team from Colombia. He did an outstanding job explaining why I was so careful, and why I could do great things for them.

When I returned, we all went to dinner. For me, the conversation at dinner was measured. It was my goal to have Latorre uncover why I knew what the hell I was doing, that I had significant resources, and that I was shrewd. But it was most important that he learn those things through his own questions and not my offerings. His discoveries had twice the power of my telling him the same. I couldn't afford to come across as volunteering details. I wanted Latorre's takeaway to be that I was assessing this relationship as either a long-term association or none at all. That would be the only way to get him comfortable telling me things that he otherwise didn't want to reveal.

When we got back to the penthouse suite, I threw the ball into Latorre's court, telling him that I was all ears to hear how he thought our partnership could benefit each of us. I sat back in my chair in silence, and he started to fidget. Consistent with the advice that my undercover trainers drilled into my head many years before, my silence and active listening primed him to reveal much more than if I had tried to lead the conversation.

Initially, Latorre avoided the obvious by claiming he and Rodriguez-Castro were helping legitimate exporters bring dollars back from the States. He claimed his customers generated ten million dollars per month in cash sales. Presently, they were using fifteen teams of workers, each of which made cash purchases of traveler's checks, money orders, MoneyGrams, and cashier's checks in increments of less than ten thousand dollars. The thousands of purchased negotiable instruments were deposited into accounts at Miami-based branches of foreign banks. From there, the funds were wired to accounts in Bogotá, controlled by Latorre and Rodriguez-Castro. This was a tedious, time-consuming, and expensive process. They hoped I could streamline their process by accepting five hundred thousand dollars a day in currency and then wiring those funds to them.

I offered Latorre a serious stare. "Luis, I help clients in the US that I suspect are in the same business as yours. You need to know that, if I make a mistake and lose their money, I'll eventually be pushing up daisies."

Latorre and Rodriguez-Castro offered hearty laughs, after which Latorre returned my serious look. "Mr. Bob, I understand, because if we make mistakes and lose money owned by the people we represent, we'll be sucking up roots." We all laughed, and I knew we were edging toward a time of full disclosure, and it wasn't far off.

"Luis, when I say that my clients sell merchandise, quite frankly, I mean cocaine. I love these guys because I've known and worked with them since I was a kid, but I also know that if they ever viewed me as a risk, they wouldn't hesitate to eliminate that risk."

A knock at the door revealed a white-gloved waiter balancing a tray of snifters filled with generous portions of Rémy Martin Louis XIII cognac. As Latorre lifted a glass to his nose, I sensed he was about to let his guard down.

"Bob, my clients, who will ship cash to you, have no legal businesses. On the Colombian side, we work with many bankers that are friends of Pedro. We have to pay them off to look the other way and help us make these transactions look normal." Latorre rattled off the names of more than a dozen banks in which he had the assistance of corrupt officers.

"Luis, I need a name of one of your satisfied customers from the world of Los Duros [the Hard Ones], so my people can confirm your reputation. Not any name—I need the name of someone in the business to vouch for you."

Latorre knew exactly what I meant. "Los Duros" is a term used in the Colombian drug trade to refer to high-ranking members within cartels. In serious thought, Latorre took a sip from his snifter. Slowly his expression changed. He leaned back in his chair, grew a smile, and said the magic words. "Oh, you mean one of the narcos." He took out his pen and one of his business cards. On it, he wrote the name and gave it to me. "Bob, this gentleman is a former bank manager in Colombia who is now a money manager for many narco-traffickers. We work closely with him."

Two weeks later, we did our first deal. It bore truth to Latorre's claim: his organization used an army of workers to exchange cash for checks in increments of less than ten thousand dollars. Quino met undercover with a courier in Miami who handed over a stack of hundreds of these instruments. Most were in amounts under two thousand dollars, and nearly all of them were in odd amounts, no round numbers, so that it would appear that they had been bought to make payments for some specific, legal purpose. Latorre's courier was a middle-aged Colombian woman, well dressed and seemingly educated. She dropped off three hundred thousand dollars in checks.

Drug cartels use hundreds of methods to launder their fortunes, but this one clearly involved a particular method nicknamed by the law enforcement community as "Smurfing." In Smurfing operations, drug cartels engaged literally thousands of workers, normally relatives and friends of low-level traffickers, whose job each day consisted of meeting with a manager entrusted to collect hundreds of thousands from the sale of cocaine. In a given day, the manager might meet with ten workers (Smurfs) and give each of them a map that pinpointed the location of dozens of US Postal Service offices, money-service businesses, gas stations, and other locations that routinely sold traveler's checks, money orders, cashier's checks, MoneyGrams, and similar instruments. The manager would also give each Smurf fifty thousand dollars or more in cash and instruct them to report back after they'd converted all the cash into these instruments. In return for their work, each worker might receive a payment equal to 1 percent or less of the total cash they converted.

Agents from Tampa and Miami surveilled Quino's meet with the courier, and as promised, it was handled with the utmost care. Properly managing the surveillance work for this type of meet is an art. Too little, and the undercover operative can be at risk of death from a double cross, but too much, and the entire undercover operation can be compromised. The challenge of getting surveillance right is directly related to the professionalism of the managers that mandate surveillance protocol in a given city. Are they mindful of the reality that the cartel has operatives conducting their own countersurveillance? Do those in charge care more about how they can manipulate a local success by seizing some drug money? Are they committed to protecting the interests of the out-of-town undercover operation? Do they think they can follow the cartel courier after the money drop to a "pot at the end of the rainbow," where tens of millions in drug money are stashed? In one out of a hundred cases, that might be true, but that small chance represents a risk that should not be taken lightly. Everyone on surveillance has to respect the intelligence of the cartel's ranks and never forget that the bad guys are smarter than they are. That's not an easy pill for many cops to swallow, but ignoring that reality has destroyed hundreds of potentially great cases. Thankfully, that was not a problem when we picked up money in our own backyard, but we couldn't always control surveillance protocol in other cities.

Given the cost and time expended by Latorre's Smurfs, our money-laundering charge—for dumping all those checks into a company account and wiring the funds to Latorre—was less than it would have been if we had received currency. To make the deposits appear normal, I opened an account in the name of a check-cashing business. From there, the funds passed to our finance company, and then eventually to Latorre's account.

Clearly, this Miami pickup was a test, and if we passed, Pro-Mo would get a significant reward, as fitting as the reward Quino received for a year of stardom. The week after his first Pro-Mo money pickup, he enjoyed a long-awaited and very distinguished achievement when he was named "Officer of the Year" in our region of Florida, in recognition of his work as the narc-detective and DEA Task Force officer who had contributed more to the success of the area's law enforcement efforts than any other.

A feature article on the day we met for lunch explained why he was the best of the best. I lifted my glass. "Quino, here's to your success. What you've achieved is very special, and I'm really proud and thankful that we've partnered together for Operation Pro-Mo. I've seen it first-hand when we've done our thing with Luis and Pedro—you're a natural. Thanks for being a part of this, and watching my back. Cheers."

We toasted his achievement, but Quino was tense, stiff, distracted. Several times during our meeting, he stared down at his hands, rolling his palms over his knuckles. His mind was somewhere else.

"Quino, are you okay?"

He looked up as though I had woken him. "Yeah, Bob. Everything's fine."

Later the same day, Quino called.

"Bob, I really appreciate your support. You were right; I'm not okay. I need your help. My asshole sergeant is flexing his muscles to show that he controls me, and not DEA. I've been ordered to show up in uniform tonight, in riot gear. The Rodney King verdict has the Black community up in arms, literally. Fires have been set in a bunch of businesses, and there's a lot of looting. I'm mentally exhausted. I've been on the streets picking up money in a different city every week. Latorre keeps calling, and we've got a few pickups coming up soon. Besides, what if someone connected to Latorre sees me in my uniform?"

This wasn't what I wanted to hear. Quino needed to make nice with his office. The Cali cartel wasn't surveilling uniformed cops handling riots. They had bigger goals. Quino's own kids would have trouble recognizing him in his helmet, face shield, and other riot gear. His concern about being seen in uniform was bizarre, but I needed to tread lightly. I knew he'd just been through a divorce, his second, and he had only occasional visitation with his two young daughters. For a while, he was a suspect in the firebombing of our office, but the polygraph had cleared him. He was right about one thing: his boss at the department was sometimes an ass who felt it his mission to dissuade Quino from thinking he was anything special.

"Listen, Quino. I don't think DEA is going to cross swords with your department over this. I suggest you find a quiet place to think this out. List the pros and cons. My guess is you'll come to the conclusion that this is not a battle worth fighting. I'm counting on you, man. I need you, and if you fight this battle and lose, DEA may not be able to stop your department from yanking you out of this operation."

"Okay, Bob, thanks for hearing me out. I appreciate your advice, and our friendship."

The next day, Quino's sergeant was on the warpath. Quino not only failed to show up for roll call and riot duty, but he also didn't answer a dozen frantic calls made in an effort to find him. According to the sergeant, "This fucking idiot went to the beach, shut off his phone, and meditated the night away." I felt guilty; apparently, Quino had taken my suggestion literally and never gotten out of Zen mode.

I knew Quino had issues. His parents had divorced shortly after he was born. His mom and a boyfriend lived with Quino, adding three stepsisters to the family, until the boyfriend decided to split. Quino's mom finally settled down with a new husband, who moved the entire family from Puerto Rico to the Bronx. Not wanting any part of the newest father figure, Quino moved to Tampa on his own and eventually found his calling, first as an air-conditioning repairman, and then as a cop. During the five years before I met him, his two marriages had failed. He received the same lack of loyalty from men and women in his life that he was now delivering to his department. That's not an excuse, just an observation.

It took every favor we could offer to keep Quino's department from pulling him out of DEA. The solution: he was found in violation of rules and regulations for failure to report to work, and he received a letter of counseling. As long as he didn't disobey another order from his department, he could stay at DEA, but he had to attend regular sessions with the department's shrink. They wanted his out-of-town undercover work curtailed and asked us to begin thinking about how we might replace him if another incident occurred. The decision was measured. It showed they were willing to be patient, just as we needed to be patient with Latorre.

Latorre and his people had been evaluating us, and his verdict was delivered at 3:00 a.m. one night. My cell phone shattered my deep sleep, and I fumbled to answer.

"Bob, it's Luis. I'm so sorry to call you at this hour. I would have called earlier, but the phone company strikes caused our service to be down, sometimes for days at a time. It's back up, but we could lose it again soon." Latorre explained that he and Jaime had met with Latorre's main Cali contact the day before. Latorre was given the green light to

bring me on. Real business would start soon. Jaime was given radio frequencies through which Jaime and I could communicate when the phone
systems were down in Colombia. Latorre's tone was so full of happiness, I
could almost see his big smile. "Welcome to the family, Mr. Bob."

On the heels of that call, we were given a contract to receive a series
of four shipments of cash, three in New York and one in LA, totaling
$1.5 million—all for Latorre's main man.

Despite promises by the New York DEA boss that they wouldn't
try to surveil the cartel courier that dropped the money off to Quino,
they lied and did exactly that. One of our Tampa guys on the New York
surveillance offered his concern. "Hey, guys, I thought we agreed that
you wouldn't follow the drop-off guy. We're just getting started in our
operation, and we need time to earn credibility." The unfortunate but
typical reply came across the radio.

"Are you kidding? This is a chance of a lifetime. We're going to follow this idiot Colombian drop-off guy after he gives Quino the suitcase
of cash, and then we're on him like glue so we can follow him back to
the stash house where they've stored all their money. Then we'll take it
down."

This surveillance of the courier after the money drop was so obvious
that the courier eventually pulled his car into a strip mall, flung open his
door, left his keys in the car, and ran away. To talk my way out of this,
I had to do my best lying to Latorre. "Luis, we saw nothing. Your man's
guy in the Towers [New York] must be seeing ghosts. I had an extra two
men watching Quino's back, since this was our first time doing this for
your client. Maybe he noticed them and lost his mind."

Despite the surveillance train wreck in New York, Jaime, my
faithful eyes and ears in Colombia, marched onward through the field
of risk. He met directly with one of Latorre's Cali contacts, a man
named Jaramillo. Details offered at the meeting began to reveal how
high Latorre was in the food chain of Cali cartel launderers. Jaramillo
worked with members of the Grajales family, a clan that included some

of the most renowned Cali cartel members, and they had two million a month in cash that they wanted us to receive in New York. The Grajales family had it all: businesses that inflated the value of exported grapes, fruit, wines, equipment, and other commodities. That gave its members access to key export documents to justify the movement of narco-dollars to the corrupt managers at Colombian banks who pushed the transactions along. Their need was our bread and butter.

On one of my daily calls with Latorre, he broke the news. "Bob, can you receive [accept cash] in Houston?"

"Sure, Luis, I'll have Antonio [Quino] handle it. What are the terms?"

"We have a half ton [five hundred thousand dollars] ready for shipment. With your permission, I'll pass the details to Antonio."

"Okay. Once Antonio has the documents [cash], please fax the details [wiring instructions] to me."

The alliance between Colombia's cocaine suppliers and the Mexican cartels that exploited the porous US border made Houston a major gateway for shipments of drugs and money. This could be a difference maker, and it was. Unfortunately, what happened in New York would look like a minor bump in the road compared to what was about to unfold in Houston.

Quino and another undercover agent—Pinellas County Detective Elvin "Al" Melendez, assigned to the DEA Task Force—flew to Houston with an agent from our office who would coordinate with DEA in Houston. Al Melendez was a humble man and the type of reliable consummate professional that I knew would get the job done, even under the worst of circumstances. His mom and dad, hardworking parents born in Puerto Rico, had raised him in New York City. After serving three years as a military police officer in Okinawa, he had worked with a small-town police department in Florida for eleven years, followed by a long and decorated career with the vice-narcotics squad of the Pinellas County Sheriff's Office. He was so good at what he did that his department constantly loaned him to federal agencies and other departments to play the undercover role of a drug dealer. Although his work took some very bad people off the street, because he was constantly on the job for other departments, his own leadership repeatedly passed him over for promotions because they really didn't know him, or the quality of his skills. They rarely got a bird's-eye view of his excellence, which had resulted in so many seizures of money and other assets that, when he ultimately retired, the value of his seizures far outweighed the cost of his salary. The taxpayers got a bargain in Melendez, and so did I.

Within a few hours of arriving in Houston, Quino and Melendez were meeting the cartel courier on the street. Quino gave the courier the keys to his rental car with the understanding that the courier would bring it back with five hundred thousand dollars in the trunk.

The courier drove directly to a home in Houston where the cash was stashed. As the courier was in the house, the battle began. Our DEA agent in Houston was supposed to have notified other agencies in Houston that we were making the pickup, to ensure that we didn't stumble into a money-laundering case being conducted by another agency. There was a law enforcement clearing house through which that call should have been made. Our guy never made that call, but after we were already in the middle of the deal, he received a call from a supervisor with the IRS Criminal Investigation Division and a Houston PD captain, claiming that they had been working on that courier and his boss, Julio Vicuna, for more than a year. Vicuna, a Peruvian who owned and operated a money-exchange business in Houston, was a high-level launderer for the Cali cartel. Their surveillance agents had been monitoring the house for more than a day when they saw our rental car arrive. Through their informants, they knew more than a million in cash was sitting in the courier's home, and they were not about to let our undercover agents leave with that money.

As the arguing continued, Houston PD parked one of their marked units in front of the courier's house. The courier and another of Vicuna's workers were freaking out inside. Understandably, they jumped to the conclusion that Quino and Melendez had brought the heat on them and were either cops or informants.

In an effort to give us a slim chance of dissuading the men in Cali from thinking that Quino was a snitch, the IRS and Houston PD let the courier return to Quino with Quino's rental car. Instead of five hundred thousand dollars, he delivered only one hundred thousand. He said another car would arrive at the drop point soon with another five hundred thousand. As Quino and Melendez waited at a restaurant, Vicuna's second worker started to load boxes of cash from the house into his car. Before he could get to the restaurant, he was stopped by Houston PD. He gave them consent to search his car, which led to their discovering the five hundred thousand in cash. Then he gave them consent to search his home, which put another six hundred thousand dollars in the coffers of Houston PD and the IRS.

By the time I could report to Latorre that we'd gotten only one hundred thousand dollars in Houston, he had been visited by the Cali bosses and their sicarios.

"Bob, their guy in Houston, a Peruvian, has convinced them that you guys are feds. I know that's impossible, so here's what I've proposed." Latorre wanted us to get copies of the documents filed in the Houston courts for the arrest of Vicuna's couriers, and the one million dollars plus that was taken from them. If the court papers confirmed that it had nothing to do with Quino or me, we'd stay in business and live. This needed to happen fast, because the Peruvian was scheduled to fly from Houston to Bogotá soon to give his version of the story.

"Luis, let them know I'm hiring a lawyer to get the papers. I can't afford to do that myself. There can be no footprints from this mess back to me."

Before the documents were sent to me, Latorre reached out to Quino. "My friend, you and Bob are in the clear. Lawyers hired by the bosses sent them copies of the documents. They clearly state that the information about the Peruvian [Vicuna] and that house was received before I ever got information from them about the Houston deal."

Then Latorre called me to share the good news. "Mr. Bob, did Antonio explain why there are no more concerns about you?"

"Yes, Luis. I haven't gotten my copies of the documents, but the details are very important to me."

"Don't worry, Mr. Bob; everything is good. They want you to receive six [six hundred thousand dollars] in Houston. It's ready."

"What! Luis, with all due respect, there's no fucking way I'm letting any of my people go back to that town until I get answers. Your people could have smeared us with their problems. I need to know everything about what happened, and what Los Feos know, before I ever consider going back to any city in Texas."

Given what just happened in Houston, only an undercover agent would accept an offer like the one Latorre delivered. We had to think like criminals, and criminals are too smart to return to the scene of the crime without checking every little detail to find out what went wrong.

I made myself very clear with Latorre. I needed to know absolutely everything about their Peruvian friend, and they needed to let him know that he'd better measure what he said about us. He was trying to make himself look good by lying about us. That wasn't acceptable. I gave Latorre my bottom line. If Vicuna kept lying, we would "do what we had to do." Latorre knew that meant we would stop the lies by any means possible; otherwise, the chatter in Cali could create grave danger for me or any of the other agents working the operation.

"Bob, Bob, calm down. I'll make it up to you. I have more than one million dollars in contracts I will arrange for you in the Towers. By the time you settle those [send wires], I will be in Sarasota with my wife and son. We would like to spend some time with you."

Just as everything looked like we were back on track, I got sucker punched. Quino was missing in action again, and his department wanted him out of DEA.

5

REVEALING REALITIES

Tampa, Florida
June–September 1992

The call came from the chief of police, who had given Quino his "Officer of the Year" award the month before. "I need you guys to come downtown. Officer Juaquin Gonzalez [Quino] was a no-show for one of his scheduled sessions with the department shrink. This kid is out of control, and we need to get him rooted back in the department full-time."

"Chief, we understand how serious this appears. Please give us a day, and we'll be in your office with a full report."

I met with the department's psychologist. I didn't reveal my experience with therapists, but I'd sat across from more of them than I wanted to remember. That's normal in the life of someone asked to be two people for years at a time. Psychologists can play an important role helping an undercover agent manage stress and mental anguish, but sometimes they act like they have all the answers before they ask the questions. I tried to coax him into giving Quino a break, but he wouldn't budge.

The truth was that Quino had rescheduled a session because he was in New York making a cash pickup. He called the doctor's assistant to reschedule again, because he was still out of town, but she dropped the ball. At least that was Quino's alibi. We dodged another bullet and got a reprieve. Quino could stay on, but we needed to start thinking of other options. Lucky for us, Latorre was visiting us in two days.

I needed more props. Since Latorre was bringing his wife and son, we had to match the family affair. Having anticipated that this need would arise, DEA agent Stephanie Radwick was in the wings to play the role of my wife, and Hillsborough County detective Carmen Rivas was ready to pose as Quino's girlfriend. These cameo roles may sound easy, but the preparation required to make sure everyone is on the same page has to be taken very seriously. Both Radwick and Rivas did just that.

As was done for the undercover identity of everyone in the operation, Radwick and Rivas filled out extensive undercover profiles that included every detail about their personal background, families, education, likes, dislikes, and interests. We used them to keep social discussion going in the presence of the Latorres. Our cover would be blown if Radwick and I didn't know every tiny detail about one another. We studied each other's profiles and met several times to practice, anticipating questions and how we'd reply. Attention to detail was an absolute must. Radwick had to know where everything in the undercover residence was. If she was in Latorre's presence and had to open five cabinets to find a glass, that would definitely raise a red flag.

On a blistering summer afternoon, Latorre walked into the offices of Avid Investment Group. After warm hugs for Quino and me, Latorre explained that his wife and son were sitting outside in a rental car. I insisted that they join us, and they did. In the midst of small talk, I took Latorre aside. "Compadre, I just got confirmation that we received

$350,000 in New York on behalf of your client, and they asked that we be ready to receive another $750,000 over the next two days."

"Mr. Bob, I have some very important issues to discuss with you."

"Luis, if you don't mind, I'd like Antonio to get you checked into the hotel next door. I've taken care of everything; you and your family are my guests. Why don't you get settled, and then come over to my home for cocktails?"

Although Latorre was assessing our every move, I was doing the same. The body language between him and his wife seemed aloof, something you'd expect during a formal business trip, or from a couple that had drifted apart. But that didn't surprise me. Latorre's focus was always on money and the bling in his life. His son clearly admired him, like most twelve-year-olds do. But while we were together, Latorre had other priorities. He left his son's needs to his wife, using every minute with us to search for flaws in what we claimed.

"Luis, I live just across the inlet behind your hotel. Antonio will pick you up when you're ready. Tonight, I'd like you and your family to join all of us for a wonderful Italian dinner at a restaurant owned by my cousin, Dominic. It would be good for you to meet him, so you can get a sense of the loyalty in our group." I let Latorre know that, unless there was an urgent need to discuss business sooner, Antonio and I would meet him at my office the next morning to discuss how we could make each other a fortune.

After pleasantries at my home and Latorre's presentation of gifts for each of us, we all drove to Michelle's, Dominic's family-style Italian restaurant. It wasn't anything special, just huge portions of excellent traditional Italian dishes. It wasn't the food that I wanted Latorre to experience; it was Dominic. My mythical cousin took to the stage and offered his close parallel to Luca Brasi in Mario Puzo's *The Godfather*.

"Mr. Latorre, my cousin tells me you are an important man in Colombia," Dominic began. "You need to know that I and our people are dedicated to watching my cousin's back, and there isn't anything we wouldn't do for him, nothing whatsoever, if you get my drift." With that, he made a subtle hand gesture below table height, so only Latorre could see him pointing his index finger and moving his thumb like the drop of a handgun's hammer. "So, nothing personal, but if my cousin gives me the word, I and everyone in our family will do whatever he says in order to make things right. The bottom line is that if you or any of your people fuck with him, I'll become your worst nightmare. But if you're with us, your enemies are our enemies, and we'll make things right for you, too. Get it?" Dominic offered his death stare, and Latorre soaked it in with slightly raised eyebrows and a faint nod of acknowledgment.

By the end of the evening, Latorre knew that if he crossed me, he would have to deal with something much bigger. For my security, that was the message I wanted to send, and it was definitely received.

The next morning, I started the day with a gift. "Luis, I know it costs you a lot to use your Colombian cell phone here in the States. You're welcome to use this US phone while you're here. Just mail it back to me before you leave the country." Although Latorre thought I was being kind, his use of the phone would give us a clearer picture of his US contacts, and maybe more.

Latorre couldn't wait to spill details. He gave us names and facts about many of his contacts in the drug and money-laundering worlds, including his most important: Miguel Rosenberg, a Jewish Colombian stockbroker in Bogotá who had the trust of Miguel Rodriguez-Orejuela, the head of the Cali cartel. Rosenberg had lived in Colombia during all of his sixty or so years and had at one time owned a factory that man-ufactured soaps. Considered a brilliant businessman whose genius was obvious from his having mastered six languages, Rosenberg had started working with Latorre in the money-laundering business two years prior, after Rosenberg's son had been kidnapped by terrorists and he paid millions in ransom to have him safely released. Laundering became an economic necessity for Rosenberg to recoup his losses.

Rosenberg's and Latorre's money-laundering success was tied to their longtime friendship with an attorney in Bogotá, a graduate of Universidad Libre in Bogotá who outwardly practiced civil law, but who was also one of the most trusted money brokers for the leaders of the Cali cartel. Latorre had met the lawyer when they were both members of the prestigious El Rancho country club in Bogotá. Latorre coughed up his name.

The leaders of the cartel had other reasons to trust Latorre. Ten years prior, he had established a friendship with Miguel Rodriguez-Orejuela, when the cartel leader was the president of a bank. Latorre's message: "Bob, I'm your connection to the people at the top."

While at my office, Latorre received a call from his partner, Pedro Rodriguez-Castro. Seconds later, Latorre gave us more details. We'd been contracted to make two half-million-dollar pickups in New York within a week. Clearly, we had everyone's trust. Al Melendez had picked up $350,000 in New York the day before, and another $260,000 at about the time Latorre arrived at my office.

In the money business, codes are important. Guys like Latorre in Colombia and Baldasare in the US know that the cops are listening. So Latorre delivered the latest codes. "Boxes of fruit" meant thousands of US dollars: five hundred thousand dollars would be five hundred boxes of fruit. Latorre set codes for the key cities in which we received cash: Miami, New York, LA, Houston, and San Juan. Then, the icing on the cake, Latorre gave us the names of his contacts inside two international banks in Miami. We were to meet them and establish accounts, as he had, in the name of a BVI corporation. His bankers knew the truth of the transactions but turned a blind eye. Most importantly, Latorre wanted to make sure we knew when it was not advisable to recontact someone who had been arrested. Latorre would refer to that type of a person as being "sick," and if it was thought that the person was cooperating with the cops, he would note that the person was "contagious." In the "hospital" meant in jail.

Before Latorre and his family left for Disney World, I met with him privately. "Luis, I need to know if our relationship will become something special. We both need some time to assess, but I can't expose my people to someone who isn't one hundred percent in. Soon, you must decide if you're all in. If not, I'm out. I say this with respect, because I sense we can do great things together."

He stared. "I get it, but my life and the lives of my family depend on this decision. Give me a little more time. And by the way, my partner, Pedro Rodriguez-Castro, and his family will be visiting you here in Sarasota in two weeks. Please take care of them as well as you've taken care of us. It's important that we get to really know you, if you know what I mean." His message was delivered with a smile, but in a way that I knew was dead serious.

When Rodriguez-Castro and his wife, Alba, showed up in Sarasota with their son, daughter, and niece, Rodriguez-Castro dropped his guard. He had fewer street smarts than Latorre. In an effort to drum up business, he started calling his main contacts in Cali. Because he was a penny pincher, Rodriguez-Castro made the calls from Quino's cell phone. Now we had the key numbers in Cali from which money deals were coordinated.

Rodriguez-Castro gave us more details about the lawyer in Bogotá who worked closely with Latorre, Rosenberg, and cartel leaders. Their business was global. They had many clients with fortunes waiting to be picked up in Spain, Italy, and Germany.

Rodriguez-Castro's attention to detail was evident as he explained how he would disguise instructions sent to us by fax. The fax would reference an "invoice number." Dividing that number by five would yield the seven-digit phone number of the US-based courier holding money that was ready to be picked up in a given city, which would be referenced by code in the body of the fax.

It seemed as though we had dodged a lot of credibility bullets and were likely to get the chance to meet a few of the people above Latorre and Rodriguez-Castro in the food chain of Cali money laundering. At least it seemed that way, until we agreed to pick up more cash in Manhattan.

On the heels of Rodriguez-Castro's visit, we received two half-million-dollar deliveries on one day in Manhattan. Unfortunately, that was like throwing blood into shark-infested waters, except these sharks were the DEA agents in the Big Apple. Despite our begging, they were all over the drop-offs to Al Melendez. My plea for caution to our guys in Manhattan fell on deaf ears.

"Listen, guys. These cartel couriers are testing us. That's the word I got from my informant in Colombia. Please hold back as much as you can on the surveillance."

I hate to say it, but our people in New York either didn't care or were blinded by their perception that they were smarter than the crooks. Most of their agents on surveillance fit the cartel's warnings about the appearance of typical DEA agents. They were gringos, in good shape, in their mid-to-late twenties, wearing solid-colored pullover collared shirts, jeans, running shoes, and fanny packs that held their service revolvers. They might as well have worn uniforms. The Colombians on the street ahead of the drop picked up on our surveillance guys. They were so easy to spot that, after the drop, the cartel's countersurveillance people followed one of our surveillance agents straight back to the DEA office on Tenth Avenue in the Chelsea area of Manhattan, which they quickly reported to their bosses in Colombia.

Quino heard the ugly story directly from his New York cartel contact. "Los Feos watched the exchange. We followed a gray Land Rover from the drop to DEA Headquarters in Manhattan." That car was driven by a newbie DEA agent who hadn't learned the importance of respecting his adversaries. His fellow agents in Manhattan should have put him in check.

Worse yet, after that disaster, we asked DEA New York for permission to pick up from another courier and were refused. According to the New York brass: "No way. We know about that cartel player, and we will be taking him down in a month." We had to walk away from our deal, but a New York undercover agent met with the same courier the next day, received one million dollars, and had it laundered. It was getting hard to figure out who was betraying whom in this game. Beyond costing us all of the goodwill we'd built with Latorre, this "game" had the potential of costing us our lives. I needed to convince Latorre that if there were problems, it wasn't us.

In the middle of the night, I arranged for Latorre to call me at one of the four pay phones we routinely used when our conversations were too delicate to make from my office. As soon as I picked up the phone, I took charge. "*Hermano* [brother], from the feedback we're getting about business in the Towers, my partners and I think it is best that we shut that factory [stop accepting money in that city] for now. We think Los Feos may have been around. We need to figure out where the weaknesses are, on your side or ours. The fires aren't burning only in the Towers, but we never got details from your people about the problem in Houston. Both of those factories are closed until further notice."

Latorre confided that, although he considered me a partner, more importantly, I was his very good friend. He promised to protect and defend me against accusations that I wasn't for real. Latorre swore he was prepared to do whatever I thought was necessary to continue our partnership, but then he added his omen. "By the way, I took a lot of great pictures when we were with you in Sarasota. I'll send you copies. The ones of you and your wife came out very clear."

I recognized the message he was sending. It would be easy to dispatch someone to eliminate the problem, if the problem was me, and it would be a very ugly ending. That was the cartel's signature. No traitor died without unspeakable agony.

A few days later, at one of the pay phones, I spoke with Latorre again. "Bob, 'Pony' [code for Miguel Rosenberg] visited me at my office today. I was forced to accompany him to the office of the attorney in

Bogotá who represents Los Duros. The Peruvian from Houston, Vicuna, was there with two guys. They made it clear. They say Antonio is either an informant or a DEA agent." The Bogotá lawyer and Rosenberg had said that they and their Cali clients analyzed the events in Houston and the Towers very closely. Rosenberg was certain and unmovable on this point. They wanted Antonio to come to Colombia to answer questions, just like Vicuna had done, but Latorre was concerned that he wouldn't be able to guarantee Antonio's safety if he came to Bogotá.

"Listen, Bob. I'll be honest. I was concerned about a few things when we were in Sarasota. There weren't enough personal items in your home, but Jaime told me this is a home you just moved into ten days before we arrived, and you only use it for meetings with clients. So that makes sense. When I tested you to take more money in Houston and you turned that down, that went a long way with me. Your shutting down in the Towers until questions can be answered is reassuring. Your business roots tell me you are for real. I have to ask you a big favor. Would you have Antonio keep a low profile for a few months? Right now, he is concerning everyone."

"Luis, we are partners. I trust you." I told Latorre I'd make some adjustments and keep Antonio in the background, but I begged him to get me as much information as he could about anything that looked odd in Houston or New York. I told him we had to keep those cities closed for now, and we should instead focus on Las Playas (the Beaches, code for Miami).

Within hours, Jaime called. "Listen, Bob. I've been in Latorre's office with Rosenberg and the other main guys. Luis is being threatened by the owners of the money lost in Houston. They have serious concerns about Antonio, which has led to a lot of questions about you. I can assure you that your business and home are being watched by people they've hired in the US." Jaime begged me to be extremely careful and avoid contact with "those other people" (meaning DEA). He promised to keep me informed about developments in Bogotá, but above all, he insisted that I needed to watch my back. There was a lot at stake, including our lives.

"I get it, Jaime. I won't take anything for granted. I know the consequences. You are the one who is closest to the fire. I won't let you down. I promise."

It only took a day for the confirmation of Jaime's warning to show up on my doorstep. As I scanned the street with binoculars from my second-floor office, there he was, parked near a side street a block away. A young white male with long, dark hair sat in a Camaro, occasionally lifting a camera with a very wide telephoto lens. He appeared to take pictures of the building, cars in the parking lot, and the surrounding area. He was there for nearly an hour.

I needed to come up with a Hail Mary to upset the momentum Vicuna was having with Rosenberg. It was time to arrange another payphone call with Latorre.

"Luis, I've given up on your getting me answers about the problem in Houston, so my people have a solution. We hired a lawyer who has a man inside the Houston Police Department. We're bankrolling a favor, a copy of the reports that are supposed to tell the entire story. I should have them in two weeks."

"*Perfecto*, Mr. Bob. I have a meeting with these people. Is there anything new you can share with me now?"

I explained that our contact said the reports confirmed that the cops and the IRS were sitting on that house days before Latorre reached out to us to do that job in Houston. The cops had been watching Vicuna for more than a year.

Now I needed to turn the tables on Latorre and grab a victory from the clouds of doubt that had been cast our way. "*Hermano* (brother), I will only show these reports to you and Pony [Rosenberg] in person. You need to come to me. I'd rather meet alone with the two of you." This would be an opportunity to tighten the noose of guilt around Rosenberg's neck.

"The problem is that I've been given thirty days to get this resolved; if not, they will come for me. Before I let that happen, Bob, my family and I will go into hiding."

I told Latorre that if he had any doubts, he shouldn't come to me. I didn't want to waste his time or my own.

"Mr. Bob, I believe in you one hundred percent. *Abrazos, Pony y yo nos veremos en dos semanas.*" ("Hugs, Pony and I will see you in two weeks.")

But Latorre was holding back. There was a new reason he had concerns, a mysterious warning. Late one night, his cell phone had rung. The caller spoke in Spanish, but it was obvious he was from the States. "Luis, this is Frankie. You need to watch *The Hunt for Red October.* That movie holds the answer. That's what you've gotten yourself into with Baldasare. That's what it's all about—defectors." Latorre could hear the clanking of ice in a drink while Frankie slurred his words. The next day, Latorre watched the movie twice, but he couldn't find the message. He kept the call a secret, but it worried him deeply.

Two days before Latorre and Rosenberg were scheduled to arrive, I carried out my daily habit with binoculars, scoping all of the streets surrounding the building. I picked up on a woman in a parked car. She was coy, parked two blocks from the office facing away from the building, but she had binoculars and occasionally looked through them into her rearview and side mirrors, apparently watching the office and my car. Not good.

While my life as Robert Baldasare was becoming increasingly tense, I still had to sneak back to my DEA office occasionally to read the endless cables and other notices sent my way. After taking my car back to the garage of my undercover house and doing what I could to check for a hidden tracker, in the middle of the night, I headed back to Tampa, using every technique I could think of to shake a tail.

The next day, I flipped through cables. There it was, an important alert about two of Pablo Escobar's top people, whose money I'd moved when I was undercover for Customs four years before in Operation C-Chase. My former undercover partner, Emir Abreu, would want to know.

"Brother, this came in a cable from our DEA office in Bogotá. Do you remember Gerardo Moncada and Fernando Galeano, Pablo Escobar's two primary managers that we moved money for back in the day? Well, last month, Escobar thought they were stealing from him, so according to this cable, he had them hung by their feet, their clothes stripped away, and the skin melted off their bodies with blowtorches, before he had them chopped up in little pieces that were burned to ash. No one has been able to find any trace of them. As if that weren't enough punishment, Escobar had his sicarios murder sixteen of Moncada's and Galeano's family and associates. Their bodies were thrown around the streets of Medellín as a message to anyone thinking they could be disloyal. It sounds like the retirement benefits that Escobar gives his men suck."

"Shit, Bob, the normal world has no idea this happens every day. How are things going in your new operation?"

"I'm worried, brother. Something doesn't feel right. I have my doubts about who I can trust. It would be great if we could get together so I can explain."

"Okay. Call when it works for you. *Ten cuidado*." ("Be safe.")

Latorre called next. "Bob, Pedro and I are in Miami and will be visiting you tomorrow. The day before we left, Pony called. His wife has appendicitis, so he couldn't join us. We'll be at your office tomorrow morning."

After hanging up, I froze and replayed our conversation in my mind. There was no doubt that Rosenberg's excuse was bullshit. He didn't make the trip because he thought we were Los Feos. Latorre and Rodriguez either had to be in great fear for their lives, or their common sense was blinded by the potential riches of a relationship with Baldasare—if he wasn't a fed.

When they arrived, Latorre and Rodriguez-Castro looked shaken. They settled into the couches in my office, and the hidden video-recording system caught every word. "Bob, there's a gentleman that we call 'the Doctor' in Bogotá, whom we didn't know. We met him during the problem in Houston. He has an office in Bogotá, and he is known by all the proprietors [cartel leaders]. They call him and they tell him, 'There are five hundred oranges [five hundred thousand dollars] in such and such a place,' and he assigns the deals [decides which launderer receives the money]."

Latorre was intent on giving us insight about the seriousness of his problem. "Pony is a Jew. He usually works with a lot of dollars, and besides that, they kidnapped one of his sons two years ago, and he had to pay an enormous amount of money in dollars. I think about two million. The night that the problem took place [the money was seized in Houston], Pony called my house at eleven o'clock at night. They told me to meet them that night, in a hotel, at one o'clock in the morning, in a bar. I didn't go. I started to picture the guys with machine guns and all that stuff."

Latorre explained that he had met with Rosenberg at the Doctor's law office in Bogotá the next day. The meeting was calm, until three people who had traveled in a private plane from Cali arrived. They included "the Peruvian," the launderer based in Houston who worked directly for the owner of the funds. He was accompanied by a lawyer from Cali who was well known. This lawyer walked with two canes because he was afflicted with polio as a child. Everyone referred to him as "Dr. Death." According to Latorre, Dr. Death earned his name because "he is mean as shit and doesn't have any problem with having people killed." The third person was never introduced, but he represented the owner of the money lost in Houston.

Latorre offered more. "Dr. Death let me talk, and then he told me, 'Look, I definitely assure you that the man that works with you (meaning Quino), if he's not a policeman, he's an informant. We interrogated this man (referring to the Peruvian). We put him under pressure. We scared him. We interrogated him in a warehouse near a gasoline station, far away and stuff, and the man has perfect answers, and I believe him.'"

Latorre shook as he went on. "That day in the meeting, Dr. Death told me, 'You owe us one and a half million dollars, and you will pay it.' And you know how things are over there, like what you see in *Scarface* movies and whatnot, that's not bullshit. I left the meeting feeling very scared. During those days, luckily, there was like some telepathy, because, Bob . . . I was, we were thinking to see which way we were going to go. That was when you said you were going to get some papers."

Latorre made it clear that copies of police reports about the Houston seizure, assuming they cleared Antonio, would be the difference maker. My offer calmed everyone, including Dr. Death. The reality is, it probably saved Latorre's life. What Latorre didn't know was that I had to move mountains at DEA to get approval to show the reports about the seizure. The truth was that Quino had nothing to do with that seizure going down. These reports would eventually come out in litigation over the seizure of the money and any related criminal trials.

"Luis, before I bring out the reports, you must give me your word. I'll let you take one of them back to Colombia, but not the second one. If the second one should fall into the wrong hands, it would be obvious that it could have come from only one source. You must assure me that you will show the one report only to the people from Cali. They cannot keep it, and you must destroy it after you let them read it."

Latorre gave me his word he would abide, but I knew his promise would melt in the shadow of Dr. Death. The report was a prop, but I needed to get every ounce of value out of its use. Latorre stretched forward on the couch, fixed on my every move. I donned surgical gloves; then I slowly turned the dials of the large safe in my office and cracked the door open. With a pair of tweezers, I pulled the reports from a shelf in the safe and walked toward Latorre. "Luis, you have no idea how difficult and costly it was for me to get these." Latorre reached out for the reports like a dehydrated man in a desert grabbing for a glass of cold water. As he read them, he translated them for his partner. As he absorbed every word, his tense demeanor morphed into that of a rookie gambler who had just pulled an inside straight.

Latorre picked up on all the key points. The surveillance in Houston had begun two days before he ever spoke with Quino about picking up cash. The Peruvian had been under investigation for more than a year, and most importantly, only $1.1 million was seized. "Bob, what I conclude from all of this is that the guy [the Peruvian] knew that they were following him. He had stolen some money, because the first time I went to speak with these gentlemen, they spoke about a million five hundred." Latorre deduced that, although the cops seized $1.1 million, the Peruvian must have pocketed another $400,000 and claimed that the seizure was actually $1.5 million.

At that moment, it appeared that our credibility with Latorre and Rodriguez-Castro had never been better. They immediately made moves indicating that their trust had been restored. Rodriguez-Castro rented a phone in Miami. We knew that number, so we would later be able to subpoena records of his calls. He called the Doctor to let him know that they had the report and would be bringing it back to Colombia. After the call, Rodriguez-Castro delivered the Doctor's verdict. "Bob, can you pick up five hundred thousand dollars in New Orleans, and another five hundred thousand in New Jersey?"

I was still wearing the surgical gloves. I held up my outstretched hands and looked at them through my fingers. "New Orleans and New Jersey? Gentlemen, first we need to clean up this mess in Houston to everyone's satisfaction, including mine. When we reach that point, everything is possible, including New Orleans and New Jersey."

Latorre and Rodriguez-Castro explained that, aside from the problem in Houston, Antonio wasn't the best person to receive money from cartel couriers for an important reason that he could never overcome. He was Puerto Rican. The cartel leaders would only be totally at ease if they were handing money over to their own countrymen. But Rodriguez-Castro had a work-around. His cousin, a former university professor in Colombia, was living in New York City, where he was taking classes to obtain a master's degree in international banking. At the same time, he was working for a trafficker, receiving drug money and then using it to buy assets on behalf of a high-level guy in Cali. As the trafficker's front-man, a position referred to in the cartel as a "*testaferro*," he had bought expensive cars, an apartment, and other assets in New York. Rodriguez-Castro's cousin was open to discussing terms about becoming a courier for Baldasare's group.

They also had a second candidate, a Colombian friend living in New York, with experience working in the stock market, the son of a man in Bogotá who worked for Latorre. This candidate ran a management company in Manhattan that supervised the maintenance of several buildings.

But then came the big surprise: Latorre offered to set up a meeting with Rosenberg in Panama. This would be an opportunity for me to win over Rosenberg and dramatically increase our business. "Luis, I have a trip to Panama scheduled in three weeks. I'll be there for at least ten days. Let's plan the meeting during that trip. I have a suite at the Hotel El Panamá where we can meet privately."

Latorre was all in. "I'll set it up. I'd suggest the meeting occur in Bogotá, but it isn't safe for you to come to Colombia until the Houston problem is resolved."

Rodriguez-Castro mentioned that he needed to go to a local mall to buy some shirts. His unexpectedly replacing Rosenberg on this trip led to his not packing enough clothes. After a quick visit to the mall, Latorre and Rodriguez-Castro would meet us at my home for dinner and eventually take a flight back to Miami in the late evening. It appeared that we were rocketing our way back to success, until our friends' trip to the mall brought them face to face with someone who would nearly cost me my life.

6

THE BOMB STARTS TICKING

September–December 1992

While at the mall, Latorre and Rodriguez-Castro shook with fear as a badge flashed. "Gentlemen, as far as you're concerned, I'm Frankie. I'm relieved I caught up with you before you returned to Bogotá. Listen closely. Baldasare is an undercover DEA agent. His businesses are all part of a DEA operation. Everyone working with him is either an agent or informant. I and a group of Colombian businessmen move the same kind of merchandise as your clients. A cop's salary doesn't cut it for me."

Latorre's and Rodriguez-Castro's hearts were pounding.

"Don't worry. I'm on your side. My friends can sell as much coke as your people can deliver. I can also give you the inside scoop about Baldasare's plans. You need to feed him lies about your contacts, and make sure they don't expose anyone important. Work smart; don't cut off your business with him overnight. You need to cover your tracks."

Frankie handed them a piece of paper. "When you get back to Colombia, call me at this number. We'll talk about options. There is no limit to what we can do together." He turned to walk away and almost instantly twisted back. "By the way, this may seem like the luckiest day of your lives, but it is only going to get better from here on. I hope you enjoy the rest of your day with Mr. Baldasare." With that, he offered a little smile and a nod that said, "You're welcome."

As I opened my door with a beaming smile, I had no idea someone had compromised my cover. Latorre and Rodriguez-Castro looked like they had just stepped off a roller coaster; they were rattled. I poured them drinks and tried to put them at ease. To allay the tense vibes, Latorre nervously cracked a joke, but it only magnified his uneasiness.

Before he and Rodriguez-Castro had arrived in Sarasota, Quino and I got word that the DEA office in San Diego was taking down a big money-laundering outfit in an undercover operation. National news reports of that takedown were about to break. The timing couldn't have been worse. As we sat in my waterfront estate on Sarasota Bay, a news bulletin interrupted the cable news station that softly played in my den. The big screen stared Latorre in the face, and his eyes bulged as he looked over my shoulder. I glanced at the screen and jumped to turn up the sound. The reporter said it all. "In coordination with narcotics police in Italy, Colombia, Spain, Canada, and Britain, the US Drug Enforcement Administration has announced the arrest of 169 suspects and the seizure of fifty-four million dollars connected to a major international money-laundering operation. The arrests are the result of a four-year undercover operation dubbed Operation Green Ice. Seven of the people arrested are high-ranking money managers for the Cali cartel . . ."

Latorre turned white, jumped to his feet, and pointed at the screen. One of the people arrested was shown in chains, being escorted by DEA agents. After gasping to catch his breath, Latorre finally blurted, *"Conozco a ese hombre. Dios mío. El es uno de nuestra gente."* ("I know that man. My god. He is one of our people.")

"Luis, I am suspending all business," I interjected. "I need my lawyers to get copies of the court papers filed for this case. I'll send them to you, and we need to talk about whether there are any potential problems for you, your people, or me. We need to make sure we haven't sent wire transfers to any accounts linked to these people. I need a full report from you after you've had a chance to speak with your team down south."

After an hour or so of fretting, it was time to get them to the airport. Conversation was understandably tense. As we waited for the plane, I fumbled through my wallet, a gift from Latorre and his wife. Latorre asked to see it—no problem. He went straight for my (Baldasare's) driver's license and studied it. He smiled. "Bob, you look better than this. You might want to get them to issue you a new one."

He was testing my identity, but I wasn't concerned. My cover was rock solid, or so I thought.

As Latorre and Rodriguez-Castro traveled back to Colombia, Jaime came to the States to brief us about an entirely new group that moved dope money for the men in Cali. He had told them about Baldasare's operation, and they were eager to do business.

"Bob, I was introduced by Cali money brokers to a key player, Guillermo Segura, the manager of the Calle 72 branch of Banco Cafetero. Many of his clients are drug traffickers. He has a law degree and manages the second-largest branch in Bogotá. Segura moves chunks of drug money by disguising it as repatriated export revenue. He has an endless supply of bogus export documents. He's the manager of the branch, so as long as he gets his cut, the funds will flow. There are other employees that do this with him, so there are plenty of eyes to ensure that no whistles blow. He wants to meet with you."

"Okay, Jaime. Let him know I'll meet in Panama."

Upon Jaime's return to Bogotá, Latorre and Rodriguez-Castro called him to their office. With Rosenberg by their side, they cornered him. "Jaime, do you trust Bob one hundred percent?"

"Of course. Why not? Is there something I should know?"

Latorre took the lead. "No. It's just that with that DEA under-cover operation in San Diego, everyone is on edge. Especially since we now have deals backing up. Before we offer them to Bob, I wanted your guarantee that he is okay. Bob gave us papers about the Houston deal, but it seemed strange that there wasn't anything in them about Antonio's car. Some of the people in Cali think they might be phony."

"Luis, I trust him with my life. I've known him for years."

Little did Jaime know that, thanks to Frankie blowing my cover, his guarantee that he'd known me for years put his life in grave danger.

Despite the concerns he expressed to Jaime, Latorre later assured me that there was no overlap between his people and the recent DEA takedown in San Diego, so I agreed to resume business. In less than a week, we received more than two million dollars from couriers in Chicago and Puerto Rico. Just when it looked like things were back on track, Quino shocked me.

On one of the few occasions when I visited the Tampa DEA office, Quino approached me with an air of reluctance. "Listen, Bob. I am grateful. It's been amazing working with and learning from you. You're a great mentor and a true friend. This is a very difficult decision for me, but my department has offered me the opportunity to work in our homicide division. That is an honor given only to the best of the best, and it will really go a long way to enhance my career. Al Melendez is an experienced undercover guy who is in the perfect position to fill my shoes in Operation Pro-Mo. This will also get me out of narcotics and away from the endless head-butting from my sergeant. I hope you understand why I can't turn down this opportunity."

"Gosh, Quino, I don't know what to say. Selfishly, I wish you'd stay with me and see Pro-Mo to the end, but I understand. I'll come up with some kind of story for Latorre and his partner about why you've moved on. Let me have your undercover cell phone."

Quino looked shocked. "Uh, why do you want my phone?"

"Well, if you're out, you're out. The sooner we make the transition, the better." I grabbed the phone. It seemed odd that Quino was nervous about my taking his phone, but I didn't have time to worry about that. With Steven Richards, my source with heavy contacts in Panama, I needed to take a trip to the isthmus of greed.

After clearing Customs and collecting our bags at Tocumen International Airport, we made our way to the street. Stooping outside a black BMW 735i, admiring himself in the passenger sideview mirror as he combed his long, wavy black hair, attorney Rinaldo Laguna was probably the most available playboy in Panama City. His tailored silk suit, flamboyant tie, matching pocket scarf, Italian shoes, and Rolex Presidential announced his wealth. Forty years old, trim, handsome, very well connected, and engaging. Everyone in Panama's elite knew Rinaldo Laguna. According to Richards, Laguna's clients and friends included money launderers, corrupt politicians, and dirty bankers.

Richards took the lead, giving Laguna a big hug. "It is so good to see you, Rinaldo." He turned to me. "I'd like to introduce you to my business associate, Bob Baldasare." We shook hands and exchanged nods. I took the back seat; Richards took the passenger seat. As we glided from the airport, Laguna talked about the things that were important to him, money and women, preferably blonds with blue eyes. He had a girlfriend, and a harem on the side. He had a newly remodeled apartment in Casco Viejo (the Old Quarter), a section of Panama City constructed in 1673. His neighborhood included Club de Clases y Tropas (Class and Troop Club), a popular hangout of his old friend, Panamanian dictator Manuel Noriega.

Offering a hint about my dark side, I volunteered a story. "Noriega created havoc for me when he went to war with the Americans. I had to totally change my methods, move accounts out of Panama, and hide client funds in safer places." It wasn't smart for me, an American, to mention Noriega. It sent Laguna into a passionate rage about "the American atrocity of Operation Just Cause," the military assault on Panama that ended with Noriega being plucked from the country and flown on a US military plane to Miami. Laguna was beside himself. "The fucking Americans. When they flew off with Noriega, they left behind more than two thousand dead Panamanians in my neighborhood. More than two thousand of our people that they didn't have to kill. Most of them were civilians."

Within five minutes, he began his endless questions. "Have you been to Panama before? Where are you from? Did you hear about Operation Green Ice? Do you go to Colombia? Are you married? Do you have kids?" And then his big question, as he stared at me through his rearview mirror, "Are you a DEA agent?"

I had to get him under control. "What, are you writing a fuckin' book?"

Everyone laughed.

When he wasn't asking questions, Laguna was combing his thick, wavy mane of hair with a circular brush, after which he would shake his head and check the placement of each strand in his rearview mirror. He must have done this three times during the bumper-to-bumper drive from the airport to his downtown office.

From what I saw during the ride from the airport, Panama had an overwhelming number of people living in poverty. I later learned a tiny percentage of Panamanians grabbed every penny they could from servicing people around the globe who wanted to hide money, while the masses lived in need. I saw no signs of a middle class. At every red light, another beggar banged on the window, either pleading for money or offering to sell chicle, plátanos, or oranges. Laguna yelled them away and waved his hands in disgust. *"Ve a molestar a alguien más. Sal de aquí."* ("Go bother someone else. Get out of here.")

Nearly every building, including the McDonald's, had civilian security guards brandishing heavy weapons, usually AK-47s or Mac-10s.

We arrived outside Laguna's suite of offices, where a scrappy little middle-aged man sat outside, packing a 9mm semiautomatic under his shirt. My stare triggered Laguna's comment. "Oh, he's my bodyguard."

Laguna's interior office suites were enclosed with glass walls and upscale furniture. He shared the place with his cousin, a national political figure in Panama who proudly displayed his relationships with American politicians. The office walls were adorned with photos of him standing with US politicians: Ronald Reagan, George H. W. Bush, John Glenn, Ted Kennedy. Nothing made sense in Panama.

Laguna explained. "Listen, I just wanted you to know where my office is, and for my staff to know who you are, so they'll let you in whenever you return. We'll save discussions about business for a meeting tomorrow at your hotel, and then we'll go to dinner at one of my favorite restaurants, 1985. They have great French and Swiss cuisine."

Laguna took us to Hotel El Panamá, which would become my base of operation whenever I was in Panama City. The hotel complex consisted of a series of four buildings that formed a large square surrounding an enormous private outdoor area, the jewel of which was a massive kidney-shaped pool that hugged a big thatched-roof bar. The pool included underwater bar seats near a massive open-air restaurant constructed of dark wood beams and topped with red barrel roof tile.

The exterior of the hotel was surrounded by smaller buildings that faced the streets. They included every type of shop and office space. There wasn't anything you really needed from outside this compound, which was why I picked it as the best place from which Baldasare could operate in Panama's business district. Unnecessary trips around town weren't safe, according to the DEA agents assigned to Panama.

As I checked out the hotel's outdoor recreation area, I walked to a railing that overlooked the roof of one of the smaller commercial buildings that surrounded the complex. I was looking for a quiet area to speak to my maker. After a moment of prayer, I opened my eyes with my head bowed, in awe of what I saw strewn along the office roof below. It was in dozens of pieces, but I knew exactly what it was—a demolished sign for the now defunct BCCI. Years before, in my prior undercover role as Robert Musella, I and others had brought the famous Panama

City branch of the bank to its knees. Tens of millions in payoffs had been delivered on behalf of General Manuel Noriega to the very bankers I had dealt with undercover. Hundreds of millions of cartel dollars had been laundered through this branch. I knew this was an omen, but I had no time to contemplate it. Although I'd put off any more meetings with Laguna until the next afternoon, my cover team from Tampa and I had to meet with the DEA staff members in Panama. This was a bureaucratic requirement, to establish a line of communication between the Tampa personnel and those in Panama.

To reduce the chances of blowing my cover, our guys in Panama met us in a room at another hotel. I went there separately, to avoid being seen near anyone who looked like a cop. When I got to the hotel, I jumped on an elevator alone, got off four floors above my destination, walked down the fire exit stairwell to their floor, and made my way to the room. I was always paranoid about being linked to anyone or anything connected to law enforcement.

Two things stood out about this gathering. Our local agents advised that the attorney general (AG) of Panama, an officer responsible for investigating and suppressing crime, was flexing his muscles about being autonomous from Panama's executive, legislative, and judicial branches. Rather than disclose my undercover activities to the president of Panama, or any other elected official, only the AG would know that DEA had an undercover agent working his way into the Panamanian underworld. Despite the AG's claims of trustworthiness, our people knew enough to avoid a double cross. He was told the bare minimum, never enough to enable him to compromise the operation. Like using a shiny metal object to distract, we highlighted that most of our meetings would be with Colombian traffickers and downplayed the local crooks we expected to meet. For operation security, the AG didn't know my undercover name or bona fides.

Panamanian politicians had too many secret ties to bad things happening in the country, and we all knew it. Although it was reassuring that the AG claimed he would act as my safety net, his background suggested otherwise. Only a few years earlier, he had been the legal adviser to and a board member of First Interamericas Bank (FIB), owned by Gilberto and Miguel Rodriguez-Orejuela, the two primary leaders of the Cali drug cartel. While the AG held key positions within the bank, it became a favorite avenue of laundering for Medellín drug cartel member Jorge Ochoa. Other FIB board members were also men of power in Panama. They would become Panama's chief justice of the Supreme Court and the Treasury minister. In Panama, the leaders of the Cali cartel had friends in high places, a reality that added to the traditional deadly risks of undercover work.

The other things that stuck out at this meeting were the appearance and mannerisms of one of the Panama-based DEA agents, Richard Fekete. He showed up at the hotel room dressed in jungle fatigues, carrying an arsenal of guns, some in exposed holsters, some concealed. When he spoke, it was all about tactical issues and deadly force. When the meeting was over, the three of us from Tampa looked at each other and wondered what we'd just witnessed. Fekete seemed to envision himself on a battlefield, ready to whack the first person he perceived as a threat.

Our impression that Fekete appeared to be a walking time bomb tragically bore out a few years later when, in a drunken stupor at a Metro-Dade Police Christmas party, he was led by a fellow agent into the back seat of an unmarked DEA car with the expectation that he would be safely brought to his home. Unfortunately, after gaining semiconsciousness from a delirious drunken haze, he pulled out his 9mm semiautomatic Glock and put five rounds in the coworker driving him home, three to the head and two to the body. The agent died at the scene, and Fekete didn't realize what he'd done until he sobered up in the hospital. Crazy things like this seemed to happen more often than most of us hoped in the law enforcement world.

The next afternoon, as we sipped beers, Laguna was all about verifying. He wanted the names of my contacts in Colombia who moved Cali money. "I have a client—he's gonna be here tomorrow, so I'm going to call, okay? I'm going to ask if they know these people [Baldasare's people in Colombia]. Do you mind?"

I sat calmly. "It's okay. I understand."

He made the call, providing the names of Latorre, Rodriguez-Castro, Jaime, and their companies. According to Laguna, his Colombian contact "works for a very strong Colombian group."

After speaking with his man in Cali, Laguna started to open up. He explained that he had major contacts in the Colón Free Zone of Panama that were "laundering big-time." As the conversation got more sensitive, he leaned forward and whispered, "We have the people, the people in Miami for this. We have a guy over in . . . by the Colón Free Zone. He has a partner in Miami who is a resident down there."

Before we left for dinner, Laguna whispered more. "I'm going to introduce you to these people, okay?" Having been quickly forgotten by crooks he'd introduced to one another in the past, Laguna let me know that, although he would become dispensable after putting me in touch with his friend, he'd appreciate a decent commission for having made the introduction. This was his hope with regard to every crook he brought my way. I assured him, "You can count on it, Rinaldo."

After dinner, Laguna took us to a disco. As we walked in, he noticed a table of five ladies he knew well. He took charge, letting the ladies know they looked magnificent, and how happy he would be if we could share their charming company. They jumped at the chance. They knew Laguna was a sure ticket to laughs, long bill-free nights, and a facade of love. As we chatted over drinks, I noticed Richards was beginning to slur his words. I lost track of him, but half an hour later, I heard the crowd near the dance floor roaring with laughter. I worked my way to the commotion and was shocked to see one person on the dance floor, circled by onlookers five deep. It was Richards. He was dancing with himself, running in circles, flailing his arms like a bird, and occasionally attempting the world's worst version of break dancing. The five women had followed me to this spectacle and couldn't resist. "Bob, is this an American custom?" They burst out laughing. The embarrassment was overwhelming. In the midst of hysterics and howling, I walked out, with no idea of how to get back to my hotel. While walking in the wrong direction, I found a cab. I was fuming. This was not an image I would ever permit for anyone in business with Robert Baldasare.

The next morning, after assurances from Richards that he would refrain from further drunken B-boy acts, or anything else embarrassing, he had bad news. His plan to introduce me to a major player in Panama was delayed. Gilbert Straub, a US citizen and fugitive, was in Europe. Straub had a luxury apartment in Panama and a sprawling estate outside of London. According to Richards, Straub worked closely with organized crime figures in Italy, Russia, the US, and several other countries. I'd be meeting Straub's son, but his father was the man in charge. Straub was a former lieutenant of Robert Vesco, and a codefendant with Vesco on the US charges they had run from decades before. Vesco was hiding in Cuba, but Straub preferred his protection in Panama, where he ran a management firm that controlled a laundry list of offshore companies that hid the identities and wealth of his clients. He was happy to do the same for me and my people.

A meeting with Laguna at his office led to his forming Panamanian companies that I could use to launder. The cost was minimal, $600 per company for Laguna's time, plus $150 per year for each company. He and his office staff would front as the officers and directors of the company, so my interests were hidden. But he also gave me unregistered certified powers of attorney that enabled me to open bank accounts for the company. Added to the package were undated letters of resignation from the officers and directors of record, in case I lost faith in the nominees he used to shelter me. I had everything I needed to secretly control bank accounts for each company he formed.

Laguna was further prepared to introduce me to several bank executives and businessmen who moved dirty money, but he warned that everyone in Panama was on edge because of DEA's Operation Green Ice. Even though he would introduce me to people who trusted him, they might not talk openly. "Let me tell you something. They think like everybody is from the DEA, you know."

Of all his contacts, Laguna was certain the best for me would be Enrique Burman, a young Argentinian Jew who spoke seven languages and, with a partner in Miami, operated a successful import/export company in the Colón Free Zone of Panama. "Bob, let me call Enrique and see if we can meet with him tonight."

Knowing that Burman was as nervous as everyone else in Panama, Laguna lied and told him he had known me for five years. Burman agreed to meet us after dinner that night at Coco's, one of Laguna's favorite nightclubs.

At dinner, Laguna jumped to greet Burman as he approached our table. "Enrique, it is my pleasure to introduce you to Bob Baldasare, an old friend of mine from Florida."

"Pleasure to meet you, Bob. I must apologize for making this a very short first meeting. I have an important client here from Argentina that I must entertain. I need to focus on closing an important deal. I intend to be in Miami in the near future and would like to meet you then."

I agreed.

Burman didn't look the part. Easily mistaken for a college student, he was short, slight of build, with short black hair and a mustache. He wore the best clothes and jewelry. After he left, Laguna offered more. "His import/export company has contracts with some of the biggest manufacturers in the States. He uses those contacts as a cover and launders big money for Colombians through false invoices."

Despite the opportunities in Panama, and my eagerness to learn more about Burman, I had to get back to the US and focus on rebuilding the rapport with Latorre. Al Melendez had picked up more than a million in cash in Puerto Rico from Latorre's couriers and was scheduled to pick up more in New York, but I could feel Latorre beginning to withdraw. Fewer deals were offered. His conversations were becoming increasingly short and cold. Then the DEA office in New York seized seven hundred thousand dollars and fifty-four kilos of blow from a courier that worked for Latorre's client, further challenging our relationship. My gut told me that red flags about Baldasare were flying around in Latorre's mind.

After a short trip back to Sarasota to put out fires, my itch to get back down south became irresistible. Richards had some of the biggest fish in Panama's underworld lined up to meet me, but I would make this trip without him. Besides, I had no concerns about working undercover in Panama with little or no backup. I had a solid cover and hadn't sensed any threat. I had no idea I was walking into an alliance that would end with a gruesome murder.

7

THE REAL PANAMA

December 1992–January 1993

As I walked out of the Tocumen airport, Laguna and one of his friends were waiting for me in his luxury BMW. "Bob, this is Domingo, my good friend. I'm sorry we didn't get here sooner. We'd made arrangements for you to bypass Customs, but our guy didn't get the word in time, and your flight was early. We have some proposals we'd like to discuss. When will you be available?"

Like every other member of the underbelly of Panama's elite who thought I was a launderer, they came at me like ants on sugar, constantly offering the next best scheme. I had to stay focused.

"I'll have to let you know tomorrow. I have a lot of meetings lined up, including one with the manager of the Bogotá branch of Banco Cafetero and some other friends of mine from Colombia."

Laguna loved to joke. "Oh, here in Panama, we call that institution Banco Coke-atero." He and Domingo howled with laughter.

"I'll be here for more than a week. I'm hoping to get an opportunity to speak to your friend, Burman. Can you set that up?"

"No problem. He's eager to meet you, too. So, I'll make sure that happens."

That night, Gilbert Straub paid me a visit at the Hotel El Panamá. He looked nothing like what I expected. From a distance, his stiff gait and short, stout physique broadcast the appearance of an oncoming large penguin. To judge him by his looks would be anyone's folly. Within minutes, it was obvious that he was articulate, confident, worldly, intelligent, and very experienced. His grandfatherly air and cordial manner were curveballs that could lead to underestimating his power, but his appearance seemed inconsistent with his history. Straub was much more than just a codefendant—with his former boss, Robert Vesco, and others—in the theft of over one hundred million dollars from unsuspecting investors. Though a US fugitive, Straub was a world traveler, with connections to reputed mobsters and other criminals in an array of countries.

What grabbed me the most about him were his ties to illegal cash contributions to the Committee to Re-elect the President (Nixon), some of which were supposedly passed to hush the Watergate burglars nearly two decades before I met him. The Watergate burglary was one of the events that drove me to a career as a fed, focused on following the trail of dirty money to identify crime bosses hiding behind armies of underlings. Deep Throat, the FBI agent who famously inspired *Washington Post* reporters Woodward and Bernstein to "follow the money," captured my imagination and inspired me. Deep Throat's mantra led me to where I was at that very moment.

Straub was all about caution. His brain was wired to assess constantly whether he was in danger of being snatched by the long arm of the US government. When we met poolside at the El Panamá, he brought a friend. Both of them knew I was a launderer for the Cali drug cartel. Straub had heard that from Richards and others. After some small talk, he began cautiously dropping names. "We work for a family called Cellini," he said, a family with interests in casinos around the world.

Straub knew all of the Cellini brothers, sons of an Italian barber who migrated to Ohio. The oldest son, Dino, was an associate of mob boss Santo Trafficante and Meyer Lansky. Before Fidel Castro closed Cellini's operations in Cuba and threw him out of the country, he operated two casinos there for the mob. He also managed casinos in the Bahamas for Lansky. He later ran more casinos in Rome and London, but the obvious link to Straub was that Cellini and other members of his family were financially entangled in casinos and other ventures with the Vesco group.

To match Straub's caution and show him that we had traits in common, I leaned toward him and made a request. "I wonder if it wouldn't be a good idea for us to have a private discussion about some of my needs. I'm happy to discuss them with you . . ." I paused and slightly tipped my head toward his companion. "But I just think that it would be good for it to be a very private conversation."

Straub took my lead and gave the order to his associate. "He's a very accommodating young man. He can go inside and organize another drink for us, and then, you know, maybe look at the art gallery."

We were alone. "I apologize, Gil, but I think that's just better . . . safer for him and for me."

Straub smiled. "Apologies not necessary."

I gave him the rundown. My clients were from Cali and generated a huge amount of cash in the US and Europe. It was our job to legitimize their money, but the volume was outpacing our capabilities. We now had options to handle twenty million dollars a month, and I was looking for experienced help.

Straub's body signaled interest, but his words were measured. "I have to assume two things. Number one, that you are not, officially or unofficially, representing agents serving any government agency. And that there is nothing that we are discussing that could in any way be construed as illegal."

I knew that both my words and the reply that my body broadcast had to be unflappable. I had to act like a crook, not like an agent. I could clarify the source of my client's money in later conversations. With a slight grunt that acknowledged the silliness of his concerns, I delivered, "Whatever you want to say. It's fine with me."

That wasn't good enough. "I have to assume that this is a business conversation that goes by two conditions: this is not for the purpose of entrapment, or for the purpose of anything that could be construed in any view to be illegal, obviously. Yes?"

With a big grin, I gave him what he wanted. "Obviously."

Straub made it clear that he didn't want anyone taking a run at him. "I'm discussing it with you as a person who is coming to us with Steven Richards, somebody we like and we trust. And therefore, we're prepared to like and trust you. I've run into an awful lot of enforcement people in my life, and they're . . . they're different people."

I told him I understood his caution. "I carry a lot of responsibility. I definitely have no intention of dancing with a partner who doesn't know the steps, okay? I can't afford the problems that could come from that."

Straub was wanted in the States, a good reason for constantly questioning my bona fides. "As long as we have the understanding that you're who you say you are."

I told him he could relax; I had no secrets.

Then Straub began apologizing. "You can be a target outside the States. They have a long arm. You've got to be very careful, very careful. I mean, with the technology today, they could be beaming our conversation into Langley. You've got to be aware of that. Actually, that's why on phones I'm very careful, as I know you are."

Little did he know I was recording every word.

"Gil, someday years from now, we're going to sit back and laugh about the beginning of this discussion." I let him know that I was in no rush whatsoever. I expected to be in and out of Panama for the next few years, and at any point when he felt the time had come for us to be frank with one another, I'd be happy to resume the conversation.

That night my phone rang. It was Richards. After my poolside meeting, Straub had called him, inquiring as to how well Richards knew me. "Bob, I let him know we've known each other for several years. He sounded interested. I just wanted to give you a heads-up."

Less than twenty-four hours later, Straub was ready to meet again. Poolside, I let him know how I felt. "I got the distinct impression that you had some doubts about my loyalty, and I just—"

He cut me off. "I've got to be very careful, like everybody does."

Since Straub had major US mob connections, I needed to distance myself from claims that I had mob connections, which would be too easy for him to disprove. But I wanted to do that in a way that said, *I know about that world, and I have other serious backing.* I let Straub know that I grew up in a neighborhood on Staten Island that was a mecca for Italian American immigrants, including people who later went on to be wiseguys. But I made it clear that I wanted nothing to do with them. "I saw a lot of people working hard on the street, and a lot of them were working for guys [mobsters] who sat around in fucking social clubs and didn't do a goddamn thing. I could never understand why. But the bottom line is, I didn't want any part of their stuff." I had no intention of giving up half of what I made to "pay tribute" to a boss.

Straub liked my spunk, and I decided it was time to get something else important on the record. I had to document that he knew the source of my funds and make sure he knew that any attempt to steal money from me and my clients would come with serious consequences. My hidden recorder captured it all.

"The guys that I work with are out of Cali. They're very business-like. Um, I'm standing around by a pool; we have a moment of privacy, so I'll just say this once. They're the most gifted people you could possibly find in the cocaine business. They are not cowboys running around with machine guns. You need to understand the delicacy of some of the things that we do. I may appear at times to be a mark, but I'm not a mark, and my friends are very serious people, and I just want to protect myself by being a little bit frank."

It was important to remind him that I wasn't pushing him. "We could get to know each other," I suggested, "for maybe a year or so, and I mean, business is going to be there for a long time. I'm in no rush."

Straub was satisfied. "This position of yours is perfectly understandable, regardless of who your clients are, or what they do." Based on his own proximity to the underworld, he voiced his assessment of the Mafia. "There is no such thing as organized crime. If anything, it's disorganized crime. I've never seen such an incompetent group."

Straub began to explain how we could work together. He specialized in constructing corporations that offered anonymity. He dealt in havens all over the world, but Panama was his current home base. The beneficial owners of the companies and the funds that ran through his accounts would remain secret. These companies could be organized in a maze of transactions that would make fund tracing impossible.

When it came to animals that laundered, Straub was among the best in show. If my clients wanted to exchange cash for either gold bullion, diamonds, or shipments of crude oil, he could arrange that through his contacts in Russia. Deliveries of gold could be made just about anywhere, but Panama would be easiest.

By the end of the meeting, we shook hands and exchanged smiles. It was clear we would be doing business soon.

Just as I gained Straub's trust, I lost some more of Latorre's. Our New York office took down another of his client's couriers that was preparing a delivery of $640,000 to us. This could not go on forever. Latorre's people would eventually decide to collect their debt in blood, and they knew I was in Panama City, a mere ninety-minute flight from their stronghold.

Jaime flew in from Bogotá with Guillermo Segura, the manager of one of the Bogotá branches of Banco Cafetero. To break the ice, we met for dinner with a few of my friends in Panama, including Laguna. It was strictly casual. Business was barely mentioned. By coincidence, Enrique Burman, Laguna's hot prospect for laundering in Panama, strolled through the restaurant and pulled me aside. He named the bank through which he could move money and explained that he was highly successful because for every million dollars of dirty money he moved, he moved fifteen million dollars in legitimate export revenue. He assured me it would soon be time for us to talk details.

The next day, Jaime and I met with Segura at the El Panamá's poolside restaurant. As usual, I was wired.

Segura was a sharp dresser, in good shape, refined, and well educated. He had achieved a lot in his thirty-three years, having become an attorney, bank manager, and cartel resource. In short order, Segura confirmed that he worked directly with members of the Orejuela family, including Gilberto and Miguel Rodriguez-Orejuela, the brothers who ran the Cali cartel. At the moment, his clients had tens of millions in drug money that had been physically smuggled from the US and Europe to Colombia. They wanted that converted to wire transfers and sent to accounts in havens like Switzerland. They also routinely accumulated millions in several US cities that needed to be received and wire transferred. Segura assured me that if we could come to terms about sharing profits, he could steer this business my way. He was anxious to get started. He simply needed to hear details about my capabilities. I explained it all.

While sparring with Segura over money-laundering fees, I noticed Enrique Burman sitting four tables away, engaged in intense discussion with two Latin men who looked rough, blue-collar, and serious. Burman later came over and assured me that we would meet soon to discuss business. He volunteered that the two men with him had arrived unexpectedly. As he returned to his table, I saw him hand his business card to one of his guests. There weren't a lot of smiles at their table, but I was too occupied with Segura to garner more.

That night, Burman and I met privately at the El Panamá's outdoor restaurant. It was obvious he was very highly educated, a focused, no-nonsense businessman who was all about detail. How else could someone command seven languages? He had options for cleaning money. He worked with an individual who had accounts in the US and a relationship with four different casinos. Together they operated an international bulk precious metals company that was a front for moving dirty money. He had couriers in Miami, New York, and Los Angeles who could accept cash from cartel bagmen. Because his operation was international, and he had accounts with big balances, he could send a wire transfer in payment of a cash pickup within six hours of receiving dollars on the street. He had the same resources in Spain, Italy, Switzerland, and Japan. All of his records were maintained on password-protected computers programmed to erase all data if the proper password wasn't used. He had no phone books, simply storing all phone numbers and passwords in his head. He had a photographic memory.

Burman also had couriers who would move cash from the US to Panama. They worked with corrupt Customs officials and charged 6 percent to move money between countries. Burman had a private pilot's license and a relative who worked in one of the major global accounting firms that helped him launder. With worldwide operations, there wasn't much he couldn't do. He credited his success to the fact that 95 percent of his money movements were legit. His cover was a relationship with major international manufacturing companies whose products he bought and distributed.

As we talked, I noticed two guys at a nearby table who looked thick, muscular, and menacing. They seemed to be paying more attention to us than normal. To flush out the connection, I turned to Burman.

With a furrowed brow, I leaned my head in the direction of the thugs, winced, and quickly glanced my eyes toward them. He got the message.

"Bob, I've come alone. The sooner we start business, the sooner I'll believe in you."

The next day, I sent a message to Burman to order a fax machine for Jaime in Colombia. Burman called. "Bob, I got your note. I'll send a runner to your hotel to pick up payment. Tell your friends their fax will arrive in Bogotá shortly."

"Enrique, soon I'll send you details about what will hopefully be our first of many deals. Please call me after you get the instructions."

Within hours, Burman went radio silent. Over the next two weeks, I made repeated calls and sent repeated faxes in an effort to reach him at his home and business. They all went unanswered. Was my cover blown? That would have been better than the reality.

Around the time of my last attempt to find Burman, a persistent flutter of vultures around the historic Corozal American Cemetery near the banks of the Panama Canal caught the attention of local authorities. Many of the birds were inside the charred remains of a high-end late-model Mercedes sedan. What the authorities found under the feasting birds was the skeletal remains of Burman. He had been kidnapped, and his skull had been crushed with some sort of blunt instrument. He had been doused with gasoline and set aflame. All that remained were charred body parts and shreds of expensive clothing.

Within days after the confirmation of Burman's fate, our office in Puerto Rico gave Latorre and his people another red flag of doubt to pin on me. A courier that had occasionally dropped cash off to Al Melendez in San Juan was taken down. The seven hundred thousand dollars in his car was seized. I tried to reach Latorre or his partner by phone, but as had been the case for nearly ten days, their secretary claimed they were either out of town or in a meeting. Clearly, there was some reason Latorre didn't want to speak with me. Before I could figure out my next best move, it happened—another kidnapping.

8

BAIT AND SWITCH

February 1993

Latorre's Cali contacts apparently didn't link us to their seven-hundred-thousand-dollar loss in Puerto Rico. They came back with another San Juan deal, this time for $1.2 million, which needed to go through smoothly or the cartel would surely retaliate. Al Melendez made the pickup.

Taking cash from cartel couriers in San Juan, Puerto Rico, in the early 1990s was more treacherous than in any other city. The per capita murder rate in Puerto Rico was five times what it was in the United States, and the only way to enhance Melendez's safety was to increase the number of officers covering him. On this occasion, there were nineteen cops on the street, trying to blend into the city's movements. Some of the officers were feds, but some were from the Puerto Rico Special Investigations Bureau (SIB).

Melendez was surprised when the cartel courier showed up with two bodyguards who were clearly packing semiautomatics in their waistbands. "Amigo, why the company and the heat?"

"Señor, this fucking town is crazy. Last year, when I met with a guy like you, he and his friends tried to jack me up and steal the money. That'll never happen again. They shot me up good, but unlike them, I walked away from the fight."

Melendez could see the scars of bullet wounds on the guy's face, neck, and arms. He wore them like medals of honor. The drop went smoothly, and Melendez eventually met up with his cover team to turn over the bags of cash. As he related his conversation with the courier, one of the SIB officers spoke up. "I hate to say this, but it's the truth. That guy is my cousin. I knew he got shot last year, but I had no idea it related to this kind of shit." The jaws of the rest of the cover team dropped, but that kind of story had become pretty common in Puerto Rico. Things were so bad on the island that anyone who wanted to get rich quick jumped on either the train to wealth, or the one to death.

That night, as Melendez relaxed on the balcony of his hotel room, he heard it—pop, pop, pop, pop—the unmistakable sound of a semi-automatic. As he peeked over the balcony wall from two stories above, Melendez saw what turned out to be an off-duty cop killing an intended car jacker. Sadly, the good people of Puerto Rico had been enduring this for years. Despite the significant danger Melendez faced picking up many millions from cartel couriers, he remained a rock of confidence on the street.

Once the funds were sent to me, they flew through Avid Investment Group, then through Latorre's front companies, and ultimately to a cartel account at Banco Cafetero. Everyone was pleased, so pleased that Latorre and Rodriguez-Castro were invited to meet some new clients in Cali.

When their flight arrived, they were picked up by Carlos and Juan, two men who worked with Dr. Death. As the SUV rumbled down the highway, it became obvious they were being taken out of town. This had never happened before. Exchanging nervous glances with Rodriguez-Castro, Latorre spoke up. "Carlos, where are we going?"

"Luis, these guys never meet downtown. We're going to their farm. We should be there in thirty minutes. Relax. You're lucky they trust you. They have tons that need to be moved."

Latorre chain-smoked half a pack of cigarettes as his imagination took over and he began to sense that this might be a one-way trip. As they approached the farmhouse, heavily armed guards were everywhere. Latorre and Rodriguez-Castro were escorted to a room and told to sit together on the couch. Moments later, they heard a sequence of thuds and scrapes, which repeated ten times before the door opened. Then they watched in fear as Dr. Death struggled, thudding his canes forward and then dragging his braced legs toward the couch.

He was in a rage. The semiautomatic tucked in his waistband was a clear sign of what was to come. This was all about the money lost when Quino and Melendez were in Houston. He spoke in a growl. "You lost our fucking money, and I want it back." He leaned into Latorre's face, his eyes bulging and his neck veins popping. "We hired a lawyer in Houston for the Peruvian. The lawyer now has an official report from the police department. It says the same thing as the report you got from your partner in the US, except it has one piece of new news. There is an informant, and it has to be Antonio, the guy your partner in the States sent to get the money. Luis, until we get our money, this is your new home. We want Antonio here with the Peruvian so we can ask them both questions and solve this, one way or another. You need to call your partner in Sarasota and give him my message. Send us our money or Antonio."

Latorre tried to talk his way out of the jam. "Doctor, please," he pleaded meekly. "With all my respect, I say I will make this right. I vouch for Baldasare and Antonio, one hundred percent. We've done business with them for a year, and we've never had any other problems." Whether he believed it or not, Latorre knew he had no choice but to dissuade Dr. Death from thinking that either Antonio or I was disloyal, because Latorre was responsible for bringing us into their circle. The cartel didn't tolerate mistakes.

Rodriguez-Castro was allowed to return to Bogotá, where he could try to raise funds for his partner's release, but Latorre wouldn't be going anywhere.

After getting word of Latorre's plight, I called Jaime. "My friend, tell Pedro to pass the word. I agree to meet, but it has to be in a neutral country. I'll bring Antonio and proof of our innocence to Grand Cayman, but Luis, Pedro, and the owner need to bring the Peruvian."

While Latorre sat in the farm outside Cali, Rodriguez-Castro met in Bogotá with one of the owner's men. He quickly learned they were adamant. Either Antonio or the money needed to be in Cali, and soon.

It was time to call in a favor. Through Richards, I had been negotiating to do business with another player in Cali named Jorge Sanz, a freighter captain who moved loads of coke for the Cali cartel. Richards had known Sanz for years, and Sanz trusted him. While we arranged for Sanz to put in a good word for us with Latorre's captors, I had Rodriguez-Castro call in my last offer.

"Baldasare says he'll meet only in a neutral country. If you kill Luis, the rat that made this happen in Houston will live on, and you'll never get your money. If you let Luis go, Baldasare will try to get more details about what really happened in Houston."

The combination of Sanz's help and my plea worked. Latorre was released, but rather than showering me with thanks, he went underground and wouldn't return my calls. His silence made no sense. If not for me, he could have easily met the same fate as Burman. Regardless, the problem was solved, at least temporarily.

I couldn't wait to get back to Panama to find out more about Burman's murder and what my friends in Panama had in store for me. Jaime added a bonus: he was bringing one of the Colombian businessmen who was part of Guillermo Segura's laundering team.

Since Laguna volunteered to pick me up at Tocumen airport, I decided it would be wise to start a new protocol after walking through Customs in Panama. From this meeting on, I always made a stop in the restroom before I met Laguna on the street. In the privacy of a toilet stall, I pulled a recorder and extended microphone from a hidden compartment in my briefcase and wired myself. The recorder went in my crotch, held in place by an Ace bandage around the very top of my thigh. Then I used medical tape to secure the wire of the extended mic to the back of the seam with buttons in the front of my dress shirt. Between the shirt and my tie, the mic was well concealed. I'd done this hundreds of times while working undercover, and I could do it in my sleep in about a minute.

After the traditional Latin *abrazos* (hugs), I threw my bag in the trunk and jumped in the passenger seat. As expected, Laguna immediately shared what he learned about Burman's murder. There were conflicting stories about the motive, he explained. He'd spoken with Burman's business partner in Panama, who warned Laguna not to place any calls to personal or business numbers linked to Burman. As a favor to Laguna, the partner had already destroyed all faxes and messages that Laguna and I had sent to Burman during the ten days Burman was missing, and there were many. No doubt this was done with a lot of Burman's other "special associates." By the time the cops got access to Burman's apartment, it was almost completely empty.

Burman had been accepting checks with questionable endorsements and associating with a known trafficker who had been released from a Panamanian jail. This guy ran up a sixteen-thousand-dollar bill on Burman's credit card. When I told Laguna that Burman had opened up to me and explained his laundering resources, Laguna confirmed.

"Bob, he had workers who accepted cash from dealers in Miami, New York, LA, and other cities. Much of that money went through a Swiss-based bank owned by a Brazilian family. He was the real deal."

Later that night, Laguna took me to El Pavo Real (the Peacock), a local restaurant and pub frequented by wealthy Panamanians and influential expatriates. This quasi-British watering hole was another of his favorite hangouts because his deceptive Casanova charm feasted off the herd of unsuspecting young *gringas* who came there simply looking for a good time. Many of the expats were employed at embassies. Laguna introduced me to Javier Maradona, an Argentinian diplomat assigned to Panama who played a role in the investigation of Burman's murder because Burman had been an Argentinian citizen. Maradona's take was that Burman was a victim of the Cali cartel, because eight months earlier, a trafficker Burman worked with had misappropriated three hundred thousand dollars of cartel money sent to Burman for laundering. Burman refused to take responsibility. Without knowing what Laguna had told me during the drive from the airport, Maradona volunteered that Burman's partner had destroyed all the faxes and messages that I had sent to Burman, as had been done also for communications with anyone connected to Burman's dirty business. Some of the destroyed records hid the flow of about fifteen million dollars in drug money that Burman and his partner had laundered for the Cali cartel during the past six months. "No one should be shocked that Burman was laundering," Maradona smirked, "because eighty percent of the money flowing into Panama is dirty."

The next day, Jaime brought another Cali man to my doorstep. I'd met Alberto Siabatto six months earlier, when he visited my office in Sarasota, and he had talked big then, but nothing had happened since. Now he was ready to work with me. According to Jaime, Siabatto was involved in both cocaine shipments and laundering for the Grajales family in Cali. Siabatto revealed his money-laundering methods, which included the same system used by Latorre: illegal export documents covering the influx of cocaine profits to Colombia. Siabatto knew I had recently met with one of his partners, Guillermo Segura, the manager of the Bogotá branch of Banco Cafetero. "Guillermo is an old friend of my brother, fifteen years. Guillermo is very smart."

Like most of the launderers I had met, Siabatto was highly educated. He had two graduate degrees, one in international marketing and the other in international transportation. He had been a professor at Jorge Tadeo Lozano University for three years and later became a professor at the Universidad del Rosario, a prestigious Colombian university founded on Roman Catholic principles, and one of the oldest universities in Latin America.

Siabatto had made some changes since I first met him. He was no longer laundering with the colleague he had brought to my Sarasota office. That guy had become a liability because two of his accounts at Swiss Bank Corporation had been seized by DEA in connection with Operation Green Ice. The guy was too hot for Siabatto's liking. This explained Siabatto's going radio silent for half a year as he waited out the storm created by Operation Green Ice. But he was now confident that the clouds had passed.

I explained my laundering system to Siabatto, who was full of compliments. He described the system as "rather extremely wise" because it offered great commercial camouflage for the movements of narco-dollars from the US to Colombia and other countries.

His clients had cash sitting in Miami, New York, and Madrid. He offered several initial test deals in the range of one hundred thousand dollars each. Provided everyone was happy, he'd arrange weekly cash shipments of half a million dollars. I agreed.

Within a day, Jaime called. "Bob, let's meet. I need to share something."

Over poolside coffees at the Hotel El Panamá, Jaime let it be known. "Bob, Siabatto mentioned that he had a concern about your paying his expenses during this trip. He said that was something the undercover agents in Operation Green Ice did with the Cali launderers they took down. I told him you're just a generous guy, but that rattled him. He asked a lot of questions about how you and I first crossed paths, and now he wants a copy of your résumé. I know that isn't a problem, but you need to know. I can assure you; you'll be very closely investigated by Siabatto and his clients."

We met with Siabatto again to negotiate our respective fees and the timing of transactions. With regard to money received in Miami, he felt we needed to make a concession and charge less than in other cities. "There are people who will pay pilots four percent—and I have evidence—to take sixty, seventy thousand dollars in a suitcase." These couriers were primarily pilots and flight attendants employed by major international commercial carriers that flew from Miami to various Colombian cities. In Spanish, he told Jaime the source of his information but warned him not to reveal the name to me.

"No le digas que he hablado con Rodriguez-Orejuela." ("Don't tell him that I have spoken with Rodriguez-Orejuela.") That could only mean either Gilberto or Miguel Rodriguez-Orejuela, the leaders of the Cali cartel.

Although I wasn't fluent in Spanish, Siabatto underestimated me. I knew exactly what he had said. Regardless, it was all on tape.

Siabatto was prepared to start in two weeks with three smaller cash drops. We came to terms. On the same day that my courier accepted the cash, we would immediately pay out 25 percent of the total. Within four business days, we would transfer the balance. Jaime and I would be paid a commission equal to 7 percent of the total. After the three test runs, assuming that Siabatto and the client were pleased with our service, we would begin to receive shipments of cash that were each between two hundred thousand and five hundred thousand dollars.

Siabatto had plans that would minimize his exposure. Besides his home in Bogotá, he had a home in Miami and was in the process of establishing a new business, a legit company in the Kendall area that would provide cover for his presence in Florida. When speaking by phone with my courier, Al Melendez, Siabatto would refer to himself as William. He would tell his client in Colombia that the client's couriers in Miami could not also be involved in moving cocaine, but instead could work only on the money side of the business. That would reduce risk for everyone. Our wire transfers would be processed through two different laundering systems. Some would go through Guillermo Segura at Banco Cafetero, disguised as repatriated export revenue, but Siabatto would also launder with the help of other bank and stock-market contacts through the purchase and sale of "*Certificados de cambio*" ("Certificates of Exchange").

Laundering through Certificates of Exchange was complicated, the perfect environment for cleaning money. The economic concept of these certificates was created by the Banco de la República (Colombia's Central Bank) so that the country of Colombia could capture and hold deposits of US dollars. The more funds the Central Bank held in US dollars, the more the country's wealth was protected from ravaging Colombian inflation and the devaluation of the Colombian peso. The certificates were a gimmick by the Central Bank to lure exporters into keeping their repatriated US dollars with the Central Bank.

When exporters were paid in US dollars by foreign customers, they had one of two choices. They could produce a Document of Exportation proving that the incoming US dollar transfer was export revenue and immediately convert it to pesos, enabling them to use those funds within the borders of Colombia as soon as they were received. Alternatively, they could use the incoming US dollar transfer to buy a Certificate of Exchange that was a promise from the Central Bank that the institution would pay out the peso equivalent in 365 days. With a typical annual inflation rate of 28 percent, immediately converting export revenue of one hundred dollars to a Certificate of Exchange was like buying a one-hundred-dollar CD with an annual interest rate of 28 percent.

Since launderers readily used fake documents to overstate the true value of exports, most of the US dollar transfers pouring into Colombia were actually narco-dollars. Much of that money was used to buy Certificates of Exchange, so the country's Central Bank collaterally became the beneficiary of money from the drug trade. Once the certificates were bought, they could be traded on an unofficial secondary market with speculators who had legitimate money. The trafficker's representatives would sell the certificates to "honest investors," who would in turn give their "honest pesos" to the launderer. Everyone was happy, including the bureaucrats in the Colombian government.

After bidding farewell to Siabatto, I had loose ends to attend to with a few of my new friends, including Straub. Unfortunately, he was in the UK, so I met with a member of his staff. The paperwork was ready for the Panamanian corporation he'd formed to disguise our money movements. To justify Straub's steep fees, the typical "company package" came with other benefits: a PO box in Panama for "the company," officers and directors, business cards, stationery, and a local phone number. Straub's secretary, an officer of "the company," would handle any calls received or sent by "the company" in Panama, and she would prepare and notarize any documents, at my direction. I was given all the traditional unregistered powers of attorney, authorizing me to open and control bank accounts for "the company," and if necessary, take control of everything if I ever became concerned that Straub's nominees weren't following my instructions. To the few bankers who knew that I controlled accounts, I was just an "employee" of "the company." I was also welcome to use an office within Straub's office suite, and he provided me with the name and contact information for a friendly attorney in Turks and Caicos, paradise islands in the warm Atlantic waters east of Cuba. For decades, Turks and Caicos has been a key veil of secrecy for crooks with hot money. Straub's friend would form a company there, and that company could be established as an officer and director of my Panamanian company. The Turks and Caicos company simply added an additional obstacle to identify the company's beneficial owner. Straub assured me that I should have no worries. Everything was first class.

Baldasare's business was booming, and his circle of important friends was quickly growing. But what I didn't know was happening behind my back would cause me to move closer and closer to a trap.

9

DOUBLE-CROSSED

March–April 1993

As Edith Uribe walked off the Avianca flight from Miami to the El Dorado International Airport in Bogotá, she kept looking for her contact, her eyes scanning wildly as she approached baggage claim. The person was supposed to have a white handkerchief wrapped around one hand. She had followed instructions and was wearing a pink scarf with big black polka dots. She watched anxiously as the last bags from her flight rolled down the beltway and onto the carousel . . . Her suitcases were not there. Edith's concern mounted. Could a bag handler have discovered and run off with the two hundred thousand dollars hidden in her suitcases? Just as her pounding heart felt about to burst, she was tapped on the shoulder. It was a Customs officer. *"Tiene que venir conmigo, por favor."* ("You need to come with me, please.") It took all of her strength to appear calm as her mind raced for an alibi.

They walked into the examination room, and there were Edith's bags. The first officer walked out and left her with a female officer who had entered from a back door. And there it was, the handkerchief wrapped around the woman's hand. She smiled. *"Señora, puede tomar sus maletas y salir por la puerta trasera. Su amistad con Luis le convierte en amiga nuestra."* ("Ma'am, you can take your bags and go out the back door. Your friendship with Luis makes you a friend of ours.")

At that time, I had no idea that Latorre had made an alliance with Edith Uribe and her brother Harry. Once every few weeks, she and her bags, jammed with cash, flew through Colombian Customs. Over time, the amounts increased. With a million dollars accepted in New York, Edith and a friend would drag their bags through Grand Central Station and onto a train bound for Miami. An Avianca flight to Bogotá was the final leg of the trip, where Edith got her special treatment from Customs.

As she got to know Latorre better, they started having dinner in Bogotá. "Luis, how did you meet our good friend Frankie?"

Latorre had a few too many, so his tongue was loose. "Darling, he saved my life by letting me know I was dealing with cops in Sarasota. Before Frankie opened my eyes, I thought Baldasare and his team were the best thing that ever happened to me. My relationship with you and your family replaces that bastard. He and the problems he caused will be eliminated, soon." With that, his look of hatred morphed into a huge smile.

Back in Tampa, under the tutelage of Frankie, the Uribe siblings were using all sorts of tricks to move Latorre's money. With the help of a relative who worked at a bank, they quietly paid cash for dozens of cashier's checks in amounts under ten thousand dollars, in order to stay under the reporting radar. This family member also gave them hundred-dollar bills in exchange for small denomination bills, a big advantage to Edith's smuggling cash on commercial flights. At friendly money-service businesses, they bought traveler's checks, money orders, and MoneyGrams.

Thanks to their jewelry business, Harry Uribe had contacts in

Manhattan that bought and sold large amounts of gold. He worked out an arrangement to buy gold with cash, and then have his contacts immediately sell the gold to other jewelers. In return for a small laundering fee, they paid him back with checks.

There was so much cash to move that Harry recruited his other sister, Yasmin, to join their team. It only made sense. Yasmin and her sister, Edith, had a lot in common. They were street smart, well educated, professional in appearance, and disarming. And they shared something else: separately they had romances with Frankie.

A week later, as Yasmin drove a rental car from Tampa to Miami along Alligator Alley, she glanced in her rearview mirror. The suitcases in her trunk were filled with clothes and tightly wrapped bricks of cash that totaled three hundred thousand dollars. As Edith had instructed, Yasmin watched her speedometer closely and never exceeded the speed limit. With a second glance in her mirror, she could see a highway patrol car closing on her quickly. The trooper brought his car nearly to her rear bumper, turned on his emergency lights, and waved his arm to signal that she should pull over.

"Ma'am, please give me your license and registration."

Yasmin followed his instructions, but she couldn't resist asking, "Is there a problem, sir?"

The trooper examined the driver's license. "Yasmin, is this your car?"

"No, sir. I just rented this car in Tampa, and I'm on my way to visit my cousin in Miami."

"You were driving twelve miles over the speed limit."

Yasmin knew he was lying, but she didn't want to make a scene. "I apologize, sir. I was watching my speed closely to make sure I wasn't speeding, but maybe there's something wrong with the speedometer."

"Ma'am, would you mind if I looked in your trunk?"

"Not at all, sir. Go right ahead."

"Okay, please exit the car and come with me to the trunk." Yasmin opened it, revealing two large suitcases.

"Ma'am, are these yours?"

Yasmin's mind raced. She could see where this was going, but she was a step ahead of the cop. "Sir, I never looked in the trunk before leaving the rental office. I have no idea whose bags those are. They are not mine."

"Would you mind if I opened them?"

"Well, they're not mine, so I don't care."

The trooper opened the suitcase, moved some clothing, and there they were: green bricks of cash wrapped in rubber bands. He put his hand on the grip of his holstered Beretta 92FS semiautomatic pistol. "Ma'am, I need you to put your hands on the car." He moved behind Yasmin and quickly cuffed her wrists behind her back. Within minutes, a second patrol car arrived, driven by a female officer. Yasmin was interviewed for thirty minutes and never budged from her original claim. She had no idea how those suitcases got in the trunk, and she knew nothing about what was in them.

Eventually the officers seized the cash, gave Yasmin a receipt, and let her go. Latorre's problems were about to multiply. Now, not only would he be responsible for the $1.5 million loss in Houston, but he'd have to account for this three hundred thousand dollars.

In the cartel's world, if couriers can prove that a load of cash is seized by law enforcement, as long as they aren't informants, they won't be immediately killed. They have to produce copies of court pleadings to confirm the seizure, but then, if the loss is truly an innocent accident, they and the money broker that worked with them will often be given the option of working for free to pay off the debt. They can only avoid repaying a loss if they can prove that it occurred as a result of someone else's mistake or disloyalty.

A week later, Latorre's favorite Paso Fino horse turned up dead, stiff as a board in its stall. While he was at the stable, mourning his loss, his cell phone rang. It was the owner of the money lost in Houston. "So sorry to hear your favorite pony drank some poison. We know where your and Pedro's beautiful children attend school. Your mistake needs to be settled, now."

The next day, my phone rang at Avid Investments. "Bob, it's Luis. You must help me settle the matter with the owners of the Houston loss. They are coming after me. They poisoned one of my horses, and they're not going away. If you don't help me, I am giving them addresses for you and Jaime, and your pictures. You know what that means."

"Luis, I understand what you're facing, but that loss was not our fault. My attorney has gotten another report, and I can have that delivered to you. It makes the truth very clear. The problem is in the Peruvian's group. It's not me, Antonio, or anyone connected to me. The feds had Vicuna under a microscope for more than a year before Antonio went to Houston."

With DEA approval, the additional report was sent to Bogotá. Jaime sat beside Latorre and Rodriguez-Castro as they read it. They were impressed and pleased. They passed it to the Cali people and hadn't heard anything since, which was a good sign. Latorre said he would call me, and as promised, he did.

"Bob, I am forever grateful. We will resume business soon. Between what you did, and the help I got from an old Cali friend who is highly respected, I've been assured there'll be no more threats about Houston. This old friend would like your team to begin handling shipments for him in Puerto Rico. Before he does business, he'd like to meet you, and he's willing to come to the States."

I told Latorre that, before I met anyone new, I needed to meet him. I had to hear everything about the Doctor and his people so I could assess my risk. Since we hadn't done any business for months, I wanted answers about why our pickups had fizzled to nothing. Plus, he owed me fifty thousand dollars to cover half of what it cost me to get the report I'd just sent. My final message: "I can meet you in Costa Rica or Panama. I'll be there for the rest of the month."

There was silence. I could hear the wheels grinding in his head. Then he jumped to what was most likely the motive for his call. "No problem. What hotel will you be at in Costa Rica?"

The question sounded more like an attempt to corner me for Dr. Death than a true offer to meet and repair our relationship. Latorre had plenty of friends in both countries who would do whatever he asked, for a price. I knew better than to make myself a sitting duck. "I'll be staying with a friend."

What concerned me the most, though, was what *hadn't* occurred over the past couple of months. We hadn't done one deal with Latorre and Rodriguez-Castro. Something or someone must have shaken their trust in me, and since they weren't laundering with us, who had taken our place?

Despite the tension and risks, I had to appear as natural as ever during undercover meets in Costa Rica and Panama. I had to operate two brains. My Baldasare mind had to be completely natural in Baldasare's skin as others observed me playing that role. Simultaneously, my agent brain secretly had to process information while on high alert. That was critical to my survival.

In San José, I chose to stay at the Herradura Hotel. It was only minutes from the Juan Santamaria International Airport and close to downtown, where Laguna had arranged meetings with a handful of his contacts that moved money.

The views from my suite were stunning. Distant green mountains covered with heavy tropical forest surrounded the city. At a glance, it looked peaceful, but this Latin American version of Switzerland was struggling to compete with neighboring havens like Panama. Costa Rica was home to many elites looking to convince the underworld that their dirty money would be safe in their homeland. This was why, years before, Mexican drug lord Rafael Caro Quintero thought he was safe there after directing the murder of DEA agent Kiki Camarena. If you had enough money, anything could happen in Costa Rica.

While at the hotel, I used the phone in my room as often as I could to make calls to other bad guys. Laguna and his friends knew I was staying at the Herradura. There was no doubt in my mind that they were recording my calls, or at least monitoring them, to see if any conversations suggested I was someone other than Robert Baldasare, the money launderer.

After a full night of meetings, it was time to hit the sack. At 2:00 a.m., I tossed in bed, wondering if Latorre would try to track me down. Then I heard the whispering, not far from my door. There was an unmistakable thud, followed by what sounded like something being dragged or scraped across the floor. It happened five or six times, and the last thud and scrape came just outside my door. I jumped to the peephole but saw nothing. I couldn't resist unlocking and turning the knob to peek into the hall. There he was, Dr. Death, with four sicarios whose shirts bulged from handguns tucked in their pants. In seconds, they were in the room. My arms and legs were duct-taped to my desk chair as Dr. Death hovered and sneered. As the sicarios wrapped more tape around my head and over my mouth, he wore a smile of victory. He had his prey. I struggled to pull free, and one of the sicarios leaned into my face, brandishing a knife that looked the size of a sword. I tried to beg for mercy.

Then I popped up from my bed. It had been a nightmare, but it had felt remarkably real. My heart was pounding. I was in a puddle of sweat. I couldn't stop gasping. I bowed my head between my knees. I was losing it, and I had to pull myself together, because in only a day or so, I would be moving on to Panama, a much more likely place for my kidnapping. I took the dream as an omen, warning me to be at my best if I didn't want to end up like Enrique Burman.

Not long after returning to Panama, I was perched with Straub on the veranda of his plush high-rise apartment in Punta Paitilla, sharing a stunning panoramic view of the Gulf of Panama. Although Straub thought we were alone, my recorder collected every word.

It was important for him to know that I was calculating. If I was going to move money with him, I needed to know about any risks he carried from his past. "Gil, I don't mean to pry into your personal affairs, but if we decide to become a team, I'd appreciate knowing where that [meaning the warrant for his arrest] stands."

"Most of my complications from those days stemmed as a result of two things," Straub explained. "One being that I was a corporate director, a very close personal adviser to a man called Robert Vesco who became very controversial." Then Straub confessed why he was a magnet for US law enforcement. "My association with the Nixon campaign, when Richard Nixon was president and my coordination person, you might call him, was John Ehrlichman . . . I did some things at the White House. In those days, I still had International Controls Corporation, which had thirty-three plants, two of them making a very exotic kind of explosive that the air force used in Vietnam."

As his story unfolded, it amazed me that this crook had simultaneous, direct involvement with the president of the United States, the president's principal advisers, the world's biggest swindler in Robert Vesco, and mobsters.

Straub went on. "So we made, at the president's request, campaign contributions in cash, never reported. And that cash, they managed to trace back to payoffs to the Watergate burglars. So they subpoenaed several people in the Watergate grand jury, including me. And I was asked by the president not to go. Imagine that. And they took offense to that. And that continued through the Democratic administration that followed Nixon. When Reagan came in, they sort of arranged for it all to go away, with the understanding that I wouldn't go back to the States."

Although the two men had been close in the past, Straub was not happy with Vesco's latest antics. In Straub's view, Vesco did a lot of silly things and talked too much. Vesco had started mixing in Costa Rican politics, offering himself to the Russian embassy as someone who could negotiate on their behalf with the US, and he had begun smuggling a lot of high-tech hardware from Mexico. His unlicensed exportation of restricted equipment was busted by the Americans, which ultimately led to Vesco's seeking refuge in Cuba.

Straub wanted me to know that he was a stand-up guy. The feds tried to get him to cooperate several times, and he told them they were wasting their time. They took exception to the timing of his marriage. He and his wife were married on June 17, 1972, the same day as the Watergate break-in. Authorities accused him of picking that day to distance himself and some of his guests, including two of Richard Nixon's brothers, from the break-in. Later, Democrats Clark Clifford and Paul Warnke convinced Congress to open the Watergate hearings, through articles written by investigative reporter Jack Anderson, who along with other reporters had published enough smoke for the Democrats to accuse the White House of a cover-up. Clark and Warnke came to Straub and laid out exactly what they were doing, telling Straub that if he cooperated, they would take the heat off him. Straub told them to go to hell. His message to me was simple: I would never have to worry about his breaking ranks.

To put me further at ease, Straub touted his close alliance with Italian American organized crime. "I'm very close personally with some people, who have been friends of mine for twenty years, who have . . . OC after their name. They live in the States, American citizens. One guy in particular is like my brother. If he asked me for something, I'd do it."

And to put a cherry on top of his story of his criminal success, he shared pictures of his mansion in New Forest, in Hampshire, England. The grounds and building paralleled the elegance of Highclere Castle: more than a dozen bedrooms, tennis courts, swimming pool, horse stables, servants' quarters, greenhouses, a pond, and manicured grounds. He had it all.

Straub's final message was he was ready to launder through the sale of gold, diamonds, or large oil shipments. He'd come up with more options after speaking with his trusted friends.

Later that week, meetings at the Hotel El Panamá with Guillermo Segura, the Banco Cafetero manager, set the stage for the beginning of a new business. Segura, Alberto Siabatto, and several other crooked Colombian businessmen were arranging cash drops to us in Miami and New York. Those deliveries were promised to start within two weeks, and they did. The deliveries were small, in the range of one hundred thousand dollars at a time, but it was enough to buy all of them future indictments.

Like a bloodhound retrieving downed ducks, Jaime kept bringing me traffickers and launderers. "Bob, I don't think I can get this person to travel to Panama before you return to the States, but I've come across something big. This guy launders for two Colombian senators who are front men for Dario Mendoza Parra, the head of the Cartel de la Costa." Jaime gave me the name of one of the Colombian senators, which didn't surprise me. It was common knowledge in the law enforcement and intelligence communities that the cartels had a large majority of the Colombian senators in their pockets.

At the same time that our partnership with Jaime was flushing launderers and traffickers out of the woodwork, Latorre and his partner reverted to hiding from Jaime. They weren't returning his calls, either knowing or thinking they knew something about me that scared them away. Was there a mole gnawing away at my cover? I had to do something to kick-start Operation Pro-Mo, something bold to dissuade the rumors that Baldasare was one of Los Feos. And I knew what that was. I needed to go where no other undercover agent had operated in many years. I had to go to Colombia.

Latorre and the entire cartel world knew that, not long after DEA agent Enrique "Kiki" Camarena was murdered in Mexico, undercover work in Colombia for US feds had ended. Showing my face in Colombia would stun them and dissolve any doubt about Baldasare's loyalty.

The hunt for Pablo Escobar was at its height. Bombings were occurring daily. Los Pepes were hunting and murdering every ally of Escobar they could find. I couldn't wait to get there.

10

A TOTAL SURPRISE

Bogotá, Colombia
May 1993

As the Avianca flight from Miami descended, Bogotá looked like a tranquil Garden of Eden, surrounded by lush mountains topped with pluming white and gray clouds. A dense patchwork of rich, checkered terrain surrounded the airport and the city. Many of the fields were home to fertile beds and greenhouses overflowing with flowers, waiting to be harvested and shipped to the States. The beauty and peace from afar masked the grave danger that the good Colombian people faced every day from the narcos.

As I walked down the gangway, I was sure I had done everything I could to arrive safely in Colombia as Bob Baldasare. First, I had dissuaded one of my bosses who insisted that I travel using my official DEA passport in the name of Robert Mazur. "Boss, Latorre controls corrupt

Colombian Customs officers. After he learns I'm in Colombia, he'll have the people on his payroll pull entry records. If Robert Baldasare is not on record, it will raise a big red flag. Plus, if he ever asks to see my passport and Baldasare has no Colombian Customs entry and exit stamps, that's a dead giveaway. And no offense, boss, but we need to sit on opposite sides of the flight to Bogotá, not next to one another. If I were Latorre, I'd search the background of whoever was sitting next to me, and a DEA agent would be a death sentence."

He grudgingly acquiesced. It isn't easy for a new agent to debate judgment issues with any of their bosses, but when your or someone else's life depends on it, it's your duty to speak up. To stay silent because of concerns about peer pressure is cowardly.

I tried to persuade management to let me spend my nights at Jaime's house, with a cover team next door. I lost that battle. I was ordered to stay at the home of one of the DEA agents assigned to the Bogotá office, who in his bulletproof SUV with darkened windows would sneak me into the embassy's underground parking garage for daily briefings.

Things didn't go as promised. The morning after I arrived, I got in the agent's SUV. The windows weren't tinted. They were as transparent as air. We drove to the embassy, and as we approached the entrance, the agent looked at me. "Okay, get out and go through the security checkpoint."

I was in shock. The only people who get out of bulletproof SUVs at the embassy are agents or snitches. "You're supposed to take me into the underground parking garage. The hunt for Escobar is in high gear. There's no doubt the Medellín cartel, and probably the Cali cartel that is chasing him, are filming whoever is entering and exiting the embassy."

The agent was indignant. "Dude, stop freaking out. You'll be okay. You can jump from my car to the doors in thirty seconds. Let's go."

I couldn't afford to make a scene in the car. The windows of the SUV were so clear, I could just as easily be videoed in the vehicle, arguing with the agent. The agent had little respect for the intelligence of the crooks, and he grew impatient with me, whom he saw as an overthinking former Customs agent who graduated from the Academy only eighteen months earlier. Clearly, this was his turf, and he wasn't about to be second-guessed by a rookie.

I had no other option, so I made the best of it and quickstepped into the embassy as I watched the agent maneuver down the driveway and into the underground parking garage. My blood was boiling, but there would be more battles over logistics to come, so I had to let it go.

Sneakiness wasn't a common enough trait in a certain segment of the law enforcement world that overdosed on macho. In my view, too many agents failed to recognize that we were outsmarted and out-resourced by the cartels. If I were Pablo Escobar or Miguel Rodriguez-Orejuela, the heads of the two biggest Colombian cartels, my lead security man would arrange to videotape every single person walking in and out of the US embassy.

Once inside, I was introduced to the DEA agents and Colombian police that would cover me during undercover meets. The Colombian officers were heavily vetted by DEA, a process that included intense background research and periodic polygraph tests. By far, they were the best of the best. Despite the widespread reputation of corruption in their ranks, some deserved and some not, they not only put their lives on the line to honorably fight the war against the narcos, but they also put their families' lives at risk.

We reviewed what we expected would happen during my stay, and I was given two options as a distress signal during undercover meetings. If I put my glasses on my forehead, or if I took off my tie, the cover team would immediately swarm in and neutralize any threat, one way or another.

I respected our attaché's concern. "Listen, Bob. Two of our informants were killed here just a week or so ago. There's no way we're going to allow anything that causes us to lose an agent, ever."

"I understand, sir."

I really didn't care which bad guys met me in Bogotá. My goal for this trip was to look across a table at as many launderers and drug dealers as possible so the word would spread in the underworld that I showed my face in Colombia. That was the real value. It would be the antidote to the rumors that I was an agent, unless the unthinkable had occurred and my cover was blown. If that had happened, this could very well be my last trip anywhere.

After the briefings at the embassy, I met privately with Jaime at Casa Brava, a Colombian steak house nestled near the top of one of the high hills surrounding Bogotá. As I walked toward the restaurant, I couldn't resist taking one of the tens of thousands of wanted posters for Pablo Escobar that hung on every utility pole, bus stop, and corner in Bogotá. In bold letters, it screamed a solemn promise:

> Thanks to the collaboration of citizens like you, we are defeating narco-terrorism. In exchange for information, the government guarantees absolute secrecy about your identity, protection for your family, the beginning of a new life abroad, and if you have criminal problems, the Prosecutor's Office can solve them.

Pablo Escobar's picture and name appeared below, with assurance of a five-million-dollar reward. The poster read well, but corruption within the Colombian institutions of justice kept many people from giving the offer any serious consideration. The reward offered by DEA, for Escobar's head, was considerably more than the three-hundred-thousand-dollar bounty that Escobar offered for the head of any DEA agent working in Colombia. But since he had hundreds of sicarios on his payroll, Escobar thought it much more likely that he would be paying than that someone would cash in on DEA's offer.

Jaime and I had dinner on the outdoor terrace, a perch that offered a bird's-eye view of the sprawling city. "Bob, Guillermo Segura is very

pleased that everything went so smoothly on the test runs. His people
in New York and Miami gave Al Melendez high marks. I've told Segura
and a few others working with the cartel to set aside time to meet
tomorrow afternoon. They have no idea you're here. As you requested,
I will call them in the morning and let them know you want to meet.
Here's a list of everyone who might join us tomorrow, and an outline
of what they want to discuss."

Jaime peppered me with details, and it all sounded good. "Okay,
let them know you and I will hold court at the Tramonti restaurant in
Bogotá. Set them up at different times. Space them out so there's no
overlap. Warn them I have a tight schedule and can't spend more than
an hour with anyone." I sensed that Jaime was unsettled. "How are you
doing, my friend?"

Jaime said he was fine, but I looked at him with an expression
that said, *Tell me more*. Silence and active listening worked. Jaime had
been going to church and lighting a candle every day for his mom. She
wasn't feeling well, and he couldn't be there for her because of his role in
Operation Pro-Mo. He made a daily prayer offering to the Lord, asking
the saints to pray for her, hoping that God's presence would make up
for his absence.

I remained silent, with a gaze of wonderment, and Jaime finally
delivered. "Frankly, Bob, I fear that if the cartel ever figures out what
I'm doing, they'll make me watch them mercilessly murder her, and
then they'll make me watch them cut up my family, piece by piece, until
there's nothing left. I'm prepared to face my own death, but if I cause
others to be harmed, I couldn't live with myself."

Jaime was a patriot who despised the corrupt stranglehold the cartels had on every institution of authority in Colombia. It angered him
so much that he was willing to die to fight for change. His loyalty to
his country was shared by many Colombians who suffered at the hands
of the narcos. I thanked him for his bravery and promised him that
he and his family had my commitment that I would sacrifice my life

before I would allow him to suffer the retribution he feared. I meant it, and he knew that.

"Tomorrow, we'll put them all at ease when they see I'm here. Other than natural caution, they have no reason to think I'm anything but the real deal, Jaime." So I thought.

The Tramonti was a massive Italian/European stand-alone restaurant that rested near the top of a mountain covered by tropical forest. Its glass-walled views looked down a valley that opened to the picturesque city below. Its three-story wood-framed shell was covered by a one-of-a-kind massive thatched roof of palm fronds. The main dining room had plenty of room for separate cover teams of two or three to sit at tables far enough away not to draw attention, but close enough to maintain a tactical line of sight. Since the building sat higher than any other structure on the mountain, there was no drive-by traffic. Anyone arriving had to walk a considerable distance, which gave cover-team members sitting outside enough time to assess whatever risk might accompany an arriving patron.

The next morning, Jaime started making calls, first to Guillermo Segura. "Guillermo, sorry to trouble you at the bank, but I'm going to have lunch at the Tramonti later today with a very important person I'm sure you'd like to see. By the way, thanks to him, your last one-hundred-thousand-dollar test run went smoothly."

Segura was confused. "Who are you talking about?"

"*Don Roberto de Sarasota, por supuesto.*" ("Don Roberto from Sarasota, of course.")

Segura lit up. "Wonderful, Jaime. I'm so happy he's here. I'll be there by twelve thirty."

Before Segura arrived, I called Pedro Rodriguez-Castro, Latorre's partner. "*Amigo, estoy aquí. Me gustaría mucho conocerte a ti y a Luis.*" ("Friend, I am here. I would very much like to meet you and Luis.") I let him know that I would be at the Tramonti restaurant at 3:00 p.m. and that I was taking a flight out of Bogotá that night, so my schedule was tight.

Rodriguez-Castro was in disbelief. In a stuttered reply, he claimed that he and Latorre were tied up in meetings until at least 4:00 p.m. They'd get back to me soon to schedule a meet.

His tone said he was full of shit, and he was just buying time. Seconds later, Latorre got the word. But what I didn't know was that Latorre immediately called Harry Uribe back in Tampa. "Harry, you tell Frankie to call me immediately. He lied about Baldasare. There's no way he can be a DEA agent. He's here in Bogotá meeting clients. I need answers now."

Minutes later, Latorre had Frankie on the phone. "If he's a cop, what the hell is he doing here in Bogotá? Baldasare is here and wants to meet."

"Luis, that's impossible. DEA is forbidden to do undercover work in Colombia. Maybe he did this on his own. I don't know right now, but I'll find out. I'm telling you; he is a fucking DEA agent."

Unfortunately, Frankie undermined Latorre's brief rebirth of faith in me. Now Latorre was thinking about how he could sell the life of a DEA agent. He called Miguel Rosenberg, his main connection to Dr. Death. "Miguel, I have a surprise for you. That fucker Baldasare is here in Bogotá. I think the Doctor should know. Maybe this is an opportunity to give him something in exchange for our Houston debt. Baldasare is at the Tramonti."

"Se lo haré saber, Luis. Esto debería valer mucho más que el millón y medio que se perdió." ("I'll let him know, Luis. This should be worth a lot more than the one point five million that was lost.")

As Dr. Death got word, Segura approached our table at the Tramonti. He was all smiles. "Bob, it is so good to see you here. This is quite a relief, frankly." He turned to the gentleman who arrived with him. "Bob, this is one of my trusted partners in this business, Oscar Acevedo. We have a number of important matters we want to discuss. But first, let me ask: Why did you come so unexpectedly, and why are you leaving so quickly?"

"I have a longtime relationship with a client I had to meet here, and I've been here for a while. I don't like staying for long periods of time because it is a red flag to the feds. Until Rinaldo Laguna finishes the immigration work he is doing for me in Panama, I need to be careful about drawing attention." I explained that Laguna was getting me Panamanian citizenship and status as a Panamanian consulate in Sarasota. With that, I'd get a Panamanian diplomatic passport and could then frequently fly from Panama to Colombia, and the Americans wouldn't have a record of that travel. In the meantime, I needed to keep my visits to Colombia to a minimum, for everyone's safety.

"A wise strategy, Mr. Bob. I totally agree."

Segura covered his points. Going forward, my communication with him by phone had to go through Oscar Acevedo. This would reduce Segura's telephone traffic with people in the States. Our paperwork disguising the transfers as export transactions had to be kept impeccably, and we needed to use some new codes he provided to further disguise our discussions. He needed me to drop my fee a little, because he was sharing his cut with a senior officer at Banco Cafetero. Now that the test transactions had gone smoothly, the next shipment of cash would be three hundred thousand dollars. Thereafter, shipments would be in the range of six hundred thousand dollars per delivery. Besides New York and Miami, he wanted us to refine our abilities to receive cash in Europe and India.

"Guillermo, with all due respect, things have progressed relatively slowly in New York and Miami. Until those cities are operating at the volume you just predicted, let's hold off doing business elsewhere. I promise you I'll take care of you outside the US once things are rolling in the Towers and the Beaches."

After warm farewells with Seguro and Acevedo, I held court all afternoon. Cali money brokers wanted to give me seven million dollars in cash in exchange for a fleet of Russian pickup trucks, which I could arrange with the help of Straub in Panama. Another broker had control of six million dollars' worth of Spanish pesetas generated from coke shipments sold in Europe and wanted the pesetas converted to US dollars, to be wired to accounts around the world. Everyone wanted "Don Roberto de Sarasota" to filter dirty money through his systems.

Eventually, I got the sign from one of the agents covering me that they wanted things wrapped up. The meetings had already gone about thirty minutes past what was mandated in our operational plan. Although the cover team appeared calm, enjoying their meals, they were concerned that I had spent too much time in one spot. The kidnapping risk was too high, but I might never get this opportunity again. I tried to prolong my time, but the signal was clear in the look of the team leader: *Let's get the fuck out of here, now.* I reluctantly shut down.

Soon after we left the Tramonti, Jaime started driving like a maniac. "Bob, I'm concerned that Latorre and Rodriguez-Castro didn't show. They've known where you were for the past four hours. That's more than enough time to set you up. You see that big black SUV about a block behind us? He's been on us since we left the restaurant."

"Okay, Jaime, lose him, and then head to the drop point. There should be two guys there from the embassy, waiting for me."

Jaime and I had grown close. That happens to soldiers on the battlefield, trying to keep each other alive.

"Listen, Jaime. You need to watch your back. If Latorre trusted us, he would have come to the restaurant in a heartbeat. You need to promise me that you won't take chances." Jaime had grown from an underworld neophyte to a professor of money laundering, and his street sense had done the same.

"Don't worry about me, Mr. Baldasare. We're in the same boat. Don't look so serious. It makes me nervous."

We got to the rendezvous point, a restaurant in Bogotá called Mr. Ribs, but my embassy contacts were nowhere to be seen. As I sat with Jaime in the car, my cell phone rang. It was Latorre. "Bob, I'm so sorry I've been tied up. I'd like to ask a favor. Would you please postpone your flight until tomorrow? I have a deal of a lifetime for you, and my most important client would like to meet you. What do you say?"

I looked at Jaime and silently mouthed Luis's name. "I'm sorry, but I've got some urgent business to attend to in Florida. I have to leave tonight."

"I'm telling you, Bob, you will regret missing this opportunity. If you have to head to the airport soon, how about meeting us there?"

My gut told me that Latorre was desperate, and there was no way I was going to meet him at the airport, since he had Colombian Customs in his pocket. "In a couple of weeks, I'll be in Panama for quite some time. Bring your friend there and we'll meet. I'm sorry, I have to tend to something back in the States, but I'm truly looking forward to seeing you soon. *Adios, amigo.*"

Jaime and I got out of his car, looking for the embassy team. A black SUV sped down the street and came to a screeching halt a few feet from where we stood, its glass tinted charcoal black. The passenger window slowly began to open.

"Get in the fucking car."

My heart pounded as the window opened farther, revealing one of my bosses. I turned to Jaime, and we wrapped our arms around each other, proclaiming, *"Abrazos, amigo. Ten cuidado."* ("Hugs, friend. Be careful.")

In the car, I got an earful. "What the hell, Mazur? We almost stormed the place. You were supposed to be out of that restaurant a half hour before you left."

"Boss, this was a once-in-a-lifetime opportunity. I never gave either of the distress signals, and the cover team was there the whole time. They must have realized I was fine."

"Just do what you're supposed to do. Let's get back to the embassy."

As I feared, when we arrived, I was paraded in front of the entrance to the underground parking garage and through the front door. Within minutes, my supervisor was on an unsecure phone, calling the DEA office in Puerto Rico. "Hey, we'll be flying through the Dominican Republic. Can you please book two rooms at the government rate? You have my details, and I guess you'll need to put the other one in Mazur's undercover name. It is Baldasare, spelled—"

I shot to my feet. We all knew that Colombian phone company employees could be bought for peanuts. They illegally recorded calls all the time, sometimes for the good guys, but sometimes for the bad guys, too. Their only loyalty was to Mr. Franklin—Ben Franklin on the one-hundred-dollar bill.

"Boss, would you please help me out? How about putting two rooms in your name at the G-rate [government rate], and I'll pay in cash."

He shot me a wrinkled brow, but he honored my request.

After being debriefed, I was taken separately to the airport by one of the agents assigned to the embassy. I didn't want to travel with my boss, who would be using his official US government passport. As we rode, the agent made an offer. "Bob, listen. I know everybody at the airport. I can get you through Customs fast, and then into the VIP lounge where you can have free drinks."

I responded with a polite no. "Thanks a lot, Tom, but since your contacts know you're DEA, that would put me with your office, either as an agent or a snitch. Sorry, I guess I'm a little paranoid."

It hurt to turn him down, but accepting could have cost me my life.

The engines on the plane that brought me back to Florida barely had time to cool before Latorre made his next move.

11

TRADING PLACES

June 1993

"Bob, I'm at Luis's office. He and Pedro have a proposal. They want me to take over. They've asked me to put this call on speaker so all four of us can talk."

Although we spoke in code, Latorre's message was clear. "Pedro and I are indebted to you for everything you did to get us released. If you hadn't sent those reports, we would be dead. As a show of gratitude and for a second reason, we want to take Jaime to Cali and introduce him to the owners of the money so he can take the lead role. Our second reason is simple. We no longer want to take responsibility for the funds. It's too dangerous for us. We'll reduce our share of the profit and increase the payout to you and Jaime."

Jaime showed no fear and welcomed the responsibility, but when I ended the call, leaning back in my desk chair, I replayed the conversation in my mind a dozen times. What was the real motive behind

Latorre's and Rodriguez-Castro's interest in resuming business with me? Something had to have gone bad with the launderers who took over for me months ago. If Latorre and his partner trusted me, they would have reverted to our original terms. They would never take a pay cut. They're too greedy. They wouldn't give up profits because they wanted to be nice guys, and they didn't fear responsibility unless they thought that dealing with me heightened the risk of money being seized. They were putting Jaime's ass on the line because they somehow thought that reduced the chances of seizures, which only made sense if Latorre had pegged me as a snitch or an agent. Something had eaten away my credibility with them, and it had to be a mole close to me.

What I didn't know was that, days before, Edith Uribe had picked up $700,000 for Latorre's client in New York. As always, the cash was in small denominations, $5, $10, and $20 bills. After she exchanged half the bills for $100s, Latorre ordered her to have a courier smuggle $340,000 in big bills on a commercial flight to Bogotá, where his dirty Customs buddies would wave it through. Edith drove her courier, a boyfriend living with her, to LaGuardia Airport.

"Okay, Hector, Luis Latorre has passed your description along to his people in Customs. You'll have no problems. I hid the cash in some wrapped presents that are in the suitcases."

After she dropped the courier off at the departure ramp, he checked his bags and headed to his flight. As he waited, the Avianca employee at the gate made the announcement: *"Señor Hector Ruiz, por favor acérquese al mostrador de salidas para recibir un mensaje."* She repeated it in English. "Mr. Hector Ruiz, please come to the departure desk for a message." As soon as he identified himself, the attendant at the desk placed a call, claiming she needed to get the details of the message from another employee. Within a minute, the US Customs agents were on him.

"Come with us, sir." They took him to a nearby office. When he saw his bags in the corner, he knew the worst had happened. As Edith had schooled him, once confronted with the cash, he claimed he had no idea how it got in his bags. Someone at the airport must have set him up, planting those bricks of currency in his suitcases. He was ultimately released with a receipt confirming the $340,000 had been seized. Latorre's life was on the line again.

The brothers and sisters in the Uribe clan were busy crooks. One of their coke suppliers in Miami came to Tampa to sell them fifty kilos. As is common in the drug world, if you don't want to pay for all of your product up front, which they didn't, you get to take a few kilos at a time, but you have to give the supplier the cash after each small sale until you've paid in full. Then you can get the rest of the load that'll generate your profit. As Mario Uribe and his brother Hernando met with their buyer to sell two kilos, deputies from the Hillsborough County Sheriff's Office swarmed in. The buyer was a snitch.

While the Uribe brothers were held on bond, their attorney shared their alibi with the prosecutor. "Listen, my clients are registered informants with the Tampa Police Department. Their handler, Juaquin 'Quino' Gonzalez, was attending a class at the local college when this went down. They tried to reach out to him, to coordinate with the Tampa cops, but Quino had his phone shut off. My clients are warriors in the War on Drugs, trying to serve this community and law enforcement. They intended to try to reach Quino again so the Tampa narcs could take the supplier and buyer down when they went to make the second delivery. This catastrophe happened because their handler failed to stay on top of what his snitches were honorably attempting to achieve for the good of this community."

At a bond hearing, Quino confirmed the alibi. It was all a mistake, a bungled opportunity to arrest the supplier who fled into the night after sloppy police work scared him off. Quino fell on the sword. "I could have done a better job facilitating communication on this case. I apologize, Your Honor."

The Uribes were released on bond, and I immediately got a call from a forgotten friend.

"Hey, Bob, how are you doing?" Quino asked. "Sorry I haven't kept in touch. I've been swamped here at the office. Do you have a little free time? It'd be great to catch up."

We met at Valencia Garden, a legendary Spanish restaurant near downtown Tampa that had been a mecca for local power brokers since 1927. I never liked going there because it was a hangout for the big-name defense attorneys in town, lawyers that I battled with in Tampa courtrooms for decades over the acts of their low-life clients.

Quino was impeccably dressed. His dark designer suit and scarlet tie were as fresh as the styling of his thick dark hair. His mustache was trimmed to perfection. He looked like an investment banker, but he either hadn't gotten any sleep in days or had a lot on his mind. The dark circles under his eyes and tense look said he had worries. As I approached, we hugged and patted each other on the back.

"It's so good to see you, Bob. I really miss working with you. It's okay at Homicide, but the excitement of our undercover partnership was the highlight of my career. How are Ev and the kids?"

"They're fine, man. Ev's looking forward to my getting through this operation. I promised her it would be my last undercover gig, and I meant it this time."

"Speaking of the operation, did things work out with Latorre? I heard from one of the guys in the office that he drifted away from you. Did he ever come back on the radar screen?"

Why was Quino interested? This had nothing to do with him anymore. Nothing against Quino, but operational security prompted me to be vague. "We've done a little here and there, but not what we expected."

Then he let me know he had concerns. "I don't know if you heard, but these asshole snitches of mine, Mario Uribe and one of his brothers, went out of control. They were developing a case for us, and then they ran with it on their own. Either that, or they were trying to deal behind our back. They really made me look bad. Have you heard anything about that in the office?"

Quino's curiosities sent off alarms in my mind. "I'm in Sarasota at the undercover business or in Panama ninety percent of the time, so I don't hear much about shit going on in Tampa."

Over flan, we talked about old times. As he scraped his last mouthful, Quino brought the conversation back to Operation Pro-Mo. "Listen, man, somebody from your office was over at our shop. I don't know if he was bullshitting, or if it's true, but he claimed you went undercover to Colombia and met with a bunch of these guys down south." He wore a frightened look.

"Whoever let that out should have his nuts cut off. That was supposed to be under wraps. Yeah, the brass says I'm the first agent they've let do that in eight years. The guys in our office down there are on the front lines of a war zone, so I understand why they felt they had to pull my reins in while I did UC [undercover work] in Bogotá, but it seemed a lot less dangerous down there, for me, than our guys claim."

"Holy shit, Bob, that's crazy. I hope you're not planning to go there again. You know what they'd do to you if they . . ."

His voice trailed off, but the look on his face finished the sentence. Everything about him radiated deep fear, as though he had received an omen about my fate.

"Listen, Quino, I appreciate your concern. I know you're a true friend, but don't worry. I've got this under control."

Quino grabbed the check. "It's on me, Bob, please." With his nose in his wallet, fumbling for cash, he continued nonchalantly. "How much longer are you going to stay under?"

My undercover trainers always stressed that, when you're dealing with someone who's deceptive, the last question they ask at a meeting most often begs an answer to the thing that brought them to the table. That popped in my head because Quino avoided eye contact as he asked the question.

Operational security—"opsec," as we called it—demanded that I throw him a curve. The bottom line was that he didn't have a need to know, and he might unwittingly repeat it to someone that was ratting me out. So, I came up with something that pushed the anticipated takedown date months later than planned.

"You're going to love this, Quino. We've arranged for a bunch of tickets to the World Cup finals. Some of those games will be played in Orlando next June. Those will be some of the hottest tickets in the Western Hemisphere. We'll invite them to a huge gala, lodging at a Disney hotel for them and their families, and tickets to the game. They'll come like lambs to the slaughter."

"That's a great plan."

I looked at my watch. "I need to get back to my office. I've only got a day before I need to get back under. I'd really like to do something special with Ev and the kids before I leave again."

Back at the office, I heard the news. According to a snitch, before the ink dried on the documents setting terms of their release, Mario Uribe and his brother were in the wind. They'd fled to New York with false IDs.

Abraham "Abe" Marwan, one of my fellow DEA agents in Tampa, had been hunting the Uribe clan for years and was suspicious as hell about why they had slithered out of nearly every investigation. Now that Mario and one of his brothers were on the run, Marwan became the Uribes' worst nightmare.

Marwan was the epitome of a New Yorker. He called it like he saw it, no matter whom it might piss off. He was about as colorful a character as you could ever imagine, rarely politically correct, but he always told you what he sincerely believed to be the truth. He may have been small in stature, but he had a big heart, at least for those he liked. Daily workouts caused many to think he was a body builder. Because of how he carried himself and his heavy New York accent, nearly everyone assumed his ancestors were Italian, which stirred his Syrian blood, and he'd generally let you know that in colorful New Yorker language. Like my source, Dominic, Marwan was very creative with the f-word, despite being a religious man who regularly attended Bible study.

Unlike some, I trusted Marwan, and I liked him. In his own way, he always tried to do the right thing within the prism of his reasoning. He had tremendous street sense and could smell the right direction to go in pursuing the most important proof of a crime.

When it came to the alibi the Uribe brothers offered when they got caught, Marwan rendered his verdict. "I don't give a fuck what the Uribes claim about Tampa PD. I'm adopting this case into the federal system, and I'm going to use it as a club to shove up Mario's ass, and every member of his little tribe of criminals. I'm not sure where that's going to take us, but I'm going to have fun doing it."

Behind my back, a few days later, Latorre got the call. *"Hermano, es Frankie."* ("Brother, it's Frankie.") He told Latorre that he'd just spoken to another guy in his department, and then he delivered the punch line. "It will be safe for you to push money through that guy in Sarasota until May of next year. The thing will end that June."

Frankie went on. "I have an idea about how our people can do cash drops that are never seized." His plan was ingenious. He suggested that Edith put the cash in a locker at a train or bus station. She should rent a room at a nearby hotel under a fake name and leave an envelope at the front desk of the hotel for a friend who would later ask for it. She could use any name for the friend. Inside the envelope, she should put the key and directions to the box. She should call Baldasare's courier and tell him to use the name she wrote on the envelope to pick up the key and instructions at the desk. Edith needed someone to keep eyes on the locker at all times to make sure no one other than Baldasare's guy got the cash. The terminal would be crowded, so no one would be able to pick out Edith's countersurveillance guy. This method would ensure that DEA never identified who was dropping off the cash, and they would have no choice but to transfer the funds to Latorre's accounts.

Latorre was impressed. "That's brilliant. You know, you're a devious son of a bitch." They both laughed. "But, Frankie, I can't do that until it is approved by the people in Cali."

A week later, two of our undercover agents, Al Melendez and Angel Perez, were in Miami to receive three hundred thousand dollars from one of Latorre's couriers.

Like many Spanish speakers in DEA at the time, Angel Perez was born in Puerto Rico. He was raised in Humacao, a small municipality on the east coast of the island. Like me, fate brought him to law enforcement. After he got his bachelor's degree in history from the State University of New York in Buffalo, he was accepted as a grad student in history at UCLA. To make ends meet, he took a position as an aide in the state probation office during his first semester. That led to his becoming a full-time probation officer in LA, then a deputy sheriff, and ultimately a DEA agent. Angel was a deep thinker, well read, humble, and a very honest man. Our work had crossed paths five years before, when he was one of forty assault team members flown on Huey helicopters into the heart of the Bolivian jungle to raid a clandestine cocaine lab. Angel got leads about the lab from an informant, while I'd learned about it from a Medellín cartel member I befriended during an earlier undercover assignment. I was fortunate to partner with Perez in Operation Pro-Mo and to earn his friendship.

Perez was new to our Tampa office, but long in experience. In the early stages of his DEA career, while on the front lines in McAllen, Texas, his partner and very close friend, Willie Ramos, had been fatally wounded during an undercover drug buy. Ramos and a trafficker tussled over his service revolver. When the gun went off, it sent a round into the center of his chest, severing his coronary artery. He died in Perez's arms.

When Melendez and Perez arrived to meet the courier, Melendez's cell phone rang.

"Señor, go to the Berkeley Shore Hotel on Collins Avenue in Miami Beach. At the desk, using the name Santiago, ask for an envelope left for you by Maria Cortez in room 314. In the envelope you'll find instructions."

Melendez was confused. "I thought we'd meet to receive the documents [cash]?"

"I was told to do it this way. You need to call me back after you pick up the goods."

Melendez went to the front desk at the Berkeley Shore, picked up the envelope, and found two gifts inside: a written instruction ("Amtrak, 8303 NW 37th Ave") and a key to storage locker #6 at the Amtrak station. He got there, opened the locker, and pulled out a large duffel bag filled with cash.

This was a challenging tactic that we hadn't seen before. We dubbed it a "dead drop." Unfortunately, we'd see it again. Although the terms weren't the best, we were back in business with Latorre and Rodriguez-Castro.

The cash, less a laundering fee, flew through our accounts and, at Latorre's direction, was wired to a cartel account at Banco Cafetero. The last step was handled by bank officers who arranged the conversion of the "export revenue" from dollars to pesos.

Jaime was excited that the owners of the money in Cali now saw him as the man in charge. He was certain it would open doors, and he quickly learned that was literally the case. A week after the owners received their checks, there was a knock on Jaime's front door. As he cracked it open, a wave of thugs filled the room, followed by a well-dressed man who claimed to be an attorney.

"Mr. Jaime Vargas?"

"Yes, sir. That's me."

"This is a check given to my client from last week's transaction. It bounced. These gentlemen will be taking your furniture. They'll be back tomorrow to take your car, and if you don't make good on the check within a week, they'll come back for you. Have a nice day."

In days, the matter was resolved. There had been an innocent mistake, but Jaime now realized that Latorre's gift of responsibility wasn't really that wonderful. It was a curse that focused the crosshairs of the Cali cartel on Jaime's head.

To take the heat off Jaime, I asked him to get out of Bogotá for a while and meet me in Panama. I had no choice but to go there because I had been invited to meet one of Panama's most lethal moneymen—a close friend of Panamanian general Manuel Noriega—as well as spies from both the KGB and Mossad.

12

NORIEGA'S MAN

Panama City, Panama
July–August 1993

After mingling with Panama's underworld elite for a year, I discovered my reputation as a confidant of Gilbert Straub, Rinaldo Laguna, and other unsavory characters made me more attractive to onlookers who also swam in the cesspool of dirty money. Collectively, my circle of new "friends" in Panama functioned as a Trojan horse that gave others in the underworld some peace of mind when considering whether to trust me. Between my references and my potential as an earner, someone who could help them feed off a bigger piece of drug profits, it was getting easier for me to open new doors and tongues. The time had come to make a move to get close to Jorge Krupnik, one of the wealthiest and most powerful players in the country. I'd heard about him from Steven Richards, so I knew he was an ally of major criminals in town, including Gilbert Straub.

From afar, Krupnik knew I was a guy who had been accepted by some of the power brokers in town. Hopefully, Straub had told him about my role with the men in Cali. Most importantly, he had a long and strong friendship with Richards. I'd seen Krupnik months before, in strictly social settings, but had purposely held off talking business with him until I was confident that Straub had bought my act and would likely endorse me. If I tried to make a run at too many smart crooks at once, their savvy would have smelled fed.

Richards put a bug in Krupnik's ear about my having been a good friend and partner in crime for years. It didn't take Krupnik long to welcome the Trojan horse. "I've heard good things about Mr. Baldasare. I'd appreciate it if you'd bring him by my office so we can be formally introduced."

Maybe he was curious, but more likely his interest was triggered by greed.

On one of the many nights with Panama's movers and shakers at El Pavo Real, I brought Krupnik's name up with one of my crooked banker friends. "I've been invited to meet someone in town who I'm told is a person of influence. Do you know Jorge Krupnik?"

The banker wrinkled his nose like he'd smelled something foul. "He's hotter than a volcano. For me, he's too high profile. He hid Manuel Noriega the first few nights of the US invasion and used to be Noriega's man in charge of weapons procurement for the entire country. Everyone knows they were very close friends. He has some scary buddies, including Noriega's head of security, Michael Harari, a former Mossad agent who they say tracked down and murdered some of the Palestinian terrorists who held Israelis hostage at the Entebbe International Airport in Uganda in 1976. He has serious contacts in Russia, Italian organized crime, and the Colombian underworld. Working openly with him will draw attention. I suggest you proceed with caution."

I couldn't wait to meet Krupnik, but I couldn't broadcast that when I met him. It would be important for me to act only mildly impressed.

Richards took me to Krupnik's office, a massively plush man cave that consumed much of the penthouse floor of the Banco Exterior Building in downtown Panama City. His sprawling oak desk, contrasted by the gleaming blond wood floor, was positioned near a living room setting, with plush chairs and a couch that had certainly hosted many of the powerful over the years. Three floor-to-ceiling glass walls offered stunning views of the city, especially through the tripod telescope in the corner of the room. A massive spinnable globe in a wooden stand sat near one of the gleaming walls, suggesting the breadth of Krupnik's influence.

At first sight, he embraced Richards like a long-lost brother. *"Abrazos, hermano. Me alegra verte de nuevo."* ("Hugs, brother. It is so good to see you again.") He threw an admiring look at Richards and continued in English. "You haven't changed a bit. You still look like a little chubby Harvard professor, rather than the scoundrel you are." They both laughed.

"Jorge," Richards replied, "I'd like to introduce you to Bob Baldasare, a man who, for good reasons, has stayed in the shadows for years but deserves credit for much of my past success."

Krupnik extended his hand. "It is a pleasure to finally be introduced."

"The pleasure is mine," I replied. "I've heard many good things about you, Mr. Krupnik."

Krupnik was tall, dark haired with a wide girth. He spoke English perfectly, although with a unique accent that left me wondering whether his Russian, Jewish, or Argentinian roots were the cause. Although he was a worldly man of great wealth, he wasn't pretentious and seemed grounded in common sense and real business experience. His words confirmed that he was well educated, if not in a classroom, at least by the university of life. When it came to important topics, he exhibited a detailed knowledge that made it obvious that he had been there and done that.

I let him know that my attorney in Panama was Rinaldo Laguna, and Krupnik let me know he'd done his homework. "I know."

I confided. "Jorge, Gil Straub has been very helpful, establishing companies for me and ensuring my safety, but it looks like he'll be spending much more time in London and Russia in the coming years, so I'm looking for some additional help here in Panama. Frankly, since we've just met, I'm a little reluctant to talk business now. I'd like to get to know you before going down that road."

"Bob, please know you can speak freely with me. I consider you family, based on your strong endorsements from others I trust implicitly. Let me tell you a little bit about my background."

He explained that he had been born in Russia, was raised in Argentina, and moved to New York before ultimately settling in Panama. He owned a construction company and a marine terminal, as well as a company called Midland Marine that chartered freighters and tankers. He had substantial business interests in Colombia, including a partnership with one of the country's largest exporters of emeralds. Most importantly, he had major bank connections worldwide, including with Swiss Bank Corp, Banco Exterior, Union Bank of Switzerland (UBS), and Banque Nacionale de Paris.

Krupnik made sure to highlight that it isn't always what you know, but who you know. "I'm close friends with very high-ranking people in the Russian and Cuban governments." And he had a lot of projects in the making. "I'm financing the automation of two ports in Panama and one in Buenaventura, Colombia. You see, you have to control the infrastructure if you're going to do something big. Why don't you meet me here later this week, alone, so we can discuss these issues in greater detail?"

"Thank you, Jorge. It would be comforting to know more about you."

Two days later, it was just me and Krupnik in his palatial office. "Jorge, you've assured me that our discussions will be kept in strict

The author undercover as Robert Musella—standing by his private jet.

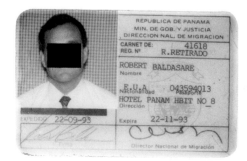

Top: The author's Panamanian Cedula arranged by Rinaldo Laguna. Middle: Condo on the Bay luxury community—location of the author's undercover residence. Bottom: View of the author's undercover marina suite and the Hatteras Cruiser he chartered.

Left: The exterior of the Belle Haven office complex, location of Baldasare's undercover companies.
Right: Front door to Avid Investment Group and Avid Mortgage Services.

Baldasare's office within the Avid Investment Group offices.

STATE OF FLORIDA
DEPARTMENT OF BANKING AND FINANCE
STATE CAPITOL BUILDING, TALLAHASSEE, FLORIDA 32399-0350   PHONE (904) 487-2583

MORTGAGE BROKER LICENSE

THE MORTGAGE BROKER INDICATED BELOW IS LICENSED UNDER
THE PROVISIONS OF CHAPTER 494, FLORIDA STATUTES.

EFFECTIVE DATE	EXPIRATION DATE
08/04/92	08/31/93

04165

ROBERT BALDASARE
327 WHISPERING OAKS CT
SARASOTA, FL 34232

LICENSE NUMBER
MB 064440632 000

AUDIT NUMBER MB 9200974

COMPTROLLER OF FLORIDA

Baldasare's mortgage broker license.

AVID **MORTGAGE**
SERVICES, INC.

ROBERT BALDASARE
President

24641 U.S. HWY. 19 N. SUITE 530
CLEARWATER, FL. 34623

(813) 799-6170
FAX (813) 797-0559

Robert Baldasare
Executive Consultant

MULTINACIONAL DE
IMPORTACIONES Y EXPORTACIONES, S. A.

Apartado 6-3246 El Dorado,
Panamá, Rep. de Panamá

Tel. (507) 69-0511
Fax: (507) 69-0580

EN-PRO TECHNOLOGY, S.A.

Robert Baldasare
Vice-President

Apartado 6-4092
R Dorado, Republic of Panama
507-23-6967
Fax 507-69-2789

327 Whispering Oaks Ct
Sarasota, FL 34232
813-379-0023
Fax 813-378-9940

AVID **INSURANCE**
SERVICES, INC.

ROBERT BALDASARE

24641 U.S. HWY. 19 N. SUITE 588
CLEARWATER, FL. 34623

(813) 725-1770

ROBERT BALDASARE
Adviser to the Board of Directors

BANQUE DE PARTICIPATIONS
ET DE PLACEMENTS
500 PARK AVENUE, APT. 25B
NEW YORK, N.Y. 10022

212-756-3550
TELEX 795119
NYREP UR

*Above: Business cards of Baldasare's
undercover businesses. Left: "Dominic",
the controlled source that acted undercover
as Baldasare's cousin and bodyguard.*
(Photo courtesy private collection.)

Low income housing in Colon, Panama.

Baldasare within the interior of the Hotel El Panamá complex.

Hotel El Panamá pool bar and outdoor restaurant.

The remains of the defunct BCCI Panama office.

The shattered BCCI Panama sign the author saw at the outset of Operation Pro-Mo.

Gilbert Straub. (Photo by Wide World, courtesy of the author.)

Heywood Manor—the mansion where Gilbert Straub resided in Southampton, England.

$ 1,000,000.00   1-27-94
From Houston, Tx.

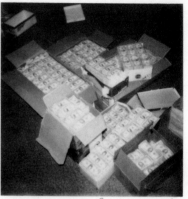

300 lbs. of Money!
$ 1,675,000.00
10-6-92 /Chicago

$ 2,000,000.00   1-27-94
From Houston, Tx.

Opposite, right, and below: Pictures of cartel cash received, with notations about amounts and cities in which they were received. (Photos by Al Melendez.)

$ 500,000.00   8-18-93
Pick up in Los Angeles, Cal.

1,279,000.00
1-21-93 / San Juan Puerto Rico

Below: DEA agent Lee Paige showing $700k in cartel cash seized in San Juan. (Photo courtesy Lee Paige.)

Gracias a la colaboración de ciudadanos como usted, estamos derrotando al Narcoterrorismo

¡No lo piense más, decídase!

Por su información, el Gobierno le garantiza :

usted pone TODAS, TODAS, las condiciones

- Absoluta reserva sobre su identidad.
- Protección para su familia.
- Comienzo de una nueva vida en el exterior.
- Si tiene problemas penales, la Fiscalía podrá solucionarlos.

PABLO ESCOBAR
"el doctor"
RECOMPENSA
$ 5.000 Millones

ALFONSO PUERTA
"angelito"
RECOMPENSA
$ 100 Millones

RECORTE Y CONSERVE ESTOS TELEFONOS

GRATIS 9800 10600 MEDELLIN 461 11 11
Desde cualquier CIUDAD 9800 19800 APARTADO 6700 461 11 12

Pablo Escobar wanted poster.

Above: Exterior of Tramonti restaurant. (Photo by Jaime Angel.) Left: Jaime Vargas, controlled source in Colombia, and the author in Bogotá. Below: Undercover agents Angel Perez and Al Melendez.

Right: Jorge Krupnik. (Courtesy private collection.)
Middle: Panamanian strongman General Manuel Noriega (© Bob Sullivan/AFP/Getty Images.)
Bottom: Robert Vesco, international swindler and close associate of Gilbert Straub.
(© Bettmann/ Getty Images.)

Above: Alvaro Garces (left) and Guillermo Segura (right) at the Bridging the Americas event in Sarasota. Left: Miguel Rodriguez-Orejuela—Cali Cartel leader.
(© PEDRO UGARTE/AFP via Getty Images.)

"Bridging the Americas"
Cabaret – Concert

October 12, 1993
The Brass Parrot • 55 Palm Avenue South
Sarasota, Florida
7 p.m. until 12 midnight

$75.00
R.S.V.P. (813) 957-4448
**This event is sponsored by the
AVID INVESTMENT GROUP** based in Sarasota, Florida.

Bridging the Americas invitation.

Ransom photo for "the Princess" during her kidnapping. (Courtesy of Tom Tiderington.
Image first appeared in *Snatched* by Bruce Porter.)

Former DEA agent Rene De La Cruz escorts General Manuel Noriega from Panama.
(© STF/AFP via Getty Images.)

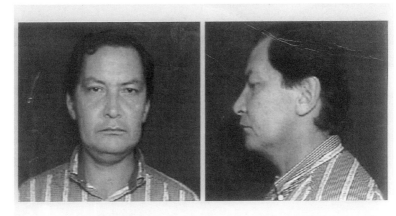

Last Name LATORRE   First LUIS

Luis Fernando Latorre.

DEA agents cuff Quino's hands behind his back.

confidence. Given the good things our mutual friends have said about you, I'd like to let you know more about my business and determine if collaborating might be mutually beneficial."

I let him know that I laundered for the lieutenants of Miguel Rodriguez-Orejuela, one of the heads of the Cali cartel, and that our work started with the receipt of large cash shipments in both US and European cities. I explained that my team included Colombian bankers and businessmen who helped disguise wire transfers, from my companies to Colombia, as repatriated export revenue and trade-based loans.

"Bob, I've dealt with these people on commercial matters."

"Well, this money needs very special handling, Jorge, because if anyone should unwrap our cover, it would expose our client's drug operations. All the money is from their cocaine sales."

For every undercover agent who has to deliver the words that will help a jury realize that the Krupniks of the world are aware of the true source of laundered funds, the next ten seconds waiting for the essential response feels like an hour. My mind raced about whether I had spoken too early in our dance of trust. While anxiously awaiting his reaction, I had to broadcast a calm and natural confidence. I couldn't offer even the slightest twitch.

He looked me straight in the eye and made no bones about it. "I would like to partner with you to provide services to your clients. I have a lot of contacts and experience that would contribute greatly to your success, providing you an impenetrable front to protect you from the feds. You need to drop your US citizenship and move here as a Panamanian citizen. That is best, not only for you, but for me, too, because no amount of money can get you out of trouble if the US wants you. On the other hand, here in Panama, we can buy whatever protection we need."

It was a challenge to wrap my mind around the fact that I was sitting in Krupnik's lair, in the same seat that General Manuel Noriega undoubtedly sat in just a few years before. Krupnik had welcomed me to join his gang of thieves. As I peered at him from across his huge ebony desk, I was in disbelief. As Krupnik talked and Robert Baldasare calmly listened, my Bob Mazur brain was raging with questions. Why was this so easy? I knew I had serious credibility issues with Latorre, but for the moment, I couldn't be distracted in the slightest. Krupnik was a very big fish in the underworld, and I didn't want to suggest anything other than that I was a big-time money launderer for the men in Cali.

"Bob, here are just a few things I can provide. I can get you large numbers of export documents to legitimize your transfers. I also have a partner in Colombia who can offer an unlimited number of Colombian pesos for dollars. Because we have a large float of funds, we can deliver those pesos right after your couriers confirm the amount of cash you receive in the States or Europe. And for those clients who want to exchange cash for goods, that's something we do all the time."

Krupnik had a bank contact in Europe who would safely provide wire transfers in exchange for cash, at a fee of 5 percent, and he was ready to introduce me to officers at major banks in Panama who would help us. He could also quickly arrange the delivery of gold bars in Panama or Colombia in exchange for cash delivered anywhere in the world.

"Jorge, I think a good start would be for us to do a few transactions and then assess how to move forward. We could immediately use your help in accepting dollars that your man in Colombia can pay out in pesos."

Krupnik was all in. He gave me his home phone numbers and the number for a private line at his office. He asked that I meet him again soon, so he could provide information about twenty million dollars in property that he owned in Miami and wanted to exchange for cash delivered in Panama.

As I left his office, I was astonished by his menu of laundering options. This man had squirmed away from investigation after investigation during the past decade, and now I had every word about his laundering capabilities on tape. My briefcase recorder got it all. This whale shark in the sea of the underworld had bought Robert Baldasare's act hook, line, and sinker, but I had an empty feeling of victory. It just seemed too easy.

A few days later, I was back in Krupnik's office. Clearly, he'd given deep thought to how we should operate to reduce risk. "Bob, we need to minimize using phones, and when we do, we need to speak in codes." He rattled off a few.

"Since we're partners, I want you to maintain a solid front. You can have a private office here with me on the twenty-fifth floor. I'll also provide space for a secretary, and I think it would be best if you became a director of Unicorp Financial Group, one of my companies."

In return for our partnership, he wanted 50 percent of our profits, and a promise that I would do everything I could to talk my clients into letting Krupnik use dope money to purchase goods for them that they could then sell around the world, giving them legitimate cover for their drug fortunes.

His partner in Colombia had offices in Cali and Bogotá, and needed only twenty-four-hour notice to provide fake export documents that could cover money movements into Colombia of two million dollars or more at a time. That was an extraordinary asset, since the Cali men thrived on laundering through a front of repatriated export revenue.

Krupnik was now willing to share details about a laundering option he hadn't previously disclosed, which he felt was a crown-jewel method of laundering. He claimed to work closely with the owners of the two largest emerald mines in Colombia, including the czar of the emerald trade, Victor Carranza. With Carranza and another emerald trader named Murcia, Krupnik could provide the perfect laundering cover. He could arrange the shipment of five million dollars in uncut emeralds from Colombia to a company I could control in the Colón Free Zone. The emeralds would be smuggled back to Colombia and continuously reshipped to my company in Colón. This carousel of emerald exports would produce all the documents of exportation we'd need to transfer narco-dollars back to Colombia, and it would also offer a perfect cover for the influx of US cash, checks, and wire transfers bought with narco-dollars and disguised as receipts from the sale of emeralds. A mountain of paper would have to be meticulously maintained to make everything look legit. If Krupnik was name-dropping, he picked the right names. Carranza and Murcia were known by law enforcement in both Colombia and the US.

And if what he had shared wasn't enough, Krupnik also had the resources to pull off another laundering trick. He could arrange for the exportation of numerous shipping containers of valueless commodities from Colombia to the Colón Free Zone that would be identified on paper as expensive goods. This would create more export documents that we could later use to justify the wiring of narco-dollars back to Colombia.

"Jorge, I'm very interested in your proposals. I need to return to Florida briefly, but when I get back, we can make a final decision about how we should move forward together. You've given me a lot to consider, and it seems to me that our alliance has countless potential." I thanked him for having confidence in me and sharing his insights. "It's ironic that you suggest I officially become a Panamanian. I guess great minds think alike. My attorney, Rinaldo Laguna, felt the same way and is working on the paperwork as we speak. I'm headed to his office to go over the documents."

When I got to Laguna's law office, I learned that there were some typical unofficial Panamanian expenses that I'd need to pay in order to expedite my citizenship and passport. He needed fifteen thousand dollars in cash, the magic number that would grease the palms of the Panamanian immigration officials who would process my applications at warp speed. That process would transpire in mere months, rather than years.

While shuffling documents across his desk, I told Laguna, "I've met Jorge Krupnik, and it looks like we may have an opportunity to help one another."

Laguna's head sprang up like a cobra eyeing a lizard. "Bob, he is well known to be in our Mafia. You need to be cautious with him. He's the only person in Panama known to have screwed Noriega and not suffered any consequences."

I told Laguna that in order to create a mirage in the US that my associations in Panama and Colombia were legitimate, I decided to take advantage of my involvement in the Sarasota Chamber of Commerce. I was sponsoring a Chamber dinner and conference entitled "Bridging the Americas" and would host twenty-five or so businessmen from Panama and Colombia to meet and mingle with business leaders in the Sarasota area. Laguna thought it was a great idea and immediately offered to make a presentation about Panamanian corporate and immigration law. Of course, I accepted.

Laguna didn't realize that I had decided to organize this event in order to comfort the crooks I'd been dealing with in Panama and Colombia about traveling to the States. It would demonstrate to any who turned down this first invitation that an offer from me to come to Sarasota wasn't a trap designed to land them in handcuffs. This first event would provide the false reassurance; the handcuffs would appear at the second event.

As my meeting with Laguna ended, I declined an offer to have his bodyguard drive me to the Hotel El Panamá. The hotel was within walking distance, and I just wanted to get off the Bob Baldasare stage. Besides Krupnik and Laguna, I'd had a dozen other recorded meetings with targets during this trip. I missed Ev and the kids. I needed time to reflect on the people who meant everything to me in my real life, and I needed a break from the charade.

The trainers at the US Customs undercover school that I had attended, before moving on to DEA, opened my eyes to a lot of the pitfalls of long-term undercover work. It was important to realize that you lived in an abnormally stressful environment, even if you were too macho to admit it. You got less sleep than you should, were immersed in a culture of people who played hard, and would be challenged to live life their way, tempted by the lifestyle of the enemy. Critical antidotes to those challenges included working out, eating healthy, maintaining contact with your real world, and remaining focused on the mission.

One of my most effective antidotes was jogging, so when I was in Panama, I didn't give it up. Despite the risks, I ran along Avenida Balboa and other roads near the water. Jogging in Panama City wasn't embraced by the locals. Anytime I had to cross a road, it was obvious that I was an annoyance to the mass of Panamanians who would rather sit in their car for an hour to nudge around town. Traffic was horrific, and joggers seemed to be targets. But that served my need, because there was no way I would make that jog without giving my surroundings my full attention. Bob Baldasare didn't exist when I ran the streets of Panama City because banishing him was the only way I could run safely, and jogging was one of the only things I could do to shut down my constant strategizing about Baldasare's next move.

By mile five, the euphoria usually kicked in, as did the endorphins, recharging my batteries and keeping me from endlessly obsessing about the outcome of every twist and turn in Baldasare's life. Absent strenuous running and periodically reconnecting with the real people in my life, the lure of the Baldasare role could become a danger. I'd seen a lot of undercover agents crash and burn, and I was never going to be one of them.

After a hard run, I decided to shower and head to a local restaurant alone. Leaving the suite was always an added security risk. I had notes, a recorder, and microcassette tapes that needed to be secured. Early in my trip, I had found a hiding spot inside the closet that housed the suite's air conditioner. It was hard to access and nearly impossible to find. Anytime I left the suite without my recorder, that's where I hid anything that might compromise me.

As I got ready to leave, the phone rang.

"Hi, Bob. It's Rinaldo. Listen, I need a favor. You met Helen, my girlfriend, the other night at the party at my home. I'm telling her that you and I are going out to dinner and have some serious things to discuss. She shouldn't call you, but if she does, cover for me. I met this unbelievably beautiful blond, and I'm taking her to dinner tonight. And more, hopefully." He laughed.

"No problem, Rinaldo. I've got you covered."

An hour or so later, as I was led to my table at the restaurant, I was ushered right past a table of ladies that included Laguna's girlfriend.

"Hi, Helen. How are you? After some intense discussions with Rinaldo and my clients tonight, they decided they needed to cover some things that were best discussed without me, so I was kicked out of my own meeting. Can you imagine that?"

The look on her face told me that she knew it was bullshit, and that Laguna was on the prowl.

Although my efforts to convince Helen fell short, my earlier pitch to launder for Jorge Sanz Sr. and his group in Buenaventura, Colombia, finally paid off. Sanz Sr. and a half dozen of his relatives were loyal assets of the Cali cartel, piloting a freighter with stacks of shipping containers used as cover to move tons of cocaine to America. Their talents also helped the cartel clean tens of millions in drug profits. Thanks to a lot of hard work by Jaime and Richards, the Sanz clan was sold on Bob Baldasare's credibility. Only five months earlier, their pull within the Cali cartel had helped us to get Latorre released from the deadly grip of Dr. Death. Since then, they had come to the conclusion that it was time to bring me an offer I couldn't refuse.

13

RIVER OF GREEN

August–September 1993

Richards had known Jorge Sanz Sr. and his son for years. They'd smuggled together in the past, so when Richards heavily endorsed Jaime and me, our job got a lot easier. Once Richards opened the door, Jaime made repeated trips to Cali to build a friendship and trust with Sanz Sr., his son, and his nephew, all of whom were named Jorge Sanz. It was easy to distinguish Sr. and Jr., and the nephew went by the nickname "Coqui."

Sanz Sr. was the captain of a freighter, the *Coffee Express*, a vessel he confessed the cartel used to transport large shipments of cocaine and currency. His son and nephew managed cartel money movements. They were trusted in Cali because they were related to several high-ranking cartel members who worked for Dennis Gomez-Patino, also known as "El Zarco," who oversaw the transportation of cocaine base from Bolivia and Peru to Colombia. Sanz Sr., his son, and nephew all revealed that, on behalf of Gomez-Patino, they dealt directly with Luis Eduardo Velez-Arias, a launderer in the upper ranks of the cartel who justified his wealth by operating a construction company funded with drug profits. During a visit to Importaciones Ltd., the Sanz clan's office in Cali, Jaime was introduced to Velez-Arias and other major players. They bought everything Jaime sold, including his pitch that I was his boss, with the contacts and means to clean the river of cash they controlled for the cartel.

To close the relationship, I spoke with Coqui and Jorge Sanz Jr. They offered options for large money pickups in Houston, Chicago, New York, England, the Netherlands, Italy, Germany, Poland, Portugal, and Japan. I had to slow them down.

"Coqui, my preference would be to do a little thing in Miami and then serve you in New York, so you can better understand the quality of our service. Then, if you'd like us to organize things in Europe, we will."

I let them know I was phasing out of the States, would soon have my Panamanian citizenship, and would manage things in the States and Europe from Panama City. I invited them to meet me there. They accepted, but they wanted to test us first by having us accept a shipment of cash in Chicago. That was a challenge, because we were spread thin. Something had mysteriously revived Latorre's interest in working with me, and he was using us again in a big way. In a period of about ten days, we received over one million dollars from his client's couriers in Miami and Los Angeles. Agents in those cities were using the intelligence from the pickups to develop cases independently. But the new door into the Cali cartel, opened by Sanz, was more promising, because unlike Latorre, the Sanz clan was introducing us directly to the leaders that owned the money. That was our goal from the start: infiltrate, identify, and dismantle the highest possible levels of the Cali cartel's command and control.

Two undercover agents posing as my couriers, Al Melendez and Angel Perez, went to Chicago and picked up eight hundred thousand dollars from cartel workers aligned with the Sanz family. We needed to get these dollars converted to Colombian pesos, the form of payment requested by the Sanz team. I had the option to use several black-market money brokers in Colombia to execute the conversion, but since Latorre and his partner were back in our fold, I took a calculated risk. My logic was that if Latorre was on the fence about whether we were DEA, what better way to dissuade him of that than to bring him new business by giving him and Rodriguez-Castro the chance to convert nearly eight hundred thousand US dollars for one of my clients. This would either bring Latorre back to being a full believer in Baldasare, or it could potentially compromise our relationship with the Sanz family.

As I weighed the decision, one major factor drove my thinking. Had someone intentionally compromised me, or were Latorre's concerns based on a guess? My conclusion: there was no way that one of my law enforcement brothers or sisters would betray me, so I chose to bring Latorre in on the deal. He and Rodriguez-Castro made the conversion, and their profit, through what they described as a banker on their payroll at Banco Uconal in Colombia, and the money flew to accounts designated by the Sanz family. On the surface, it seemed like everyone was happy. I'd bet my life and the lives of my fellow under-cover agents on my deduction that none of our colleagues were rats. If I was wrong, I prayed that any loss of life would fall to me. I couldn't live with myself otherwise.

While getting ready to leave for Panama, I missed a call from Gilbert Straub. I called him back at Heywood Manor, his mansion outside of London. As I began to explain that I had been introduced to Jorge Krupnik, he let me know how fast information traveled along the grapevine of crooks. "Well, that's funny, because my office sent me a message, and they said, 'Please call Mr. K collect . . .' Mr. K said you and Dana . . . met with him, noting you'd been referred by me, and he wanted me to tell him that you were good people. Jorge came back at me, saying, 'Hey, you're sending me these guys, and who are they?' Jorge is a very gracious host. He's a very nice person. I like him, as a person, but in a business setting, I wouldn't go near him with a twenty-foot pole. Jorge is under the eyes of every investigatory agency known to man. Any agency with an initial has got Jorge in their files, and I mean their big files." Straub shared everything he could. "Jorge is not a Panamanian. He's an Argentinian Jew. He married into a very well-known family of Catholics. He's shunned by the Catholics and the Jews alike."

"Gil, he extended an invitation for me to—"

"Bob, let me guess. He offered for you to use his office. He does that for everybody. It's always empty, and I think you know why now. He's got the highest profile of anybody I know in town."

Straub offered a better alternative to setting up shop at Krupnik's palace. "We are expanding the office in Panama, and if there's any kind of facilities that you need, like a dedicated room or something, we'd be happy to talk about it."

I was beginning to feel like a beauty queen. Two of the highest-profile crooks in Panama were competing to get me under their wing. If I were really Baldasare, my choice would undoubtedly be to nest at Straub's office. I thanked Straub for his warnings about Krupnik and let him know I would set up my shop in his suite of offices.

It was time to get back to Panama. As my flight cruised over the Gulf of Mexico, I opened that day's edition of the *Miami Herald*. The front-page story covered Amjad Awan, one of the dirty bankers I'd caught in my last undercover assignment. After I'd gained his cooperation, he testified before Congress about his laundering for Manuel Noriega. As I read and listened to music, it happened again: Richard Marx singing Ev's favorite song. Within a few seconds I started to lose it. I began tearing up, overwhelmed with simultaneous thoughts of how much I missed Ev and the kids, and how my undercover work years before had changed so many lives, putting bad guys that deserved to do time behind bars, but also bringing pain and suffering to those bad guys' families, whose loved ones I had convinced to trust me.

I struggled with the guilt of possibly destroying the lives of many

people again, in my current operation. It hurt to think about the outwardly decent people who would suffer when Operation Pro-Mo went
down. In the midst of emotion, I swore again that this would be my
last undercover job. I wanted out in the worst way. I wanted my life
back. I wanted to just be me, not this two-headed character who had
to calculate his every move, every minute of every day, and who left a
wake of other peoples' tears everywhere he went.

The ride to the Hotel El Panamá was a blur. I got a good night's
rest, because the next morning, I would have to sweeten the delivery of
what would be a sour message to my new underworld friend, Krupnik.

As we sat in his sprawling office, I did my best to persuade him
that it wasn't personal, just my being a smart crook. In a respectful way,
I let him know Robert Baldasare would be out of his mind to have a
high-profile relationship with Krupnik, regardless of how attractive that
was in the mind of Bob Mazur, the federal agent.

"Jorge, I've been giving this a lot of thought. I like you very much
and value your capabilities immensely. But with all due respect, I've
taken time to learn about your background, and how you've drawn the
attention of authorities in your country and mine. My assessment is that
it would not be in our best interests for me to move into your office and
be seen by the rest of the world as a member of your team. I want to
partner with you, but it's best for both of us that we do this in secret."

Krupnik explained that the hit his reputation had taken was
because of Manuel Noriega. Noriega had lured Krupnik into his inner
circle, offering control of arms procurement for the country. In return,
Noriega wanted 25 percent of the profit. Krupnik was fine with that
arrangement. He established relationships with arms dealers around the
world, as well as buyers. As the money rolled in, Noriega changed the
terms and demanded 50 percent of the profit. Eventually, he demanded
75 percent. At that stage, Krupnik drew the line, insisting that they split
all remaining assets equally, and Noriega would have to find someone
else to do his bidding.

Krupnik continued to cry on my shoulder. "A few days before Noriega was captured, he came to my home with twelve armed men, demanding entry. I had no choice but to let him in." Two days later, when one of Noriega's guards jumped over the wall that surrounded Krupnik's house and fled, he convinced Noriega it was too dangerous for him to stay. Krupnik suggested Noriega hide at the Apostolic Nunciature, the Holy See's embassy in Panama, and he did. Not long after, 250 US soldiers stormed Krupnik's home. They threatened him in many ways, including canceling any future visas he requested to travel to the US. They made it clear none of that would happen if he answered their questions. Krupnik knew Noriega's days were numbered. To save himself, he did what he had to and told them where to find their man.

Wanting to make sure I knew everything about his endless money-laundering prowess, Krupnik filled me in on more options. "I have very close contacts with Hasidic Jews in the New York City diamond district. For a fee, they'll take your client's money and wire the funds anywhere in the world. They move tons of cash."

And there was more. A man in the Miami Free Zone sent goods to the Colón Free Zone regularly. I had an option to deliver cash to his Miami contact hidden in commercial goods. Krupnik's man would ship the items to Colón, where Krupnik would have it collected and flown to Colombia on one of his two planes.

"Bob, these are pictures of my planes, two North American Sabreliner 40s. They're registered to Panamanian companies. I use them to fly gold bullion and cash to remote airstrips in Cali."

Offers kept rolling off his tongue. "I have contacts in Vegas. We can move a lot through casinos, and I can help you in the Bahamas. I have a contact who is a close friend of the prime minister. With his diplomatic status, he can transport cash, deposit the funds in a Bahamian government-related account, and then wire the funds wherever you'd like."

Krupnik obviously had a lot of experience.

"Bob, I can't stress this enough. You need to build a sound legal front to cover these money movements. Without that shield, your chances of getting caught are very high. Neither I nor my friends want problems, especially my friends in Italy. I move a lot of black-market cigarettes in Europe for 'the family' in Italy. They control the entire European cigarette market."

Later that night, I met with Krupnik and a mutual friend, a Panamanian banker who had his own reputation for moving dirty money. Krupnik took us to one of his favorite restaurants, Restaurante La Marina, a seafood place at Panama City's Yacht and Fishing Club. This hideaway is nestled in the marina with a picturesque view of a lavish fleet of cabin cruisers and sailboats with a stunning panorama of the gleaming high-rises in Punta Paitilla. As Krupnik crushed lobster tail after lobster tail, splattering butter and remnants on his plastic bib, he and his friend laughed and shared details about one of the best money-laundering schemes they'd witnessed in decades. A very well-known international bank based in Switzerland sold gold bullion to a Jewish friend of theirs in Panama, who arranged to have it delivered on a private jet to a remote airstrip in Cali. A string of Jeeps overflowing with duffel bags of cash met the plane. As sicarios armed with AK-47s watched, the gold was unloaded, and the bags of cash were thrown on the plane. The gold was sold to the traffickers at 15 percent above market price, pure profit for their friend. The plane flew the cash back to Panama, while the traffickers' men shredded the gold and sold it to Colombia's Central Bank, falsely claiming it was mined locally. The bank paid the traffickers Colombian pesos, completing the last leg of the laundering process. It was brilliant.

As I sat at the table, taking everything in, I was amazed by the complexity, brilliance, and broad variety of Krupnik's laundering schemes. Designing and executing them required the brain power of a Fortune 500 CEO. He could have enjoyed riches operating solely in the legit world, but he seemed to relish the rush of making many fortunes while operating without rules in an underworld of limitless power and corruption.

It wasn't just a handful of people who functioned as the underworld's moneymen. What I personally witnessed in both this undercover operation and my previous one was that a significant portion of the financial sector was involved in laundering. Some did it openly, but many more wrapped themselves in plausible deniability as they pushed money around the world in the midst of a fog of willful blindness. The horde of professionals I saw was incapable of realizing that what they did destroyed tens of millions of lives. They were blind to the consequences of their acts because the suffering they caused couldn't be seen through the sea of greenbacks that had their full attention. It became my mission to do whatever I could to help the rest of the world know this reality, which is seen only by those who earn membership in a criminal trust. Guys like Krupnik, Straub, and Baldasare are given the secret handshake, and the opportunity to see what really happens behind boardroom doors.

At Krupnik's request, I met him the next day at his office. After revealing details about laundering opportunities he was ready to furnish in Europe, he delivered his last line. "Bob, my contacts look professional. They're bankers and businessmen. They wear suits. But you should know they have people who kill for them."

I couldn't resist delivering a solemn look. I quietly said, "Don't we all?" He got the message.

Back in Cali, since we'd passed the Sanz clan's test, moving eight hundred thousand dollars from Chicago to Cali, Jorge Jr. was dispatched to Panama to meet me and negotiate a long-term relationship. This was important, because it was our opportunity to get details about the members of Sanz's team and his clients. Without acquiring details about others in his orbit, laundering money for him had no law enforcement purpose, and we'd have to shut him down. Undercover laundering is an investigative technique that can't be taken lightly. It's only justified if it gets you new evidence to prosecute other people and seize otherwise unknown assets. Lose sight of that, and all an undercover operation accomplishes is the facilitation of crime and the enrichment of cartel coffers.

As I approached a table at the Hotel El Panamá's poolside restaurant, Richards exchanged laughs with a short, young, dark-haired, casually-dressed guy whom I'd never seen before. He looked unpretentious, like a cabdriver or hotel maintenance guy. Richards turned to me. "Bob, let me introduce my good friend here, Jorge Sanz Jr. Come and sit with us."

Jorge Jr. was confused. "Oh, you are Bob? I pictured you . . . very different." He was expecting an older man.

My goal was to keep the first meeting casual. As we clanked our beers in a toast, I welcomed him to Panama, and he immediately announced his hope. "Here's to us doing a lot of business." In his next breath, he wanted to know if we could handle eight million dollars a week. His clients had large stashes of cash in New York, Chicago, and Los Angeles.

"Jorge, I think it would be wise for us both to invest a little time to get to know one another. These matters are very delicate. Let's enjoy dinner this evening and plan on having a detailed business discussion tomorrow, in the early evening? I unfortunately have meetings scheduled during the day." He agreed, so Richards, Al Melendez, and I ushered him off to Restaurant 1985, Laguna's favorite dinner place that had now become ours, too.

The next day, on the terrace of my suite, Sanz Jr. was eager to get down to business. After I explained our capabilities, he got serious. He assured me his clients were among the top people in Colombia's drug business, and they were looking for a source to move their money that would work exclusively for them. "They work in every city, so there's money in every city. In Europe, we take the money in Holland, London, Italy, Spain, and Belgium." And his clients weren't only major traffickers in Cali. The Sanz team also serviced cartels in Barranquilla and Santa Marta. "We have clients who, for example, have two hundred million dollars a year. Other clients may have forty million three times a year. It's a delicate business. We have to be very sure of what we are doing." As he put it, we could be tasked to receive three million, five million, fifteen million, and twenty million dollars in different US cities, all on the same day.

In the States, he was very disappointed that I didn't want to accept money in Houston, the biggest cash center for the cartel, where cocaine was pouring under, over, and through the border between Texas and Mexico.

As he revealed more, he fidgeted. Something had him on edge. "I will be frank. I don't know whether you guys are DEA. I don't know whether you're CIA. I don't know whether you're FBI. Deep inside, I don't know who you guys are. We started a business with trust. On my part, I have absolute trust on my side because I know who I work with. I mean, who I can do work for. Deep inside, I don't know who you guys are. The DEA, the CIA, the FBI or whoever, they have operations that may last one year, or two. And they keep throwing you a line until you trust them. I have to know you personally, see if you have families, where they live, what they do, how they do it. Do you understand what I'm saying? I'm risking my life, and not only my own, but my family's, too. If I'm putting my life at risk, you guys should put your lives at risk, too."

"Jorge, we work very hard to be professional in the community, to look professional."

"Bob, that's why we are talking." He and his people had studied our backgrounds, including all of our companies. Everything checked out, but he was still concerned. "This week, I was offered fifteen million dollars after we did our first business. I did not accept it." He wanted to make sure we could handle that kind of volume before risking his death.

"Jorge, maybe an event that I'm hosting in Sarasota soon will serve your need to know me, my family, and my business." I handed him the glossy brochure for "Bridging the Americas," my company's Chamber of Commerce–sponsored dinner and conference. "You and your father are welcome to attend as our guests."

He studied it. I could see the wheels turning in his head as he methodically weighed the invitation. The words in the brochure were designed to anesthetize the sixth sense that he and everyone in his underworld circle possessed.

> Join prominent entrepreneurs and bankers from South, Central, and North America in a celebration of international trade and democracy in the Americas. Participants from Costa Rica, Panama, Nicaragua, Colombia, the US, and other countries will attend a formal cabaret to heighten awareness of international trade among their respective countries.

It was a ploy to numb future worries when I invited him, Latorre, Segura, and all their friends to the States for a different event that would make them guests of the US Bureau of Prisons. Apparently, it worked, at least temporarily, because he then made a startling proposal.

"There is one more matter I want to talk about. I move international things, very big and very good international things. Perhaps it's a little daring to say it in the middle of this, but this is it. Is it possible for you guys to put a . . . I don't know whether you know about lines. When I say lines, I refer to, uh, to move that crap."

I knew exactly what he was asking, but I had to play dumb so he would explain himself in terms that a jury would understand. After five minutes of cat-and-mouse discussion, in frustration, he turned to my partner, Al Melendez. "Did he understand the question I asked him, or didn't he? I'd like to know whether we're talking about the same thing, whether he's understanding me. Whether he's able to transport you-know-what . . . for blocks to Panama or the United States."

He still couldn't bring himself to say kilos of cocaine, so I continued to play dumb. "What do you mean 'blocks'?"

Finally, he whispered the word in Spanish. *"Cocaína."*

I replied from my Baldasare brain. "Oh, oh, oh! No, no, I don't want to get into that. The blocks could be done, but I don't want to be involved myself directly. I would have somebody else do that. One of the things that I have been directed by our group to make sure of is that I only get involved with the green stuff [cash]. It's best never to mix blocks and green."

Junior found humor in my feigned handling of his hot-potato question. In the midst of laughter, he assured me that laundering hundreds of millions for his group was more than sufficient. I knew I could always come back to the topic of transporting coke loads in the future, but I had to play my best Baldasare to seal our deal to handle their money. If I had jumped at the idea of transporting cocaine, too, all of Sanz's fears of our possibly being DEA, FBI, or CIA would resurface when he later evaluated our discussions. Only federal agents offer to participate in any and all crimes. Real bad guys have limits.

As we talked about secure communications, Sanz had something else to share. "Right now, Search Bloc is in Cali looking for Pablo Escobar. Escobar is in Cali under the protection of Gilberto Rodriguez-Orejuela." The Sanz clan knew that Search Bloc illegally tapped hundreds of phones in Cali, and they were concerned that our relationship might be exposed through careless phone calls. We agreed to keep the calls to a minimum, to communicate primarily by fax, and always to use codes consistent with people involved in legal commerce.

I knew of Search Bloc, a collective effort by three different units of the Colombian National Police, created with the sole initial objective of apprehending Pablo Escobar and his associates. I also knew the man Junior had just referenced, Gilberto Rodriguez-Orejuela, one of the Cali cartel leaders. The Sanz family was aligned with the cream of the Cali cartel's crop.

A few days later, we headed back to Sarasota. It was time for "Bridging the Americas." Some of my Colombian friends were bringing new contacts, their bosses. Most importantly, I was just about to receive a very special gift from a real princess: my life.

14

THE ROYAL SAVIOR

Sarasota, Florida
October 1993

As soon as I got back to Florida, the Sanz clan lit up my phone. Sanz Sr. was first. "I am calling you very urgently because we have two containers, forty foot [meaning two million dollars]. It's Spanish product in Spain [Spanish pesetas in Madrid]. Our idea is to know how much per case or box [the laundering fee]?"

I offered to do the job for 15 percent and tried to squeeze more out of the deal by offering him a lower exchange rate. They wanted the pesetas converted to pesos. We haggled, so he took my offer to the owners of the money, for their approval.

Then it was Sanz Jr.'s turn. He had one million dollars he wanted picked up in Chicago. I closed the deal. Al Melendez made the pickup, and I had Latorre handle the conversion from dollars to pesos. Things were moving fast with the Sanz clan, and I wanted to take one more shot at repairing Latorre's loyalty, so I approached the head of our Tampa office for a favor.

"Mike, I know it was a big deal to get approval for me to operate undercover in Colombia four months ago, but could you pull some strings and get me cleared to go back to Bogotá? If I can meet the Sanz family, their clients, Latorre, and a lot of our other targets face to face, it will boost my credibility and open a lot of doors."

"Listen, Mazur. You're pushing the envelope, but if you want this that bad, I'll see what I can do."

"Thanks, Mike. I think it'll be a difference maker. I know there are risks, but we all live with uncertainties every day on this job. No one knows that better than you."

As I began to make final arrangements to welcome my guests from Colombia and Panama to the Chamber of Commerce "Bridging the Americas" event, Latorre was busy behind the scenes.

He was confused. "Baldasare invited me and Pedro to this Chamber of Commerce event he's hosting in Sarasota. Frankie, is this a scam to lure everyone to the States so they can be arrested?"

"Maybe this is something new, Luis. The last word I got is that the arrests are set for the World Cup in June 1994. I'll make some calls and confirm."

He came back to Latorre the next day. "We got this from one of the female cops working with Baldasare. This is not the takedown, so it'll be safe to move cash through him until May. That's when they'll start holding money to seize as much as they can before the takedown."

It seemed that Frankie was keeping his cohorts in crime one step ahead of the feds, until a high-speed chase through the streets of Manhattan ended with US Marshals collaring Hernando Uribe in Abe Marwan's case, which charged Hernando and his brother Mario, Quino's informants, for their two-kilo deal in Tampa.

After getting word of Hernando's fate, Marwan leaned back in his office chair, threw his feet on his desk, and wrapped his hands behind his neck. He trumpeted his prediction like a town crier. "One down, and one to go. Once we get Mario, we'll have two shots at rolling the rock and catching the cockroaches of corruption in this town. This is going to be fun. I can't wait to turn the screws on these fucks."

Marwan had a plan: encourage the Marshals to pump more resources into finding Mario, and then, with both Hernando and Mario in a Tampa jail, bargain their potential life sentences in exchange for their deepest secrets.

As Hernando Uribe was being bussed in shackles to Tampa, my guests were traveling first class to the festivities in Sarasota. Guillermo Segura brought a colleague, Luis Alberto Garay, a higher-ranking officer with Banco Cafetero who worked with Segura laundering dope money. Garay coordinated the export repatriation activities of 60 percent of the bank's branches in Colombia and had responsibility over roughly two thousand employees.

Garay made clear that he was in a position to ensure that dirty money movements through Banco Cafetero went smoothly. He and Segura also had two surprise gifts they hoped I would accept: Miguel and Alvaro Garces, Colombian businessmen who lived in Tampa and claimed to launder about two hundred thousand a week. They wanted the Garces brothers to join our team. Segura vouched for them. He'd known them for more than twenty years, having grown up with them in Colombia.

My private meeting with Alvaro and Miguel Garces quickly confirmed that they were small-time launderers with big-time connections. Their clients' needs clearly outweighed their resources. They managed five accounts but couldn't safely push more than two hundred thousand dollars a week through them, they claimed, but I sensed that claim might be an exaggeration. They were too eager.

They saw an alliance with Baldasare as a way to move a lot more for Cali traffickers. They revealed that their Colombian bank connections were far greater than just Segura and Garay. They also had laundering contacts at Banco Ganadero, Banco Industrial Colombiano, and Banco

Union de Colombia who would be eager to work with us. Together, we would work to serve two cartel leaders with whom they worked directly.

"I know these people down there, and he is in jail right now," Miguel Garces admitted. "You might know him, Ivan Urdinola?"

Urdinola was a powerful member of the Cali cartel who helped develop their heroin trafficking capabilities. Miguel Garces knew him, his wife, and their adopted son well. He had lived with them at their home for nine months.

"Bob, he loves me and everything. He wants me to teach him English and Portuguese. Somehow, he knew I was in Cali, teaching English down there. I went to the house. There were like thirty people in the house, I mean, bodyguards. He's getting out in four months. I mean, he's not in jail. He's like in a palace."

Urdinola's compound impressed Miguel Garces, with its four tall turrets that served as perches for armed guards. The mansion had three levels of underground parking that housed 150 luxury cars. While Miguel was living with the Urdinolas, they had introduced him to Ivan's partner, Miguel Rodriguez-Orejuela, one of the top leaders of the Cali cartel. The Garces brothers had the capacity to eliminate any other brokers on money deals with Urdinola and Rodriguez-Orejuela, so our cut for laundering would be higher than normal.

Since I already had a long history with their trusted friend, Guillermo Segura, they were comfortable introducing me to their contacts at other Colombian banks the next time I traveled to Colombia. The Garces brothers had already met with Urdinola's money managers in New York, Miami, and Los Angeles. Through them, we would initially receive about six hundred thousand dollars a week, but that would likely increase over time.

Despite their optimism about our futures, Miguel Garces felt it was necessary to state the obvious. If we didn't handle these delicate matters as promised, both Urdinola and Rodriguez-Orejuela were very capable of having us all killed.

The Garces brothers and a dozen of my underworld friends from Colombia and Panama attended the Chamber of Commerce conference. Some made presentations at the event. Being pillars of their Latin American communities, they had no problem convincing Sarasota businessmen that they were gifted lawyers, bankers, and businessmen. Their organized crime connections fit well under their suits.

That night, at a dinner and dance for about a hundred people at the Brass Parrot, Jaime and two of the Bogotá-based launderers headlined the entertainment. If they ever decided to get out of the laundering business, they had a future competing with the Three Tenors. They were that good.

The day after the cabaret, our VIP guests joined us for a tour of Sarasota Bay and the Gulf of Mexico on a forty-four-foot Grand Banks yacht, fully catered and adorned with a huge glass basin of ice that chilled a case of champagne. As the corks popped and flutes were filled, Jaime and I strolled off to a corner of the deck. Our conversation was muffled by the roar of the boat's engines, giving us total privacy.

"Bob, I didn't want to bring this up sooner because I didn't want to distract you from the importance of the past two days. I had some serious discussions with Jorge Sanz Jr. in Cali. He and his father didn't come to the conference for very specific reasons. There were things about his trip to Panama that made him uncomfortable about you. He felt you were working hard to take him to too many places, introducing him to too many people. He thinks Richards looks like a DEA agent. He didn't like Al Melendez because he looks like a *traqueto* [low-level drug dealer]. Melendez wears too many gold rings and bracelets. Looking like that, he is likely to be followed, because he doesn't look professional. When Junior told a friend about your invitation for him and his father to come here, the friend said this is similar to parties thrown in Barcelona and the US where everyone gets arrested. Bob, he stared into my soul and very solemnly asked me if I was sure you aren't a DEA agent. I told him you're a very cautious man who takes a very detailed approach, that your lawyers got copies of all the Green Ice indictments, and you've made lists of names and accounts so you know who in Cali is on DEA's radar. I told him you never want to deal with anyone on those lists, or even anyone linked to them. He seemed to understand, but he's nervous."

"I understand, Jaime. I'll back off as much as I can, but DEA wants results. I have to ask Sanz Jr. hard questions about his clients to learn more. We can't just launder money in a black hole for 'the unknown'; otherwise we'd just be helping the cartel."

The next morning, Laguna and I met privately in my office. As the video recorders collected every word and movement, our conversation drifted to his intention to run for office in Panama. He explained his strategy. "I need, at least for my campaign, like a hundred fifty to two hundred thousand."

I handed him a check for five thousand. "That's just from our little company here."

"I appreciate it." As he looked at the check and laughed, he confirmed what I was buying. "Panama is a place where the best investment is sometimes in politics. If we are in the government, we control Customs for, you know. They just caught a contraband of dollars in Panama. Like I'm never gonna go like, 'Hey, let drugs pass through' or something like that, no way. But there are a lot of things that we can help with, you know."

"Money especially, Rinaldo?"

"Yeah."

As he prepared to leave Sarasota, Laguna assured me that, if elected, he was ready to provide my clients with a green light to smuggle currency in and out of Panama, especially if, through me, they could help finance his campaign.

After my guests left town, I reflected on the developments of the past few days. It was clear to me that I needed to expedite my request to return undercover to Colombia. It was my only chance to calm the concerns of Sanz Jr., Latorre, and Latorre's partner, Pedro Rodriguez-Castro, but it would also be an opportunity to meet all of the bank contacts collected by the Garces brothers.

Unbeknownst to me, Rodriguez-Castro had embarked to the Colombian coral island of San Andrés, a speck of paradise in the Caribbean Sea. San Andrés is 470 miles northwest of the coast of Colombia, a playground for many of Colombia's biggest narcos. They shuttle there on private jets to enjoy holidays and relish luxury. This trip was one of the most important of Pedro Rodriguez-Castro's life.

He was lodged in one of the suites at the Palace Hotel, an opulent resort that offered every imaginable amenity. On this beautiful autumn day, he was sitting amid narco-trafficker royalty. To his left was the owner of the hotel, Carlos Alberto Renteria, also known as "Beto." Renteria was one of the strongest and most organized of the Cali cartel leaders. He was from Tuluá, in the heart of Valle del Cauca.

To his right was Juan Carlos Ramirez-Abadia, also known as "Chupeta" and "Lollipop." Ramirez was probably the most important man in the Cali cartel, and he was well known for his violence. At his direction, many informants fell victim to a unique extermination. Sicarios cut their chests open, filled them with rocks, sewed them up, and dumped them in the Cauca River.

Ramirez had the cartel's smuggling route from Colombia to Puerto Rico. It was his money that we laundered in Puerto Rico for Latorre and Rodriguez-Castro (and sometimes seized). One of Ramirez-Abadia's money managers, Miguel Rosenberg, was the money broker who brought Latorre and Rodriguez-Castro on board. Ramirez-Abadia was also in the process of developing a smuggling route from Colombia to Cape Verde, an island country off West Africa. From there, his coke shipments would move to Germany, and then throughout Europe. He was as smart as he was violent.

Rounding out the list of cartel royalty was Carlos Herrera, a major transporter of cocaine for the men in Cali. But the last person in the room was the most enchanting. Most people knew her as "the Princess" or "Pilar."

The Princess was the pampered child of parents who were part of the upper class in Cali. Her relatives included a former president of Colombia, and she had attended the best private schools in Colombia and Europe. Her childhood days had been filled with music lessons, horseback riding, tennis, and swimming. She was gorgeous, delightful, refined, and competitive, as evidenced by her having previously been adorned with the "Miss Colombia" title. Despite her status, and against her father's wishes, she became a flight attendant for Braniff Airways, frequently traveling between Colombia and the States. Her marriage to her first drug-trafficking husband led to her getting involved in his business, muling larger and larger amounts of cocaine. She later married another drug trafficker and amassed a fortune, including a seaside villa on the Mediterranean island of Majorca and many expensive toys. Her life-long friendships included Juan Gonzalo Rodriguez Gacha, a.k.a. "the Mexican," one of the leaders of the Medellín cartel and a stone-cold killer. Now, she was one of the most trusted money launderers in the organization.

The Princess mingled with the cartel royalty as everyone discussed laundering strategies and boasted about money movements around the globe. Cocktails loosened the men's tongues, especially when the Princess was in the room.

When I was with him, Pedro Rodriguez-Castro always seemed like the classic geek who wanted to be accepted by the "cool kids" in the class. This day would be no different. As his partners in crime sipped away, he announced why he, too, was powerful.

"We've been able to move a lot of money safely because Latorre and I have a special contact in Tampa. Our boy Frankie is a lifesaver. Thanks to him, we have eyes and ears inside DEA. He put us with a Colombian family that works for us. He is really a good guy and someone we trust completely. He saved our asses. He's actually a Tampa cop who was assigned to DEA. He was working undercover with a DEA agent who had set up an operation in Sarasota. Thanks to Frankie, we learned that the guy in Sarasota (Baldasare) is actually a DEA undercover agent running a money-laundering sting. If it wasn't for Frankie, Luis and I thought the guy in Sarasota was for real."

As the Princess moved away from the men, she heard only parts of what else they said about the Sarasota operation, but a few points were clear: "Now we have to get rid of him. Yes, we have to finish him up. He's going to cause more problems."

While in San Andrés, the Princess snuck from the Palace Hotel to a pay phone. She glanced around nervously as she placed a call to Joe Salvemini and shared what she had learned about Frankie and the DEA agent running the undercover operation in Sarasota. Baldasare had been betrayed, but so had the cartel. Salvemini was the DEA assistant special agent in charge of the Fort Lauderdale District Office.

Yes, the Princess was DEA's eyes and ears inside the highest levels of the Cali cartel. After being pressured by agents in Fort Lauderdale to cooperate, she and they came to terms. She would provide them with the highest-level intelligence about the activities of the Cali cartel leadership, but her identity could never be disclosed. She would never testify, and she could never surface as a witness in any way.

On one of the few days I visited the Tampa DEA office, I received a call from a DEA supervisor in Fort Lauderdale. "Bob, we just got important news from the Princess." He told me all about her pay-phone message to Salvemini, identifying the Tampa cop who once worked undercover with me as a launderer and was now working with Luis Latorre and Pedro Rodriguez-Castro. There was no doubt. The only person who fit the description was Quino.

Quino had gone dirty. He was now on the take, and a major asset of the Cali cartel.

The Princess was highly reliable and had been working undercover with some of the agents in Fort Lauderdale, including Rene De La

Cruz. De La Cruz was another agent Abreu warned others to avoid, because it was Abreu's suspicion that De La Cruz was dirty. He had first heard rumors about De La Cruz's dark side years before, from a DEA agent we'd both worked with in Costa Rica.

When the Princess's revelation about Quino's corruption was disclosed, I stared into a vacuum of darkness, hearing nothing but an echo in my mind: *Quino's dirty. Quino's dirty.* I dropped the telephone receiver and froze, mentally and physically. How in the world could Quino have done this to me, and to every other agent working undercover in Operation Pro-Mo? He could have caused any one of us to be kidnapped, tortured, and murdered, and I was selfishly devastated by the thought that all the work we had put into this undercover operation was lost, forever.

At the same moment, I was overcome with shame. If I had pushed harder at the start, when Abreu tried to warn me about Quino, this would probably never have happened. Although Abreu was forced by his front office to keep his mouth shut about Quino, he secretly told me what his bosses wouldn't let him tell DEA brass. Abreu's suspicions were not a general concern about Tampa cops—they were about Quino. "Bob, I'm telling you, man, you're going to get fucking killed. I know this Quino asshole is dirty as hell. I only have a few pieces of the puzzle, but I'm certain he's the one that outed me to the Uribe family. My bosses at Customs don't give a shit if you get whacked, but I do."

That's what Abreu had told me, way back when, but I knew I couldn't violate his trust. I shared his concern with the front office, but there were no takers. Besides, Abreu's view about the superstar "Officer of the Year" was mostly driven by his gut. He had no hard evidence. Worse, I didn't want to believe Quino was bad, because I was given an ultimatum. I had to work with Quino, or the operation would never have launched. I was blinded by my addiction to go back undercover and prove that the underworld had a ton of help from bankers and businessmen around the globe.

And I had underestimated Quino. I thought that even if he did somehow play both sides of the street, as long as he had a chance to be a star in Operation Pro-Mo, he'd remain loyal. When his department pulled him off the operation, I knew I was fucked, but I refused to accept it. On that fateful day eighteen months earlier, when Quino told me he was leaving Pro-Mo, I had searches done in what was, until Edward Snowden's unlawful disclosures, a very secret database of global phone records. I found two calls from Quino's home to Latorre. They made no sense, because even if Quino had had a brain fart and accidentally used his home phone, he generated no reports of phone calls to Latorre on those days.

I had confronted him back then, and he claimed he had in fact had a brain fart. In the midst of his nervousness from not really having long-term undercover training, Quino said, he used his home phone by accident on two occasions. His story was that the calls were both less than two minutes in length, and that he must have only reached Latorre's secretary, who told him Latorre wasn't in the office. He didn't feel those types of calls warranted reporting. I passed his alibi on to my bosses. That should have been a huge red flag for all of us, but it wasn't enough to overcome the law enforcement phenomenon of giving other cops the benefit of the doubt, especially the "Officer of the Year." Suspicion that a fellow cop is a criminal unfortunately requires a lot more proof than for someone who doesn't carry a badge.

I betrayed my instincts, my colleagues, and my common sense. Now I had to find that one in a million shot to overcome insurmountable odds. We needed to take down as many of the Pro-Mo targets as possible, but more importantly, we had to take Quino down—hard. We needed him behind bars and off the street, because in time, his corruption would undoubtedly cost lives, most likely the lives of brothers and sisters in law enforcement. Getting irrefutable proof of Quino's corruption became my obsession.

I snapped out of my daze of guilt and self-pity when our boss, Mike

Powers, marched into our group's meeting area and slammed the door. "All right, I want everyone's attention." He had been briefed about the message from the Princess, and it was time to share it with everyone involved in Pro-Mo. As the story unfolded, Abe Marwan yanked his feet off his desk and jumped to attention, pointing around the room. "I told you, I told you fucking Quino was bad. I can solve this problem in one night. Just let me track his fucking ass down, and I'll garrote the bastard with piano wire. This piece of shit needs to die."

Powers looked at Marwan with disgust, his coal-red eyes fixed on Marwan like lasers. "You shut the fuck up." He didn't need to say more. Marwan sat down like a third-grade class clown that knew he had gone too far.

The boss went on. "Listen, consider this information Top Secret. You are not to tell anyone outside of this room, not your wife, your husband, your kids, or even your cat. This has to stay totally under wraps. For now, we will not share this with Quino's department, or even other personnel in this office. Mazur, Brunner, your supervisor, and I will figure out how we're going to handle this. We'll meet again soon, when we finalize a plan."

We were in a dilemma. We knew Quino was dirty, but we had no admissible evidence against him. The agency's oath to the Princess forbade her ever surfacing as a source. Quino had burned us with Latorre, Rodriguez-Castro, and probably a handful of cartel players close to them. That meant that the Sanz clan may have been warned by Latorre that I was an undercover agent.

"Mike, as bad as Quino hurt us, he couldn't have outed me to ninety percent of our targets," I proposed. "He knew only Latorre and Rodriguez-Castro, and they have a connection to only a couple of the two dozen launderers in our crosshairs. The only way we can get solid proof to take Quino down is if I stay under. If we take Latorre and Rodriguez-Castro down now, everyone will scatter. At best, we might get some of them to testify against Quino, but that won't cut it. Any half-assed defense attorney will claim the government made deals with devils who are now making up stories about the 'Officer of the Year.' We need recordings of Quino in the act, and we need documents that will confirm he's a launderer. He's not doing this for free, so there's got to be records linking him to cash he can't explain. I can manipulate Quino, Latorre, and Rodriguez-Castro with disinformation while we put our case against Quino together. At the same time, we can come up with a plan to take everyone down within four months. To pull this off, I need to go through with this undercover trip to Colombia. Our office can cover it as tight as they think they have to. You see . . ."

All of a sudden, the coals in Mike's eyes started to redden again, and the veins in his neck began to bulge. "Are you out of your fucking mind? There is no way on earth that you are going back to Colombia—nada, *fini*, over, done. Do you hear me? You and Brunner get together and figure out how we can keep this operation afloat until we can take these yo-yos down. You can still work UC in Panama and do your thing in Sarasota, but you need to be covered, more than you have been. Quino is now a subject of this investigation. He's a coconspirator with Latorre and the cartel. As far as I'm concerned, he is the most important target of them all. It's up to you guys to figure out how to make it happen. Pro-Mo has to be over in ninety days."

The ship was sinking. Quino had lied to everyone in his real life just as I had been lying to my cartel friends as Baldasare. But now I had to deliver a big fat lie to Jaime, the man in Colombia whom I was indebted to for watching my back over the past two years. I needed to let him know he was in grave danger, but I couldn't divulge that Quino was on the take. To do that would be against operational security. We couldn't risk any chance of the cartel or Quino discovering that we knew about his treason. The lie I delivered would haunt me forever.

"Listen, Jaime, I'm convinced we have been compromised. Right now, it's almost one hundred percent confirmed. Our people have been listening in on Latorre's phone calls. From what I'm told, he somehow knows I'm a DEA agent. Since you introduced me to him, they must think you are a snitch. We need to put something out that will confuse them. We need to make it look like, if I am a DEA agent, you, too, were duped. That may be a hard sell, because you told them you knew me for a long time, but either way, you need to take every possible precaution until this is over."

"Bob, tell me this isn't true. I'm not worried about myself, but I have a family. If anything happens to my wife and children, I couldn't live with myself. Then there's my mom, and our extended family. You know how these people are. They could take us all and make me watch them torture my family before slowly cutting off my fingers and toes, followed by my head."

"If you want us to pull you and your family out now, Jaime, consider it done. But if you want to try this plan, the wait-and-see game, we can do that, too. I can't promise you anything other than that I will do whatever you want done to ensure you and your family's safety."

He wanted to hear my idea.

"However Latorre and Rodriguez-Castro came to believe I'm with DEA, they need to question whether the person who convinced them is lying. You could tell Sanz and a few others, in separate meetings of strict confidence, that you have concerns about me. Tell them I told you that Quino tried to introduce me to a jeweler in Tampa who turned out to be a DEA informant, and that I also learned that Quino was heard saying, in a drunken rage at a party, that he was going to destroy me by falsely claiming that I'm a DEA agent, unless I pay him two hundred fifty thousand dollars. Tell them I think Quino is out of control and that I'm planning to have him killed. Add that you are scared to be drawn into this. You oppose any violence. For good measure, tell them someone told me that there is a snitch inside Latorre's office that is selling information to the cops. This should confuse the shit out of everyone and buy us some time. We need only ninety days. If you don't think this is a good move, just tell me what you'd like to do."

"Bob, this plan is so crazy, I think it could buy us time, at least for a while."

"Okay, let's go with it, Jaime. It's you and me, brother. We'll either make it or break it together."

I felt terrible, but it was the only way I could keep the Princess out of the picture. Jaime needed to know he was in grave danger, and he either needed to get out of Colombia or use a story to deflect suspicion back on Latorre and Rodriguez-Castro. I was beginning to have trouble living with myself. Lying to both the bad and the good guys was already tormenting me, and then I learned that another DEA agent was dirty.

15

SURVIVING TREASON

October 1993–February 1994

Unbeknownst to me, the acts of a cartel courier in the summer of 1993 brought more betrayal closer to my doorstep that fall. Unlike many money couriers who worked secretly with the Cali cartel, this one was Cuban. Nearly six feet tall, with dark hair, a dark mustache, and olive skin, he spoke perfect English and Spanish and was college educated. He was under the radar of the feds when at least $760,000 in cash was handed to him in a Houston parking lot, and he embarked on a path that often leads to death. He never passed a penny of that money back to the bosses in Cali. Instead, he took it to his home in Fort Lauderdale, hid it in safe deposit boxes, and was now in the process of making repeated deposits of less than ten thousand dollars into personal accounts.

When he walked into the branch of a US Bank in San Diego, he was a little nervous. He'd made three trips there that week, depositing a total of twenty-five thousand dollars in cash. Red flags rose in the mind of the bank cashier. When questioned, the courier produced DEA credentials. It was Fort Lauderdale DEA supervisor Rene De La Cruz. He claimed he was conducting repeated small transactions as part of an official undercover operation.

Having serious doubts, the banker called a friend at the local IRS Criminal Investigation Division office. His suspicions were confirmed. There was no undercover operation connected to these transactions. In due time, when confronted by DEA Internal Affairs, De La Cruz confessed.

A few months earlier, he'd gone to Houston to pick up several shipments of cash that were monitored by DEA agents who were managing the cooperation of the Princess. These pickups would be pure profit for DEA because there was an outstanding arrest warrant from another case for the money broker who engaged De La Cruz, in his undercover capacity, to receive the cash. The official plan was that, after these DEA-monitored cash deliveries, De La Cruz would lure the broker to Aruba for a meeting. On arrival, the broker would be arrested on the outstanding warrant. That would empower De La Cruz, in an undercover capacity, to claim the broker's arrest led to the seizure of the accounts in which he'd started to launder the funds. In the end, DEA would keep the money, and the cartel would be none the wiser.

De La Cruz followed the plan and, under the watchful eye of his DEA colleagues, received one delivery of one million dollars. After the first pickup, De La Cruz claimed the broker refused to authorize a second delivery of one million dollars until the first was laundered. That was a lie. After his colleagues left town, he secretly met alone with the broker's courier and received the second cash shipment. In his devious, conniving mind, De La Cruz saw an opportunity to stuff his pockets. Pieces of the puzzle caused some to think this may not have been the first time he'd dipped his hand in the till. De La Cruz never reported the second pickup to anyone, neither to the feds nor to the owners of the money in Cali.

In accordance with the official undercover plan, De La Cruz arranged an official undercover meeting in Aruba with the broker, the only person who could otherwise confirm De La Cruz had received two shipments of cash. The broker was arrested, locked up in an Aruban jail, and remarkably died in that prison. The broker's passing created a dead end that buried the truth. Everyone was allegedly the victim of the broker's stupidity. No one in either the good-guy or bad-guy world was the wiser until De La Cruz was tripped up by an astute banker in San Diego.

These transgressions in law enforcement are more common than any of us like to acknowledge. In an effort to resolve the mess with as little publicity as possible, De La Cruz was offered a two-year prison sentence and required to forfeit a little more than what he stole, and his wife, who was also a DEA special agent, was forced to resign. Through her attorney, she would later claim to have known nothing about the three-quarters of a million in cash, portions of which had been deposited into accounts for which both she and her husband had signature authority. Her claim of innocence was hard for some to accept, since her specialty at DEA was conducting money-laundering investigations.

As a result of his being caught stealing cartel profits, De La Cruz's reputation in some circles went from "Great American Hero" to "lying common thief." Only a few years earlier, while De La Cruz was stationed at the embassy in Panama, photos of him arresting Panamanian general Manuel Noriega had appeared in newspapers and magazines worldwide, crediting him as the DEA agent who arrested Noriega. Photos of him escorting Noriega on and off a US military cargo plane and into the hands of American justice were seen around the globe. Noriega was now behind bars in the US, and De La Cruz would soon become one of Noriega's fellow federal inmates.

This was proof positive that Emir Abreu's instincts were superhuman. He was right on both counts: Quino and De La Cruz were both despicable thieves whose paths had crossed mine. Quino's betrayal was potentially lethal. I wasn't certain how much De La Cruz had learned about our operation, but he certainly had the opportunity to know a lot, if he'd chosen to do a little digging. Unfortunately, I needed to continue the life of Robert Baldasare for another few months, regardless of the risk.

Back at the DEA Tampa District Office, Abe Marwan was in rare form. "Can you imagine, Bob, De La Cruz turns out to be as big of a crook as Quino?"

It was clear to me that it was time to make an alliance. "Abe, you are homing in on Quino through the Uribe brothers, and I'm homing in on Quino through his partnership with Latorre and Rodriguez-Castro. Let's join forces. We both want to take Quino down. Your street smarts are better than mine, and my attention to detail doesn't compute for you. If we combine our talents, Quino's fucked. What do you say?"

"You're crazy, Mazur, and I like that. Let's do it." Unlike the view of some of his colleagues, I saw Marwan as a man with good intentions. The claims of others that he was crude, rude, and worse were understandable, but that was just Marwan's veneer. One thing was sure: he hated police corruption, and with help, he would be a lethal force against Quino.

Almost immediately after Marwan and I joined forces, his earlier plea to the US Marshals paid off. Mario Uribe was tracked down in Manhattan. Another deadly high-speed chase through the city's streets led to Mario being collared. He was headed back to Tampa on what we called "Con Air" (Convict Airlines), a commercial airline service managed by the US Marshals Service that moves prisoners around the country via the most inconvenient connecting flights possible. Getting from one city to another often took weeks and required three or four "connecting" Con Air flights.

While I was waiting for Mario Uribe's arrival, it was time to start collecting the pearls of truth that would confirm the Princess's claims. I queried the massive database of telephone records, a move that yielded the first pearl on the string of guilt. During the past year, phones at Definsa SA, the offices of Latorre and Rodriguez-Castro in Bogotá, were in repeated contact with the Uribes' jewelry store, pay phones in the vicinity of Quino's home, and even phones subscribed to by Quino's wife. All of this happened many months after Quino was no longer involved in our undercover operation. The Princess's warning was undoubtedly true, but phone records alone wouldn't put Quino behind bars.

In the midst of my obsession with nailing Quino, I had to weave an end to Operation Pro-Mo. Although it was important, I would have traded the evidence against every Pro-Mo target for rock-solid proof of Quino's betrayal.

The Sanz clan kept knocking on my door. They had more than five hundred thousand dollars ready for pickup in Los Angeles. The owner of the money, Dennis Gomez-Patino (a.k.a. El Zarco), previously mentioned in connection with the transportation of cocaine base from Bolivia and Peru to Colombia, was a rising star in the Cali cartel. Al Melendez and Angel Perez made contact with Gomez-Patino's courier by phone, and the cash was left in the trunk of an older-model brown-and-tan Chevrolet Caprice Classic parked at a McDonald's. We'd have no face-to-face contact with the couriers. Gomez-Patino's men would be watching in the shadows from a distance to make sure nothing went wrong. Melendez jumped in the car and sped off, hoping to frustrate any efforts by Gomez-Patino's men to follow him. The cash was passed to the cover team, but before Melendez returned the car, he punctured the radiator hose to discourage the cartel from continuing this technique. It didn't work. This was their preferred way of covering their tracks and keeping their couriers away from the eyes of Los Feos, and it worked.

Now that I had the half million dollars, it was time to let Jorge Krupnik do what he'd been asking me to let him do for months—launder. I transferred the funds to several of his Banco Exterior accounts in Panama so that his partner in Colombia, David Kuschner, could convert the funds to Colombian pesos and put them in Gomez-Patino's hands. Krupnik delivered, sealing both his and Kuschner's fate as future defendants in a money-laundering indictment.

In the midst of our first deal, Krupnik took me back to Restaurante La Marina in Panama City. "Bob, I need you to be as careful as possible and deal only with people you've known for many years. If you have the slightest doubt about someone's loyalty, take a pass."

"Listen, Jorge. The payout you're doing is going to one of Miguel Rodriguez-Orejuela's lieutenants. This deal was referred to me by a long-time friend who is an officer at Banco Cafetero. I've got our back, I promise."

As the food and wine began to disappear, Krupnik opened up. "Bob, I've traveled to Russia over the past eighteen months. I've developed what one might call a 'close relationship' with a few fine young ladies who have very important friends. We all run in the same circles with several high-ranking Russian generals and the head of the KGB. One of these ladies is a secretary to the most senior KGB officer in Russia." As Krupnik shared his secrets, including names, he showed me photos of himself with uniformed KGB officers and some very attractive companions. His message: "I can do very big things for you and your clients in Russia."

At this time, during the early 1990s, every crook on the planet was making a beeline to Russia to buy as many of the Soviet Union's assets as the Kremlin was willing to sell, and they were selling everything. Wealthy guys like Krupnik jumped headfirst into Russian privatization, giving birth to today's oligarchs.

Despite Krupnik's promises, the payout to Gomez-Patino's people was slower than pledged. "Timing is important, Jorge," I insisted. "You and Kuschner promised the pesos would be in my client's hands by now, and they haven't arrived. There's a lot at stake. This client has offered ten million dollars a month, if everything goes smoothly. Now that's in jeopardy."

"Bob, I don't like to work under unreasonable time pressures. What are the consequences for this delay?"

I was dead serious. "Jaime's life."

He leaned back in his chair with a frown. "You know, Bob, I don't really know you. I need to satisfy myself that you're okay in every respect, if you know what I mean."

I knew exactly what he meant. He wanted to be 100 percent certain I wasn't a fed. "I know precisely what you mean, Jorge. You have nothing to worry about." I had to let him know I was as cagey as he was. "Do I have anything to worry about with you?" With that, we slowly grew smiles, clinked our glasses of wine, and toasted our future.

Krupnik was unique, but not quite as unique as a new friend that Gilbert Straub sent my way. Straub knew I had been approached to launder money through casinos in St. Martin, including some controlled by Rosario Spadaro, a guy some people accused of being a member of the Sicilian Mafia. Straub had what he thought was a better option. "Bob, I have a very dear friend here with me at the mansion, Bobby Cellini. He knows the lawyer you mentioned who is close to Spadaro. I'll let Bobby explain."

Through Straub, Cellini knew the needs of my Colombian clients. I was eager to hear what Cellini had to say, because members of his family were very well known to the FBI, CIA, and others. Bobby Cellini was the brother of Dino Cellini, who ran casinos for New York mobster Meyer Lansky in Havana, Cuba, during the late 1950s and early 1960s. Dino later ran casinos in the Bahamas and the United Kingdom, some of which were connected to Straub's old boss, Robert Vesco.

Straub passed his phone to Cellini. "Mr. Baldasare, I know the guy close to Spadaro who approached you. My take is that he can't be trusted. I'm somewhat familiar with your needs and very comfortable operating in Kenya, where I control a number of casinos. I've also got casino interests in Russia. I'd like you to be my guest in London or Kenya so I can explain how I can help you and your clients."

Two months later, Bobby Cellini was sitting across from me in my Sarasota office, with no idea that the meeting was being videotaped from several angles by hidden cameras. He confirmed that his long-time friend and financial adviser, Gilbert Straub—an adviser to several members of the Cellini family—had briefed him about my background and needs.

I set the stage for our candor. "Bobby, I represent a number of clients in Colombia who conduct transactions that generate large amounts of currency in major US cities. They're also active in Europe and generate cash in Madrid, Milan, and Rome. One of our next responsibilities is to accept about ten million dollars in US cash in Zurich on behalf of a Colombian client. Like all my clients, he can't offer a legit source for his cash. In return for a ten percent fee, I provide a service integrating that cash into the banking system and building a front that makes it look like export revenue. My clients are particularly interested in moving a lot of money in the near future because they need to hide their fortunes before they close a deal with the Colombian government to surrender and do short stints in jail. I'm sure you recently heard the news about my clients' counterpart, Pablo Escobar, being tracked down and murdered by the Colombian police and DEA. It's my guys' hope to avoid that type of a messy ending, but they need to hide their assets before working out the details."

Cellini explained he was looking for investors to partner with him in a Moscow casino. I let him know I might consider it, provided it would give me a resource to move money for my clients.

"Mr. Baldasare, I suggest you visit me at my casino in Kenya so you can gain firsthand knowledge about how efficiently we operate."

"Well, Bobby, I'll be in Europe in late February to move my client's ten million dollars into Switzerland. If you're in London during that time, we can meet there. After that, I can visit you in Kenya in either March or April."

Cellini welcomed a meet outside the States.

I told him about the ten-million-dollar deal in Europe in the hope that Cellini would share the story with Straub, because that was the cheese I intended to offer Straub to get him out of his hole in Panama and into a country that would arrest him and send him to the States in chains. He'd undoubtedly want in on the fees for cleaning ten million dollars, and I'd offer him a chance to have that money moved through one of his Swiss bank contacts. If he flew on his normal route from Panama to Heathrow to get the job done in Europe, the Brits could take him down at the airport.

As badly as I wanted to romp with Cellini in his Kenyan playground and document his proposals, I knew the bureaucratic and security obstacles perceived by DEA Headquarters would be insurmountable. It would have to be coordinated with Kenyan authorities, and the risk of Cellini hearing about it in advance, through his government contacts, would be high. And given that I would be Cellini's guest in the bowels of a casino with no backup, the agency would surely kill the plan anyway. If I were calling the shots, I would have sent myself alone to meet in Kenya, with no recording equipment. I could always orchestrate meetings later in London or other countries where recordings could be done safely. My request for fast-track approval to meet Cellini in Kenya, before our planned arrests in late February, died a quick death seconds after it left my desk.

To set the February trap, I had to start weaving stories with our targets that would get them to travel on the same date either to the US or to a country that had a strong extradition treaty. While meeting with Laguna in his office about my Panamanian residency and passport, I cast my lure.

"Rinaldo, I'm seriously thinking about buying a small bank in the US and having the legal work done to get a license to expand into Panama. Would you have an interest in being a part of the legal team to develop the Panama side of that equation?"

"Of course, Bob."

"Okay. I'm organizing an important meeting for our team that will handle this project. Can you plan on being in Sarasota during the third week of February?"

"Absolutely. I'll be there, but now we need to get over to the Panamanian immigration office. My friend is ready to issue you your passport and cedula."

Foreigners who establish residency in Panama can get a cedula, a national identity card giving them rights under Panamanian law. That usually involves a lot of time and paper. A few weeks earlier, Laguna had delivered the most important paperwork, an envelope of cash, to an official in the immigration office who was married to one of his relatives.

In anticipation of going with Laguna to speak with his immigration contact, I had a hidden recorder in an eyeglass case placed in the exterior breast pocket of my suit. To the unsuspecting eye, the open top of the case exposed a sliver of a set of designer shades and looked perfectly normal, but if anyone pulled the glasses from the case, the jig would be up, because the glasses were cut in half to leave room for a tiny recorder in the lower half of the case.

As we entered the government building, my eyes nearly popped from my head when I saw the guards, the magnetometer, and the X-ray machine. There was no turning back, but what the hell was I going to do? I approached the guard, my innards churning in a panic, and put my eyeglass case on the conveyor belt that pulled it toward the X-ray machine. A second after I passed through the magnetometer, the guard handling the X-ray machine shouted, *"Señor, ven aquí, por favor."* ("Sir, come here, please.")

My heart stopped as I turned toward him to face the verdict.

"Sir, you almost forgot your glasses. Here, I think these are yours."

I was clear. When he went back to his station, the thing that saved me became obvious. He was talking with a very attractive young female security guard who had far more of his attention than the screen of the X-ray machine.

Given Laguna's status, we were ushered to a private room ahead of everyone else crammed in the waiting room. In minutes, I had my Panamanian cedula and passport, and we were on our way.

Continuing to guide the paths of our targets toward their February arrests, I met with Alvaro and Miguel Garces at my Sarasota office. Before I could offer the bait, they insisted on briefing me about their recent trip to Cali. They'd met with Ivan Urdinola, one of Miguel Rodriguez-Orejuela's lieutenants.

"Bob, he's a mafioso, a *traquetero* [drug smuggler]. He had bodyguards around him at all times. They have a big organization in New York. They're moving two to three million per week."

The Garces brothers were ready to connect me with Urdinola, but Urdinola wanted a person in Colombia who would be "the responsible person," someone with big bank balances that they could kidnap and force to pay for any unexpected losses in the States. Since Jaime didn't pass Urdinola's "responsible person" test, I gave the brothers my personal and business financial statements, along with copies of some recent bank statements. I volunteered to be "the responsible person." As I would soon be living full-time in Panama, I'd be only a short flight from Cali. Urdinola could grab me there easily. They took the documents and agreed to try to close the deal.

While I was with the Garces brothers, at my request we called Guillermo Segura, our main Banco Cafetero contact in Bogotá. It was time to invite him to the takedown.

"Guillermo, I'm negotiating to acquire a small US bank. Once that's completed, we want to start working on getting a license to operate in Panama, and maybe eventually in Colombia. I need someone on our team with knowledge about banking in Colombia. Would you consider taking a consulting position?"

"Absolutely. This sounds interesting."

"I assure you, Guillermo, it will be. We are planning a team meeting during the third week of February. We'll cover your travel expenses, plus a consulting fee. Can we count on you to attend this important meeting in Sarasota?"

"Count me in, Bob. Don't you think that Alvaro and Miguel Garces could be assets to the team?"

"Great minds think alike, Guillermo. I'll get them on board, too." No sooner had I hung up the phone than the Garces brothers were on board to attend as translators, since some of the planned attendees spoke only Spanish.

Now it was time to see if the brothers had an interest in meeting a new demand delivered by the Sanz clan. "Guys, Jorge Sanz Jr. wants our team to use only native Colombians to pick up money from his boss's couriers. Do you guys want that job? We'll have deliveries of five hundred thousand to two million dollars in New York and Houston in the near future. If you want the job, you'd need to pick up the funds and deliver them to us here in Florida."

They wanted in but bickered about their fees. They wanted 2 percent of the gross pickup. I offered 1 percent, and we settled on 1.5 percent. "You'll be getting all of your directions from Al Melendez. He is your boss on these pickups. He'll coordinate with the Sanz clan in Colombia and their people on the street in US cities. You guys need to follow Melendez's every command closely. Agreed?"

They had experience as money couriers, and they welcomed the work.

A week later, they came to my office with a huge green army duffel bag stuffed with nearly two million dollars in cash they'd received from Dennis Gomez-Patino's couriers in Houston. The handoff went smoothly. As I got ready to write the checks for their services, Alvaro Garces gave me instructions.

"Bob, my brother, Miguel, has a driver's license in another name, Eric Martinez. We'd like his checks made out to that name. You can make mine out to my real name."

I let Gilbert Straub in on this deal. He passed some of the funds through an offshore trust account to keep my companies from being repeatedly connected to these transfers. His help and fees for providing those services would later buy him a ticket to a US prison.

Sanz Jr. kept lining up cash pickups on behalf of Gomez-Patino. Al Melendez received more than $1 million in Manhattan, giving our office in New York new leads on couriers in the Big Apple, while the Garces brothers picked up $1.5 million in Houston, feeding us with intelligence about addresses, phone numbers, and descriptions of couriers they met.

The Sanz clan was diversified. Besides bulk cash couriers delivering to the Garces brothers and Melendez, they had dozens of people working in the New York area who were buying hundreds of thousands of dollars' worth of cashier's checks, money orders, traveler's checks, and MoneyGrams in major cities. Each check was purchased in small odd-numbered amounts between $950 and $2,500. This army of Smurfs was buying these negotiable instruments with cash. Sanz had weekly FedEx boxes containing hundreds of these negotiable instruments shipped to me so I could deposit them and then send him the total of each shipment in one wire transfer. These checks and money orders were purchased at banks, convenience stores, money-service businesses, and post offices throughout New York, predominantly in Colombian and Dominican neighborhoods in Queens and Manhattan. I had no choice but to agree to accept these shipments. We were too close to taking the operation down, and I couldn't make unnecessary waves. My highest priority with Sanz and his family was building their confidence so we could hold and seize as much of their money as possible during the last two weeks of the operation. Although it wouldn't be easy, I'd also try to lure at least one of them to the States at the time of the takedown.

In the midst of this, Abe Marwan and I got a gift, another nail for Quino's coffin. We had passed on information about Edith Uribe to our New York office. They and Customs agents put the pieces together and developed enough probable cause to get a warrant to search her home. They hit pay dirt. She had a tough time explaining the sixty-three thousand dollars in cash in her closet, but an even harder time explaining the half kilo of cocaine hidden in her bedroom. She was arrested, made bail, and fled to Colombia. But we got copies of every piece of paper in her house. Those records offered the dots that connected Quino to the underworld. Her address books had contact information for Latorre, his partner Pedro Rodriguez-Castro, and Quino. There were copies of records confirming big transfers of funds to accounts controlled by Latorre and Rodriguez-Castro. Edith was on the run, but there were several reasons she'd eventually want to talk with us: her young children. They were US citizens who very much wanted to grow up in the land of opportunity, and Edith didn't want them relocating to Colombia.

Abe Marwan couldn't help but crow about the mounting opportunities to flip witnesses that could expose Quino. "Oh yeah, baby. Quino's fucked. Our Uribe trifecta will deliver a big payday. Quino's going down. It's only a matter of time."

Two weeks before the big takedown, Sanz Jr. called in a panic. "Bob, I need you to reroute the one point five million your people received in Houston. You must not send any more funds to the accounts at Banco Uconal."

"I'll try, Jorge, but it may be too late. The instructions you gave me were executed a day or two ago."

"And, Bob, I need your people to pick up two tons [two million dollars] in Houston as quickly as possible."

"I'm sorry, Jorge. My warehouses [accounts] are full. I can't take any invoices [cash] until next week, but then I can take as much as you can send my way."

My claim was bullshit, but it was the only way I could postpone money deliveries until the last week before the takedown. Every penny we took from Sanz, or anyone else, from that point forward would go into US coffers.

I knew the accounts at Banco Uconal were controlled by Pedro Rodriguez-Castro, Luis Latorre's partner. Rodriguez-Castro and Latorre had to be in big trouble.

The same day, the Princess was threatened by the owners of more than three million that had been seized and was supposed to be moved by Rodriguez-Castro and the Princess through a Swiss bank. The owners told the Princess that Rodriguez-Castro and his partner had been kidnapped, and she should take note of what they were going to do to them, because she would suffer the same consequences if she refused to help settle the debt.

Since I had arranged for Latorre and Rodriguez-Castro to convert dollars into Colombian pesos for the Sanz clan, it was quite possible that Sanz's clients were the kidnappers. This raised the risk for Jaime and me greatly. If Rodriguez-Castro outed us to the Sanz clan's people in the midst of torture, Jaime would never see the light of day, and my upcoming trip to Panama would be riskier than ever.

"Jaime, in two weeks, this whole thing will implode. You'll be contacted tomorrow by one of our people from the embassy. He and one of our people in Tampa will coordinate getting you and your family out of Bogotá. From this point on, we need to stay in close contact until you leave. At a minimum, you need to call me every morning, and I will call you every night. You need to let me know every single thing you see, hear, and smell down there. If the shit hits the fan, get your ass and your family to the embassy immediately."

"Bob, we've been talking about this for a while, so I'm totally ready. There's nine of us that your people need to move to the States."

"Nine? There were only eight on the list a month ago."

"Well, the ninth is my dog. I'm not leaving here without her. You've got to get that approved."

An asylum request for Princesa the fino hound flashed before my eyes. "Please tell me you're joking. You're giving me ulcers, man."

But he wasn't. To Jaime, Princesa was one of the most important members of his family.

While the paperwork to extract Jaime and his family was flying through our embassy in Bogotá, I was on my way to Panama to herd my underworld friends to their arrest. This trip was riskier than any other. Latorre was desperate and in the hands of killers. If he thought some of his boys in Panama could corner me, he would try. Getting ransom money to settle his losses was his highest priority. His friends in Panama had experience kidnapping, torturing, and killing. Despite my best efforts to keep a low profile on this last run to Panama, not long after I checked into my suite at El Panamá, a death threat was delivered, personally, nose to nose.

16

OFFERS THEY COULDN'T REFUSE

February–March 1994

The cabin bounced and lurched as we made our way through heavy clouds over the Gulf of Mexico. I barely noticed. I was in a trance, concerned about whether this would be a one-way trip. The betrayal of Quino had signaled alarms around Robert Baldasare's world. My "friends" in Colombia and Panama knew I was on my way, and for the first time in my career, I had serious concerns about safety. My mind was tense, and my internal barometer was spinning out of control, which I couldn't allow my underworld friends to sense. I had to be natural. I had to fight this off and let it all hang out. I had to commit to winning it all, though I could still lose big. There was no outcome in between.

Just before I left the States, DEA brass let me know the plan they and the US ambassador to Panama would soon execute. Shortly before I was scheduled to depart Panama with some of our targets, our attaché and the ambassador would brief the president of Panama about our operation and the imminent arrests. If he didn't already, he would soon know details about what I'd done in his country over the past two years.

Laguna, Krupnik, and Straub had high-level contacts in Panama's elected elite. What if they were told? Laguna certainly had "close contact" with people in Panama's royalty. I'd spoken with the daughter of a high-ranking official close to Panama's president when she occasionally jumped, in her skimpy white nightgown, from a limo into Laguna's apartment. He was also a longtime personal friend of Marcela Endara, the daughter of Guillermo Endara, the current president of Panama.

Then there was the message that Krupnik left for me just before I began this last journey to Panama. "Bob, I'm glad you're on your way here. I need to meet with you urgently. We need to hold off doing any new business for a while. I've been given the word. Something big is going to go down here in the next few days. Please call me as soon as you arrive."

There was no way I was going to accept that invitation. We had enough evidence to indict Krupnik. We'd just have to hope that the Panamanians would send him to the States, which was highly unlikely.

Then there was the pressure to keep the Sanz clan calm. The week before, I had been given the order from the front office. "Hold and don't launder any more money that comes in from Sanz or anyone else. We're seizing everything you can back up over the next two weeks."

Backing up cash sounds simple, but the deal with Sanz' clients was that I'd clean their cash within four days of receiving it. Two weeks without seeing a nickel would have them nervous as cats. We were already a day late on $350,000. Over the next two days, we'd get another two million dollars. If they smelled a rat, they'd pounce. They kidnapped Jaime in Panama once before, and they had people who knew exactly where to find me.

I had no choice, so I began planning my best lies for the Sanz clan. But there was a bigger lie to create for Gilbert Straub. I had to get him out of Panama at the same time that everyone else was arrested in the States.

Near the end of my first day back in Panama, I went to Chartered Management Group and walked into Straub's office. His eyes lit up as he offered me a big smile. After the traditional *abrazos* (hugs), I began to lay the bait, using a truth about Krupnik to make it all seem logical.

"I think Jorge [Krupnik] is feeling pressure from somewhere. He was going to do something with us, and he wanted to talk to me. He said he heard from his contacts that there are, as he put it, 'two corporations [law enforcement agencies] from the other side' who are apparently active. He said he needs to slow down, take it easy."

"Well, Bob, you know Jorge has been hot as a pistol for years. I mean, first it was the North Koreans that he was dealing with; then it was the Russians; then it was the Cubans. Jorge is involved with every anti-US interest group around, all right?"

I explained that Krupnik had left me at the altar with nine million dollars in cash. The money was stockpiled in Geneva, but Krupnik was reluctant to deposit and transfer it until he was sure that agencies weren't watching his every move.

Straub shared a story about a meeting with Krupnik and some of Krupnik's "guys" in Italy. "Bob, he wanted me to stop and spend the night with some of the most absolutely delightful hijackers. These were criminals, guys who were hijacking trucks, a whole hijacked load of sunglasses, designer sunglasses. They were hot as a pistol. Jorge sold them into the street in Miami. I think he sold them to Kmart."

Straub offered to pick up Krupnik's slack. He had couriers and bank connections in Russia that he felt would be ideal for my needs.

"I mention Russia because there are two things in Russia that fit your system. One is that everything is US dollars. Second, everything is cash. It's not illegal, all right? You can declare it [the cash]. Secondly, we have people there who are KGB, to look after you."

Straub suggested we work out the finer points of the deal during a meeting at his mansion near Southampton, England, where we could talk freely. "You know, nobody is going to have eyes on us there. For now, Bob, what are your plans for tonight? Are we on for dinner?"

I accepted and agreed to meet at his Panama City apartment later that evening. He preferred a private dinner in the comfort of his home, just him and me, so we could speak openly.

Later that night at his posh high-rise, after pleasantries with Straub's wife and son, we were alone. No one could hear us discuss our secrets, except the recorder hidden on my body, which captured more details than Straub had ever offered before.

For starters, for a fee, he could take as much cash as I could give him and wire the funds anywhere in the world. He'd established sources to do this in Russia, Geneva, and several European cities, and he'd put those systems in place to service the needs of the Cellinis. He had a special message about them.

"I'll never give them up. So, Bob, if you're a government agent, you can forget the idea of me providing information about them."

He was expressionless. He'd delivered that line to analyze how I'd handle it. I had to be equally unfazed. "Well, that's good to hear, and I'd expect you'd do the same for me, Gil."

Straub confessed that he had worked for organized crime figures for decades. "I've primarily handled financial matters for them, but I've killed for them, too. Remember this, Bob. I'm very capable of murder."

I smiled and made sure I didn't blink. "Good, Gil. When I need that done, now I know I have someone I can trust. It's nice to have so many friends with that talent." I wanted him to know that, as hard as he thought he played the game, I had friends that played just as hard.

As I got ready to leave Straub's home, it was agreed that he would depart Panama on Saturday, arriving at Heathrow on Sunday morning. I was to arrive at Heathrow from Florida at about the same time, and we'd travel together to his manor near Southampton. For me, that was perfect timing, because the takedown in Sarasota was scheduled to occur shortly before Straub's flight departed from Panama. He'd be in the air before any publicity got out about the arrests.

The next day, Laguna drove me to the Tocumen airport. I'd booked flights for him and several other targets so they could travel back to Sarasota with me to attend "business meetings" related to the bank I claimed that I would soon purchase. Everyone showed up at Tocumen as promised, and we were soon on our way to Miami. After clearing US Customs, we took a quick limo ride to a private jet terminal within Miami International Airport. There was nothing but smiles as we boarded what they thought was my private Learjet, compliments of DEA.

That night, they were pampered. After an elegant dinner at Ristorante Bellini in downtown Sarasota, agents posing as drivers escorted them to their rooms at the Longboat Key Club resort on the Gulf of Mexico.

During business meetings the next day, I introduced a couple of the Panamanian bankers to a person who I explained was the co-owner, along with his Cali-based partners, of the tens of millions sent to me in cash. Unbeknownst to the bankers, that person was actually DEA special agent Cesar Diaz, one of the most gifted undercover agents in the agency, with years of experience posing as a money launderer and drug trafficker.

These bankers already knew it was my job to get the cash into the banking system in a way that made it look legal. Upon learning that Diaz had obtained US citizenship, the bankers explained that their branch in Panama wasn't officially opening accounts for US citizens, but with the help of financial service providers outside the bank, structures could be purchased and put in place for the money to be held in accounts in the name of foreign trusts. Despite those veils of secrecy, Diaz and I would control the accounts by providing our instructions orally, not on paper.

Diaz gave them the bottom line. "We have to be absolutely guaranteed that I and the other people will never show up in anything. I mean, that's a hundred percent guaranteed?"

The banker's reply said it all. "We prefer it that way, although from time to time, when you are talking about these kinds of money, the client wants to meet me and say, 'I'd like to measure these people.' But what I'm trying to say is that, if there is anything that is irregular, I don't want to know about it, so I prefer that you keep me in the dark about these things and just let me do my job managing the money."

The bankers from Panama offered interesting advice about our use of computers, cell phones, and beepers. "I warn you, though, the computer is becoming . . . I suspect Bob is even sleeping with the goddamn cellular phone. He's on the plane; he's on the phone. He's at the restaurant; the phone is on the table. Other guys have beepers. The technology is really taking over, and it's great to have it, but a lot of people can be listening in on these frequencies. So, the more that we use technology, the more we open our legs to disclosure. And the only place that has disclosure is the United States of America. The rest of the world keeps their legs crossed and their mouths shut, and they tell only the people who have to know. And that's the way you should handle your money."

Not the kind of speech that a banker would share with regulators. He was probably a pillar of the banking community in their eyes. Minutes after our meeting ended, he and a co-officer from the same bank were arrested. As they sat, handcuffed, in the back seat of the arresting agent's car, one of the bankers confessed. "I'm guilty and ready to pay the price, but part of Baldasare must be a bad guy, because he was very convincing."

Although arresting as many of our targets as possible was important, it was far more important to use the arrests as a tool to flush out Quino. As far as he knew, the arrests wouldn't go down for another four months. We decided that, at the same time as the arrests, the man in charge of our Tampa office, Mike Powers, would call Quino and ask him to come to the DEA office. Quino would be told that unexpected developments in the case mandated that we make arrests that very evening, and we intended to hold a brief celebration in the bar of a nearby hotel. Since Quino had played such an important role, we all wanted him to join us in the revelry. Powers would also tell Quino that one of the cartel money brokers he dealt with, Pedro Rodriguez-Castro, would be arrested later that night when he arrived at a Miami hotel. With that bait, we would use air and ground surveillance to see whether the rat would run to the trap.

Back in Sarasota, a dozen or so of the money launderers were transported by agents posing as chauffeurs to what they thought would be a business meeting. When they got out of their limos, agents posing as greeters took them down. I hoped that everyone would be treated with respect, but unfortunately, that wasn't the case.

Abe Marwan was Rinaldo Laguna's driver. Laguna got in the front passenger seat, impeccably dressed as always, with matching tie, pocket scarf, and an overbearing scent of cologne. Laguna didn't like cigarettes or any other kind of smoke. As Marwan got a block from the arrest team, he lit a stogy, took a deep drag, and blew the smoke in Laguna's face. As Laguna held his breath and grabbed for the door handle, Marwan chuckled. "Rinaldo, this is the start of a very bad day."

As each of my smiling guests arrived, their expressions slowly turned to confusion as they were handcuffed. When the limo carrying Guillermo Segura and the Garces brothers rolled up, they were told to get out of the car, but they froze. Abe Marwan was their driver, too. When they wouldn't move, Marwan pulled his semiautomatic 9mm Glock and shoved it toward Alvaro Garces's face. "Get the fuck out of the car." All three immediately jumped out, into the hands of the arresting officers.

At the same time the Sarasota guests were being carted off to jail, Julio Vicuna was arrested in Houston, Jorge Sanz Sr. was arrested in

New Jersey, and we seized three million dollars in drug money we'd received over the past two weeks in New York, Houston, and Sarasota.

Search warrants were executed at offices and homes in Panama, Tampa, and Houston, but both Luis Latorre and Pedro Rodriguez-Castro were safe from US law enforcement in Colombia. They couldn't be arrested, and their offices couldn't be searched. Members of the Colombian Congress, many of whom were on the payroll of the cartels, refused to allow the extradition of Colombian citizens to the States, and we weren't about to try to go after them under Colombian law. Besides, the Princess was still undercover, dealing with Latorre and Rodriguez-Castro. There would likely be more opportunities to grab them later.

It was time to set the trap for Quino. As requested, he reported to Mike Powers's office.

"Hi, Quino. Great to see you," Powers said to him. "Listen, a bunch of shit changed our plans. We had to take Operation Pro-Mo down earlier than we hoped. We bagged a bunch of the assholes in Sarasota earlier today. Mazur conned them into making a trip to the States. Unfortunately, Latorre is in Colombia, but we just got word that his partner, Pedro Rodriguez-Castro, is on the East Coast. We had no idea he was there, but Customs alerted us when he entered the country. He's scheduled to check into the Doral in Miami in the next few hours. We've got a team on the hotel, so we should bag him, too."

Quino feigned approval. "Congratulations, Mike. Finally, after two and a half years, it looks like things have paid off for you guys." The news seemed to shake Quino to the core, but that was magnified by a new fear. Were things starting to point at him?

"This is a big victory for all of us, Quino, you included. You were a big part of getting this operation off the ground. We're all heading over to the Hyatt in an hour for a round of victory drinks. It would mean a lot if you'd join us."

The wheels in Quino's mind spun. Was there some other reason behind Powers's outreach? Quino glanced at his watch and squirmed.

"Gee, Mike, I'd love to join you guys, but I have a stack of overdue paperwork on the latest homicide case that dropped in my lap. I'm going to have to take a pass so I can get back to my office at Tampa PD and finish those reports."

Quino had no idea there was an army of agents and aircraft in the shadows, waiting to follow his every move.

A half mile away from Quino's car and thirty-five hundred feet above, DEA pilot Paul Pitts was behind the controls of a Cessna 210 retractable single-engine airplane. Although he was only a speck in the sky, his and the second aircraft were critical to the surveillance of Quino.

Pitts's aircraft was unique. It had a large cabin and powerful engine that allowed it to fly at a slow enough airspeed to follow vehicles and people on foot. Slow fuel flow and large fuel tanks enabled long surveillance time.

Pitts was an ace in the deck of surveillance resources we'd rolled out, a fearless, highly trained pilot who had been throttling all types of aircraft for a decade. Although he had logged thousands of hours flying for DEA in the States, he'd also flown for months at a time on missions in Colombia, Peru, Bolivia, and several Central American countries. He'd operated in and out of jungle airstrips, supporting raids on clandestine cocaine labs, and logged tons of time on missions in Medellín, Cali, and Bogotá with agents who were hunting Pablo Escobar. Pitts's close calls had him prepared for anything, the closest coming in Medellín when, in heavy clouds and pouring rain, an air traffic controller put him on a course that unexpectedly brought him face to face with the side of a mountain. He had pulled out just in time.

Pitts's efforts were complemented by a TwinStar AS355 chopper equipped with a Gyrocam. The Gyrocam was unique in its time. From thirty-five hundred feet up and a half mile downrange, it offered video quality that could produce a clear image of a license plate, and the images captured by the Gyrocam fed into a recorder that enabled a jury to evaluate every piece of the truth later on.

Then there were agents Quino didn't know, whom we had borrowed from other offices and who drove cars that Quino had never seen before. To all of us, there was nothing more important than proving our case against the "Officer of the Year."

As Quino's car pulled out of the DEA parking lot, he made a beeline to a pay phone. We'd get the records of that call later. After several minutes, he jumped back in his car and drove to another public phone. After making at least one call there, he went to a third pay phone and made more calls. Eventually he drove to a Burger King and stayed in his car. A few minutes later, we hit pay dirt. Harry Uribe walked up to Quino's unmarked vehicle and got in the passenger seat.

"Fuck, Harry, we need to move on this fast. I just left DEA. They told me they're making arrests in their undercover operation today and that Pedro is in the States. They know Pedro has reservations at a hotel in Miami, and they're going to arrest him the second he shows up. We've got to get word to him. You need to call your sister Edith now and have her warn Pedro. We can't let DEA get their hands on him. If he flips, he'll take us all down."

"Are you fucking kidding me, Quino?" Uribe responded. "Think about this. You haven't been involved in that operation for a year and a half. Why the hell would they tell you this? In the midst of everything they've got to handle right now, do you really think they would take time out to share this with you? What, are you stupid or something? They probably fed you this bullshit to see what you'd do with it. I bet they're out there right now watching us. You'd better come up with a story about why you've done everything you've done, from the second you left them until right now."

Quino and Harry stayed in the car for forty-five minutes. Quino was animated, flailing his arms. After Harry Uribe got out, Quino started driving like a maniac. He went through fast-food drive-through lanes but never bought anything, opened his sunroof, and looked up for aircraft surveillance while driving in circles, and eventually drove at a snail's pace on a highway while looking in every possible direction. Eventually he drove to his home. He never went back to his office to "finish paperwork," another nail that would help us seal his coffin.

About the time that Quino worried himself to sleep that night, Detective Constable Colin Smith of the Metropolitan Police calmly watched as passengers disembarked from Gate 16 in Terminal 4 of Heathrow Airport. As the first-class passengers emerged, he saw his man.

"Sir, are you Gilbert Straub?"

"Yes, I am."

"I am Detective Constable Smith from the Organized Crime Branch at Scotland Yard. I have a warrant issued on behalf of the American government, by Bow Street Magistrates' Court, for money laundering in Florida."

Straub was in shock. He could only manage one word. "Okay."

Smith took Straub into custody, escorted him through the airport's immigration checkpoint and on to the Charing Cross Police Station, where he was advised of the charges and his rights. His worst nightmare, extradition to the States, was underway.

Straub's lairs were searched, including his home and office in Panama and his mansion in Southampton. Documents seized by the cops confirmed that he'd formed and managed offshore companies for a boatload of crooks. Straub was furious, but not as furious as some of Baldasare's friends in Colombia.

Proof of their outrage was undeniable, thanks to a wiretap by the Colombian National Police. While speaking with a New York lawyer representing two of the money launderers charged in our case, a major Cali trafficker revealed that Miguel Rodriguez-Orejuela authorized a two-hundred-thousand-dollar partial payment of the launderers' legal fees. The lawyer confirmed that Jaime Vargas was the DEA informant in the case, and DEA agent Robert Mazur was the primary undercover agent. The trafficker then shared the word he'd gotten from the Rodriguez-Orejuela brothers. "They say a contract has been issued. Jaime Vargas will be hit."

Wiretaps and body wires produce recorded conversations, the type of powerful evidence we would need to ensure that our case against the "Officer of the Year" would stick. To get that proof, Abe Marwan and I mapped our plan. He would get Mario and Hernando Uribe to cough up the truth about Quino. That would give us leverage to convince Harry, the only Uribe brother still on the street, to work as our snitch. We'd need him to record meetings with Quino and help us lure Latorre to a place where we could arrest him. I'd work on developing probable cause for a warrant to search Quino's home. I'd pulled facts together in dozens of affidavits for search warrants that got us into the homes of money launderers, and Quino's would be no different. With recordings and the paper trail, we'd have him in checkmate.

In the prison interview room, Mario Uribe sat as calm as ever in his orange jumpsuit, thick white cotton socks, and rubber shower shoes. Marwan wasted no time, leaning into Mario's face while a prosecutor and another agent sat nearby. "With your record, Mario, you're looking at the rest of your life in this shithole. He's your key to freedom. Give him to us, and things will go a lot easier for you."

Mario smiled calmly. "Who? Who, Abe? I don't know who you're talking about. What's the name you're after?"

"Don't be coy, asshole. You know who I'm talking about, the wolf in sheep's clothing."

This banter went on for nearly an hour. Marwan didn't want to give Quino's name to Uribe, fearing how that might be portrayed in court. Even a newbie defense attorney would scream foul and claim that Uribe had been coached to implicate Quino.

Eventually Uribe caved. "All right, all right already, I can tell you all about how Quino compromised your office's undercover operation, and all the money he and my family laundered for Latorre."

Marwan was all smiles as he went into his classic *I'm the smartest guy in the room* pose, leaning back in his chair, throwing his feet on the table, and folding his hands behind his neck. He turned toward the prosecutor and smirked. His body language said, *Your witness, Counselor,* as he soaked in the silent applause.

Mario Uribe was the leader of the pack of thieves. Once his brother Hernando realized Mario was on board with the government, he quickly followed.

When he got back to the office, Marwan couldn't wait to share his trophies with me. "They fry Quino, but Harry and Edith Uribe are the keys. They did a lot more shit with Quino and Latorre than Mario and Hernando did."

"Abe, I've subpoenaed Quino's, Edith's, and Harry's phone records, plus we've got details from the mega-database about calls by Latorre and his partner. The five of them were in constant contact. We just got a court order to put a pen register on Quino's home phone. As we speak, it's logging the phone numbers of all his outgoing and incoming calls. He and Harry Uribe are burning up the lines. Harry's the key. We need to get him on our team."

The next morning, at the crack of dawn, Marwan and I sat in an unmarked car, sipping coffee and taking turns with binoculars as we watched Harry Uribe's home from a distance. A few hours later, the door cracked open, and Harry made his way toward his black Mercedes. Marwan and I jumped out. Marwan circled to the left, and I came at Harry from the right. We pulled our badges, identifying ourselves, hands on our holstered semiautomatic 9mm Glocks.

Marwan took the lead. "Good morning, Harry. We're with DEA. We're offering you an opportunity to get out of here quickly and quietly, but you're coming with us one way or another. You can volunteer to speak with us at our office, where your brother Mario is being held, or we can drag you out of here in cuffs, because we have more than enough proof of what you, your sister Edith, and Quino have done. What's your choice? Mario has been a big help."

Uribe was stunned. "Yeah . . . yeah, I'll go with you. I'm all right with that."

"Good. You're making good choices, Harry. I'm going to jump in your car with you, so no one gets excited about your car still being here. Bob is going to follow us to the DEA office. I promise you, Harry, if you do anything stupid, I'm gonna do what I gotta do. Understand?"

Harry knew that meant he'd be shot.

When we got to the office, Mario Uribe was allowed to stick his head in to confirm that he was cooperating. "Harry, they know everything, man. They know about Quino being in on all three of those loads of money handled by Edith and Yasmin. You should tell them all about that."

Mario was rushed off, and I was pissed. Mario's speech sounded like an alert, limiting what Harry should disclose. Sure enough, Harry gave us all the details about Quino flipping, and his role in the laundering of three shipments of cash for Latorre, a total of about one million dollars that was wired to Latorre's accounts. That didn't sit right with me, but for now, I was willing to take what I could get to see Quino behind bars.

Now it was my turn with Harry Uribe. "It's great that you and your brother are telling us what you know, but in the end, a jury will never believe you over the 'Officer of the Year.' You need to work with us. We need to wire you up and have you record conversations with Quino. Absent that, none of this is going to make a difference for you or your brothers."

Harry was smart. "I get it. Let's do it."

But before we got the chance to wire Harry Uribe, treason struck. We were betrayed again.

17

THE WALLS CLOSE IN

Tampa, Florida
April–June 1994

Tampa's Ybor City neighborhood grew from the toil of its blue-collar Cuban and Sicilian immigrants who migrated there beginning in the late 1880s. Its cigar factories, now converted to restaurants and office space, put bread on the table for the ancestors of what became some of the most prominent families in the city, including those of crime bosses Ignacio Antinori and Santo Trafficante Jr.

As Quino stood inside what once was the largest cigar factory in the world, now housing the Spaghetti Warehouse, his beeper signaled a call-back number, followed by a 911 code. He responded. "You beeped me?"

"Yeah, it's Manny. I need to see you immediately. Do you know what it means to be under the gun?"

Quino knew damn well what that meant. He had testified in a trial against one of Manny's clients and explained that the term meant that the government had someone in its crosshairs.

Manny was impatient. "Where are you now?"

"I'm in the Spaghetti Warehouse, waiting for my wife."

"Leave your wife. Go outside. I'll be there in three minutes. It'll be the most important investment of time you'll make in your life."

Quino went outside. Minutes later, he saw a familiar white Mercedes slowly approach. As it pulled to the curb, he jumped in the passenger seat. Once the door closed, Manny turned the radio volume up so loud, the speakers rumbled.

"Quino, do you have a dollar?"

"Yeah, why? Here, take it."

"Okay, now I'm your lawyer, and this conversation is privileged."

Then Manny cupped his hand over Quino's ear and whispered. "You are under investigation by the feds. Mario and Hernando Uribe are going to do you. Make sure you get a good lawyer. You can take what I've told you to the bank."

Quino's world was crumbling. He was so scared, he began to shake, and the terrified look on his face was so startling that it sent shivers through Manny.

There was nothing else to say. Quino stepped from the car and literally staggered to the curb in shock. He knew Manny wasn't bullshitting him. Manny Machin was a well-known criminal defense attorney who'd been of interest to the feds himself. The FBI became especially focused on Manny after his close friend, attorney Charles Corces, introduced Manny to Vincent LoScalzo, a man accused of being the successor to Santo Trafficante Jr. as the head of Florida's organized crime.

The next day, Quino reached out to Harry Uribe. He wanted to meet, and it had to happen fast. As Harry got in the passenger seat of Quino's car, the "Officer of the Year" followed his consigliere's protocol. He turned up the radio and whispered in Harry's ear.

"I was contacted by an important source and advised that your brothers, Mario and Hernando, are cooperating with DEA. I know they're going to give up what I've done with you and Edith. You're probably going to be contacted by the feds."

Quino handed Harry Uribe a small folded piece of paper. "Here's the name of a defense attorney. Contact him."

What Quino didn't know was that Harry was wearing a transmitter. Abe Marwan and I had one of our techs wire him up before the meeting. We recorded the conversation, but the noise of the car radio made it impossible to make out most of what was said.

When Harry Uribe got out of the car, Quino drove like a maniac, using a lot of the same techniques he'd used after meeting Harry to warn him about our takedown. Quino went through fast-food drive-throughs without making purchases and drove at about twenty miles per hour on a six-lane highway, peering through his sunroof, looking for aerial surveillance. Although he didn't notice, DEA aircraft videotaped all of his crazy maneuvers.

A week later, Marwan and I met Harry Uribe at a pay phone. "Listen, Harry, to avoid Quino's radio blasting, we want you to use this equipment to record a call with him now." We schooled Harry about what we wanted him to say, and he dialed Quino's pager, followed by a code that let Quino know it was him.

The callback came in seconds. "Quino, you were fucking right, man. They came at me with a grand jury subpoena, and they're trying to get me to give you up."

"You don't have to answer their questions, Harry. You can plead the fifth. They can't put you in this unless you trip up talking to them."

"Okay, Quino, I'm with you. I won't say a word. This subpoena says I need to show up in ten days. Maybe I can get my lawyer to come up with an excuse to get it pushed back. That'll give us time to think out the best way to deal with this. I'll get back to you soon."

We gave Harry the microcassette recorder and extended mic to record more phone calls, just in case Quino unexpectedly tried to call him. We didn't want any unrecorded communication between them, but we didn't want Harry to initiate anything until we figured out our next step.

Marwan and I thought we needed more to corroborate the testimony of the Uribe brothers. Prosecuting the "Officer of the Year" required overwhelming proof. We wanted one more recorded face-to-face meeting, and it had to be a homerun.

But we faced resistance from our immediate boss. "Listen, you two. I don't want Harry Uribe recording any more conversations with Quino. I think he smells a rat, and all you're going to get will be self-serving statements by a dirty cop who will try to cover his tracks."

Marwan and I knew damn well that the only way we would surely put Quino behind bars would be with a smoking gun. Harry Uribe was our best option.

We met with the prosecutor handling the case, Assistant US Attorney Bobby O'Neill. Bobby was an agent's prosecutor. He'd fought in the trenches for decades, first as an assistant DA in the Manhattan District Attorney's Office, and then as a federal prosecutor in Miami and Tampa. He grew up on the streets of the Bronx, the son of parents who migrated from Ireland and Germany. His parents worked hard all their lives as laborers and lived in their truth, setting honorable examples inherited by their four children. Although Bobby's family was poor, he had earned a scholarship to Regis High School, got his bachelor's degree at Fordham, and graduated with honors from New York Law School. Everyone knew that Bobby lived to do the right thing. He took leadership seriously and had a knack for letting everyone know that their voices were important and heard. Being an Irish American from the Bronx, he wasn't shy about fighting for the truth or himself. I'd been with him on occasions when he offered an unethical defense attorney, who'd made false claims in court, an opportunity to get his ass kicked out in the parking lot—a far better course of action than a bunch of motions. And besides being brilliant, Bobby was also the most down-to-earth guy you'd ever meet, a man not afraid of being himself, even in his mullet haircut and polka-dot socks.

Abe and I told Bobby about our concerns and difference of opinion with our supervisor. Bobby saw it our way, and before you knew it, we had the green light to set up Harry Uribe with one more meeting. This time, in anticipation of Quino's whispering and the blasting radio, we placed the transmitter mic in the left collar of Harry's shirt, just below his ear.

We gave him his marching orders. "Harry, you need to make sure you get in the passenger seat. That's the only way this mic will pick up Quino's whispers."

Harry asked for another meeting, and luckily, Quino invited him into the passenger seat of his unmarked cop car. The plan worked. After Harry showed Quino his grand jury subpoena, Quino whispered directly into the microphone.

"This is the only thing I ask of you, Harry. I ask it as a personal favor. Look, if the shit comes down, right, and we both get charged, the only way that we can help each other is if we stay with the same story. I've given this a lot of thought, brother. We can save ourselves. If you go before the grand jury, you tell those people, if they ask you questions about you, and it's going to incriminate you, you say, 'I refuse to answer that question.' Look, your attorney cannot go in there with you. If you stick your foot in your mouth, they're going to get you. I am confident. I know they don't have anything. What they have is a weak case."

Quino knew that, under the worst of circumstances, he might try to mitigate his punishment if he could get us to believe that he had simply lost it, psychologically. But if his motive could be shown to be greed, he was fucked.

"What's really important, Harry, is that if the shit hits the fan, you never gave me any money, right?"

Once Harry agreed to lie about the money, Quino spelled out a blueprint for his defense. He'd never been trained by DEA to do deep undercover, and he was scared. He didn't want to admit to his fears, so he tried to scare Latorre away by passing him off to the Uribe family to have them handle the laundering.

Quino was obsessed with making sure Harry never disclosed that he had stuffed his pockets with laundering profits. "If they ever ask you if you delivered money to me, you tell them, 'No. That I never did.' Okay? Everything is hinging on me and you sticking together. What they're trying to do is break us apart."

His parting words were the bottom line. "I'm telling you, the only thing that you don't tell them is that I took money . . . We've got to minimize."

Marwan and I were sitting together a block away, in our unmarked car with heavily tinted windows, listening to and recording every crystal-clear word that Quino whispered into Harry Uribe's ear. We couldn't resist celebrating, exchanging high fives and smiling in relief. Marwan proclaimed the verdict. "We've got the motherfucker, Bob. He's done. We did it."

"I get it, Abe, but there's one more smoking gun we've got to get. I need a week to organize the probable cause to search Quino's home. As soon as the magistrate approves the search warrant, we need to deliver two big punches at the same time, Quino's arrest and the search."

I subpoenaed the home and cell phone records of Quino, Harry Uribe, and all of Harry's siblings. Those made it clear that they were all working closely with Latorre and Pedro Rodriguez-Castro in Colombia. The calls coincided with specific deliveries of cash by cartel couriers to Edith Uribe in New York.

Quino admitted making laundering profits during his recorded meetings with Harry, so as long as I could establish probable cause that there were records in Quino's home related to his purchases and expenses, I'd get the warrant. We put a mail-cover on Quino's home, a process in which the US Postal Service confirms the sender's address of every piece of mail sent to Quino's home. It proved that creditors were sending bills to his home. We pulled Quino's trash in the early-morning hours, before the garbage truck was scheduled to arrive. The trash contained discarded envelopes from creditors. I pulled his credit reports, which showed the address to which banks and his creditors sent him mail. The results—undeniable proof that there were records of Quino's financial affairs in his home.

Just for icing on the cake, we got proof that he had purchased a home computer during the time that he laundered for Latorre. It was probable that there were files corroborating his wealth on that computer.

After a short visit with US magistrate Thomas McCoun, who reviewed the application for the warrant, it was approved. Judge McCoun and I established a deep respect for one another over the years. I first met him a decade before, when he was an attorney defending one of eleven defendants in a drug case that involved the prosecution of a dirty lawyer who financed drug deals. In addition to being a gifted lawyer, McCoun was a person of immense integrity and fairness. As he signed the warrant, he looked at me and said, "You're a lucky man, Mr. Mazur. You could have easily gotten whacked."

"I know, Judge. I no longer take any day for granted. Thank you for your service, Your Honor."

With warrant in hand, Marwan and I mapped out the plan. He would handle Quino's arrest, and I would lead a team that would search Quino's house. Arresting Quino would be dangerous. Like all of us, Quino always carried at least one gun.

Quino was a witness in a pending drug case handled by Assistant US Attorney Mark Jackowski. We had Jackowski call Quino and tell him that he and another agent involved in the case, Bob Davis, had to come to Mark's office to assist in trial preparation. Unlike the other prosecutors, Jackowski had a private office in a corner of the first floor of the federal building. There would be no innocent bystanders if something went wrong. There was also a second small room within

Jackowski's office, so Marwan and another agent, Lee Paige, could leap out at the right moment to make the arrest.

Lee was a former NFL football player. Quino would be no match for his size and strength.

As Quino and Davis entered Jackowski's office, Jackowski, knowing he was the only one in the room without a gun, leaped and hid behind a file cabinet filled with papers. It was the safest hole he could find for what he knew was about to happen. While Quino was in a confused daze, Abe Marwan, Paige, and Davis pounced, but Marwan was not going to be denied the privilege of cuffing Quino. As he slapped the cuffs on, Davis steadied Quino and Paige frisked him, removing the service revolver hidden in Quino's ankle holster.

Marwan's eyes raged. "Hey, Quino, you fucking rat bastard, we've been watching you on video. We know everything. Why'd you do it, Quino? Why'd you do it, you piece of shit?"

Quino only hung his head in shame.

Marwan went on. "Listen, we've got a search warrant for your house and an entire search team out there now. We're either going to knock your door down, or you can have your wife go to the house and let us in. Which is it?"

Marwan called Quino's wife. "Hi. This is Abe Marwan with DEA. We just arrested Quino, and we have a warrant to search your home. The search team is there. If you'd like to go there and open the door, we'll wait. If not, we're knocking it down."

Quino's wife, a sharp woman with a law degree, also had a sharp tongue. "If they knock down that door, they'd better not let my fucking cat out. I'm headed there now."

Quino was moved to a small room with only a table and a few chairs. Paige joined him, and Bob Davis positioned himself at a distance, by the door. Davis was uneasy. He had worked closely with Quino for years. At times, he was like a father to Quino. Unlike Marwan, he wasn't enjoying himself, but he knew this had to be done. He internalized his outrage.

Davis was an extremely honest, humble, and genuine man of faith. His moral compass made it difficult for him to fathom Quino's treason.

Paige and Quino were two of very few agents of color in our office. Because of that, they were repeatedly used, and many say abused, to work undercover in cases that required someone to pose as a drug dealer. Paige had spent many hours on the road with Quino, consoling him when he complained about the bigotry that he and Paige had endured in the workplace. Quino felt his colleagues refused to acknowledge his accomplishments. They didn't show him the type of respect he thought he deserved, and he had come to feel he was more respected by the "bad guys" than the "good guys."

Paige, once a punishing defensive back for the Florida State University Seminoles, was a gentle giant who always treated everyone kindly and with respect. He'd occasionally watched my back in Panama when I worked there undercover, and he did the same for Quino during money pickups in New York and other cities. Now that he was alone with Quino, he tried to settle Quino down by playing "good cop" to Marwan's "bad cop," in an effort to get Quino to confess.

"Hey, man, are you going to be all right?"

"Thanks for asking, Lee. Please make sure they don't treat my wife badly, and if they break into my house before she gets there, would you please make sure they don't let the cat out? It's an exotic cat, and almost like a child to us."

"Okay, Quino, I'll make sure of that."

"Thanks, man. I'm sorry. I'm so, so sorry. All I can say is I'm sorry. I know how the people in our office think everybody on the other side in this war is a bad guy. I've seen a lot of people treated like they're pieces of shit. You know, not all of them are bad guys."

"Quino, I think you'll feel a lot better getting some of this off your chest. You know that, if you come clean now, the road you'll have to travel to make amends will be a lot less bumpy than if you don't talk."

"No. I want to speak with my attorney before I do anything."

Marwan leaned his head into the room. "Yeah, just like a criminal. We're wasting our time here. Davis and I will take this scumbag to the county jail. You can join Mazur and the search team at this shitbird's house."

Marwan and Davis led Quino out of the federal building with his hands cuffed behind his back. The workday was ending, so there were dozens of agents and support staff in the lobby and outside the front door. They were in shock. Most of them knew the "Officer of the Year" and were buzzing in speculation as Marwan threw Quino in the back seat of his car.

As Marwan drove toward the Pinellas County Jail, he flung a Bible in Quino's lap. "Here you go, Quino. You're going to have a lot of time on your hands, asshole. You ought to make the best of this next decade behind bars and read that Bible, you piece of shit."

Marwan lit a cigar and repeatedly took deep drags, blowing clouds of cigar smoke toward Quino's face, again and again. Quino didn't say anything. He wouldn't give Marwan the pleasure of his complaining. Marwan became so distracted, relishing his punishment of Quino, that he wasn't watching the road. The locked breaks and screeching tires turned every head in the neighborhood as Marwan desperately tried to avoid having his car T-boned. He ran a red light and barely escaped a deadly crash.

Once at the county jail, Marwan rushed to the back door so he could march Quino into the lockup. As he led his prisoner, he moved his hand down to the handcuffs and began to jerk and twist them, bruising and cutting the skin around Quino's wrists. Quino turned to Marwan and yelled. "So, that's the way you're going to be? You wouldn't be doing that to me if I wasn't handcuffed."

Marwan leaned in Quino's face as veins popped in his neck, his own face red from anger. "You fucking rat bastard. You're a piece of shit; you're not a cop."

Quino looked toward his former mentor, Bob Davis. "Bob, you see this, right? Abe's a big man here. I'm handcuffed."

Davis put an end to Marwan's antics. As Davis handed his prisoner off to the deputies at the jail, he looked at him sincerely and offered a simple promise of optimism that rang in Quino's mind for many years to come. "Quino, there will be better days."

As Quino entered the jail, on the other side of Tampa Bay, his wife raced from her car and stomped toward me. Betsey Gonzalez was the daughter of the lead attorney in one of the most powerful law firms in Tampa. She'd followed in her father's footsteps, earned her law degree, and previously worked as an assistant state attorney for the county. As soon as she came on the scene, she announced her role. "I'm my husband's lawyer until Bennie Lazzara, the only lawyer that'll be representing him, gets here."

I knew Bennie very well. He represented one of the senior officers at the BCCI who had been indicted as a result of one of my prior undercover jobs. He'd questioned me repeatedly on the witness stand during the three months that I testified against his client and other dirty bankers. Bennie was a total gentleman and an extraordinarily gifted lawyer. I respected him immensely. He and his family had a long history in Tampa, including the unfortunate fact that his father was the victim of a gangland killing in 1959, the last year of Tampa's Mafia wars, which came to be known as the "Era of Blood."

"Betsey, we've arrested Quino and have a warrant to search your home. We didn't want to break down the front door, so we'd like you to unlock it."

She was indignant. "I need to go in the house before you start. I need to put my cat in a cage."

I had to take control. "Betsey, when you unlock the door of your house, I and another officer will have to accompany you while you secure the cat. When we're in the house, if you'd like to show us where your husband normally keeps his personal files, that might get us out of there quicker."

While we were in the house, she showed us Quino's office and confirmed that only he used the computer on his desk. As soon as the cat was secured, two Florida State Troopers swept the house with canines trained to sniff out drugs. There were none.

Once the dogs were out, two agents began taking photos and video of every room. They drew diagrams of each floor of the house, and assigned unique numbers to every room, closet, and other area, on each floor. Whatever was seized would be put in a box marked with the number assigned to the area where it was found, and the agent assigned to that room was identified on the box as the seizing agent.

As we went through our pre-search protocol, Quino's wife grew increasingly anxious. "What the hell are you people doing? Why are you in there with cameras? How long is this going to take? Where is my husband? Does he have a lawyer with him, one that represents him? I want a copy of the search warrant, now!"

A female agent gave her some advice. "Listen, honey, you don't realize how hard you're making this on yourself."

I gave Betsey Gonzalez a copy of the warrant.

I hadn't seen Betsey since I invited her and Quino to have dinner with me and my wife at our home. My angst was with Quino, not her. Knowing she would eventually read the affidavit in support of the warrant, I felt compelled to explain. "I apologize for any personal problems it may create, but when you see the affidavit for the search warrant, I just want you to know that I had no choice but to include details about Quino's romantic relationship with two of the Uribe sisters. It was relevant to his committing crimes with them. I didn't want that to be a surprise."

She threw me a look that said, *Oh, how naive*. "A surprise to who? Listen, Mazur, I'll leave if you'll make sure the cat won't be let out, and you'll feed her."

"No problem. You have my word."

Minutes after she left, the home phone rang. It was Quino, calling from the county jail. He knew it was me. His voice quivered. "Bob, please, please, I'm begging you. Please tell me where I can contact my wife. I need her here with me. Please."

"She's with her brother, and I think they're on their way to see you at the jail. You take care, my friend."

"Thank you. Thank you, Bob."

With Quino's wife out of our hair, agents worked tirelessly for six more hours, meticulously searching every inch of the house. By the time we were done, we had twelve boxes of damning records and Quino's computer.

What we found provided the final nails sealing Quino's coffin: bank records revealing repeated deposits of cash in increments under ten thousand dollars to his personal accounts; copies of cashier's checks and money orders he'd purchased with cash, in amounts under ten thousand dollars, throughout the Tampa area; an address book with phone numbers acquired by Latorre and Pedro Rodriguez-Castro after Quino had stopped working on Pro-Mo; records of large cash purchases, including a motorcycle and the deposit on a condo he set up as rental property; boxes of police files, including four photos of a DEA informant in social settings with the Uribe brothers, the informant's head circled in each picture. Presumably, the Uribes had given the pictures to Quino so he could warn them if the man whose head was circled was either a snitch or an undercover agent.

The most damning thing we found was probably worth about a million dollars to Latorre's friend Miguel Rodriguez-Orejuela, who shared leadership of the Cali cartel with his brother, Gilberto. It was a thirty-three-page Narcotics and Dangerous Drugs Information System (NADDIS) printout containing all of DEA's intelligence and case work related to the Rodriguez-Orejuelas. Details in that report, if read by the Rodriguez-Orejuela brothers or their chief security officer, would have given them a road map identifying DEA informants around the world. It was hidden in Quino's attic, under the insulation.

The day after his arrest, local media outlets were on fire about Quino's fate. His unveiling shocked the conscience of the city. Tampa PD deputy chief of police John Cuesta provided an on-air description of his firing of the "Officer of the Year." "He was very teary-eyed. He was emotional and had a very difficult time maintaining eye contact with me."

After he appeared before a US District Court magistrate, Quino was held without bond. He wasn't going to see the real world for many years to come.

Now it was time to capitalize on the cooperation of the Uribe family. Abe Marwan and I sat down with Harry Uribe and explained how he could help his sister Edith.

"Harry, Edith has young kids who continue to live here in the US while she's on the run in Colombia. There's no doubt she'd rather work out a deal to come back and help raise them. She'll eventually get that opportunity if she helps us lure Latorre to a country where we can grab his ass and bring him here to face charges. Reason with her. Let her know we can be trusted. You've seen what we've done for you, Mario, and Hernando. She can get the same honest help if she does the right thing with Latorre."

"I'll call her, Bob. I can't promise anything, but I'll try to make this happen. I know it would be the best thing for her, and for my nephews and nieces."

Before the ink was dry on the paperwork that denied Quino bond, I was on the phone with Edith Uribe.

"Listen, Edith. We won't negotiate any terms regarding your outstanding criminal charges until you surrender yourself here in the States, but if you want to volunteer information without a promise of leniency, we will accept that information and evaluate what's possible."

"Bob, Harry tells me you and Abe have been honest with him. That's good enough for me. I want to be with my children. I don't want them to have to grow up in Colombia, so I'll talk with you now, knowing there's no promises."

She gave it all up.

"Before Quino came to me with the offer of working with Latorre, I'd never been involved in any drug trafficking or money laundering. Quino offered me and Harry a three-way partnership to launder. The three of us split a fee equal to eight percent of any money Latorre had the Cali cartel send our way. Things went fine for a while, but when money got seized, the cartel forced us to take lower fees. Latorre and I are still on good terms. He lives in Bogotá with his girlfriend. He left his wife and son. He has approached me about helping him to get false identification, but even without that, I think I can get him to travel with me outside of Colombia to meet a potential new client. Pedro Rodriguez-Castro is now in hiding. Both Colombian law enforcement and the Cali cartel are hunting for him. Pedro lost two million dollars of the cartel's money, and they want either their money or his life."

Although I thought what she'd already said had value, she continued to deliver.

"Latorre works directly with the biggest traffickers in Cali and has high-level connections in Colombian law enforcement, the Colombian money-laundering hierarchy, and traffickers in Panama. Bob, his guys in Panama were outside your office the last time he met with you there. He'd given them orders to kill you if he didn't return to them by a certain time, and you were three minutes from being blown away. That's a fact. He told me the whole story."

"Edith, would you work with us to sell Latorre a lie that will bring him to the Dominican Republic? Would you lie and tell him that you have a new client in Santo Domingo who needs his help and has tens of millions to launder? Would you put your life on the line?"

Latorre would never be brought to justice otherwise, because at that time, Colombia wasn't honoring extradition requests from the States. Edith just needed to bring Latorre to Santo Domingo. Once they arrived, we had contacts in the Dominican Republic who would help us get Latorre to the States and her to Florida. I promised her we'd do right by her, and I meant it. I couldn't promise she wouldn't serve time, but I assured her that we'd tell the judge assigned to her case that she put her life in the crosshairs of the cartel to help us get Latorre.

"I have to do this for my family, Bob. I have no choice. Count me in."

During my law enforcement career, I'd had this type of conversation with people in Edith's shoes a hundred times. In a life of crime, turning on others can have major consequences, but Edith's choice was epic. Her decision ended one life and saved three others.

18

FACING JUSTICE

June–October 1994

"Luis, this is Edith. Please call me back. I've come across an opportunity that can help all of us. I know you're being cautious, but we may lose the chance of getting some big business unless we act quickly."

Latorre was lying low. He and his partner, Pedro Rodriguez-Castro, had just gone through the terror of being kidnapped on the orders of Carlos Alberto Mejia, a major Cali trafficker who supervised a clandestine cocaine lab on behalf of the Rodriguez-Orejuela brothers and Orlando Heano, a former Colombian police officer destined to become the leader of Colombia's Norte del Valle cartel. Latorre knew the men wouldn't think twice about tracking him down again.

Just three months earlier, when Latorre and Rodriguez-Castro had been cornered, Latorre thought he would be killed immediately. But a sack was thrown over his head and two carloads of sicarios whisked him away. While held at gunpoint, he was given one of two choices. If he didn't comply with their demands, he would be signing death warrants for himself, his wife, his son, and his girlfriend. On the other hand, if he and Rodriguez-Castro signed over all of their assets, they would be allowed to go free, provided they found ways to pay off more of their debt after they were released. They turned over everything they owned. Eight properties, three luxury cars, valuable artwork, bank balances, and more—gone. Now they needed to earn to stay alive.

Latorre and Rodriguez-Castro were desperate. They'd burned their bridges with Carlos Alberto Mejia (a.k.a. Beto), who—along with stockbroker Miguel Rosenberg—had given them the opportunity to clean tens of millions for the cartel. Carlos Mejia had the trust of the leaders in Cali, but he no longer trusted Latorre.

When he got Edith's message, Latorre envisioned light at the end of a tunnel that would otherwise surely lead to his death. This was his chance to make more laundering profits and finally get the cartel off his back.

Edith gave him the bait. "Luis, before I went on the run, I was moving money for some Dominican traffickers in Queens. Their boss in Santo Domingo is prepared to have me move fifty million dollars for him, but much of it has to be sent to Colombia to pay for product [cocaine]. I'm willing to handle this in partnership with you, but you have to handle the conversion in Colombia. I'll work with you only if you show your face to him and accept responsibility for the funds, after I pass them to you. He has agreed to meet in Santo Domingo next week. Can you join me there?"

"But what about Los Feos, Edith?"

"Both the owner and everyone else I've spoken to confirm that the Dominican Republic has no extradition treaty with the States. We have nothing to worry about. Plus, the owner has a very strong influence with Dominican generals. They run the country. I would never go otherwise. We've been guaranteed safety."

Edith wasn't lying, at least not about everything. The Dominican Republic had no extradition treaty with the States, and it was true that her contact had influence with a Dominican general. The detail she didn't share with Latorre was that her "contact" was DEA.

"I know from my people that what you're saying about the Dominican is true," Latorre agreed. "Thank you for this opportunity to work with you again. Rest assured, my bank contacts in Bogotá can easily handle the fifty tons [fifty million dollars]."

When countries have no extradition treaty with the US, sometimes there are "work-arounds" that can still get the job done. We wouldn't break the law, but we would build relationships with decision makers in countries like the Dominican Republic who, fortunately for us, would make decisions resulting in our success. In this instance, DEA had established a good working relationship with a general who had the authority to declare someone attempting to enter the country as "undesirable," refusing entry and forcing the "undesirable" to take the next available flight back to the country from which they arrived. Because Latorre had been indicted in Tampa, if he should attempt to enter the Dominican Republic, the general would be on solid ground in declaring Latorre "undesirable."

Following our plan, Edith scheduled Latorre's supposed meeting with the Dominican "godfather" at a time when there were no nonstop flights from Santo Domingo to Bogotá. They all made a stop in Miami.

The night before Latorre was scheduled to arrive, Jeff Brunner and Abe Marwan flew to Santo Domingo and met with our agents stationed there. Everything was in place.

With the hope of building a relationship with Edith's contact, Latorre strolled off his flight into Las Américas International Airport, just outside of Santo Domingo, arm in arm with Sandra Garay, his twenty-two-year-old girlfriend, who was twenty-five years his junior. Many eyes turned toward Latorre, mainly because Garay was stunning: thin, tall, with thick waist-length black hair and the looks of a beauty queen.

It wasn't long before the Dominicans had Latorre in custody. They took him to a room where he met Brunner and Marwan.

"Hello, Luis. How are you? My name is Abe. We understand that the military here is putting you on the next flight back to your country. What a coincidence—that happens to be the same flight we're taking. What do you know, that flight to Bogotá stops in Miami."

The Dominicans cuffed Latorre's hands in front of his waist and put his jacket over the cuffs, so it appeared that he was simply carrying his coat. Latorre grew nervous, mentally struggling with his fate. Then the American Airlines pilot and crew were briefed, and the plan began to unravel.

"Listen, as the pilot, I'm responsible for everyone's safety. If this guy resists in any fashion, I'm not letting him on board."

Brunner took the lead. "We understand, sir. This guy has been declared by the Dominican authorities as undesirable. Under their law, he is being put on the first available flight that will take him back to Bogotá. Once this flight lands on US soil, we are going to exercise US law, take him into custody, and remove him from the plane. With your permission, we'll sit on either side of him during the flight, in the back of the plane. He's already resigned himself to the fact that the Dominicans want him on this plane. There's an outstanding arrest warrant for him back in the States. Here's a copy."

"Okay, guys, but if this guy shows any resistance after takeoff, we'll return here and give him back to the Dominicans."

While the other passengers waited at the gate, Brunner, Marwan, and Latorre boarded the flight and sat in the last row. Brunner and Marwan did everything they could to keep Latorre at ease, talking about anything other than the charges waiting for him in Tampa. For Brunner, the lead on this detail, the two hours of flight time felt like it would never end, but finally, they were wheels down at Miami International Airport.

Customs and DEA agents met Brunner, Marwan, and Latorre at the gate. Latorre was whisked to the local US Marshals office, photographed, fingerprinted, and shuttled to county jail where he was held pending his initial hearing. For Latorre, it was over. The plan had succeeded. The laws of two nations were followed, but some jokingly referred to the process as "extra-napping."

Within two weeks of his arrival in Miami, Latorre was in the Hernando County jail, one of many county facilities in the Tampa Bay area that contracted with the US government to house federal prisoners pending trial or sentencing. We visited him, and he was willing to speak with us about Quino.

"Bob, when Quino was alone with us at the mall in Sarasota a few years ago, he told us everything about you. Pedro and I were in shock. We felt Quino saved our lives, because we were otherwise convinced you were for real. Quino told us he worked closely with a Colombian family in Tampa that moved dope. He wanted us to get them supplied so they could sell big shipments. I kept telling him that wasn't our thing. We just wanted help laundering. Eventually, he brought Edith and Harry Uribe into the picture, and the three of them helped us move money for more than a year. When we were deep in debt because of the seizures and had no other choice, the Uribes sold dope for us in New York. The narcos in Cali would have killed us otherwise; they wanted payment, one way or the other."

Days after we left the jail, Latorre ran into an old friend at a jail-house Bible study. "Hi, Antonio, or should I call you Quino now? I heard you were here. I need to speak with you."

"Luis, I'm here to serve the Lord and study the Bible. I don't want to talk now."

"Can we talk later?"

"When Bible study is over, I'll meet you outside in the yard."

An hour later, they were outdoors, in the inmates' concrete exercise yard, surrounded by a twenty-five-foot fence topped with barbed wire. The second Latorre opened his mouth, it was obvious that he was afire with hate and bent on revenge.

"Listen, my friend. I've decided that those fucking Uribes, Harry and Edith, must die. I have the means to make that happen, and I will. They betrayed us. I will never forgive them."

Quino's heart pounded. He didn't know what to think. Was it possible this meeting was orchestrated by DEA agents, as a setup? "Luis, man, I've made peace with God. I just want to do my time. I've already forgiven those people. I can't live the rest of my life with that bitterness."

"I will never forgive them, or anyone else who betrayed me. If you won't help me with the Uribes, I have another offer. Do you know anybody that has a helicopter?" Latorre gestured around the yard. "This place . . . we can easily get out of here. I can get the money to pay for the chopper. You're from here, in the States. I'm sure you know someone who can help us. If you do, I can help you. Once we're out, we'll be taken to a small plane. I can fly us to Mexico. We'll be free to enjoy the rest of our lives."

"Luis, first of all, I don't know anybody like that. Second, I'm not interested. Like I told you, I've forgiven these people. I just want to do my time and get this nightmare behind me."

"I'm sure you know DEA visited me. News of those kinds of things spread like wildfire in here. I had no choice, Quino. I had to tell them everything, about how you came to us and everything else. If I can't escape, I have to get the best deal possible."

Quino winced, knowing that any chance of his winning in court was over. He stared into Latorre's eyes. "Luis, do I have anything to worry about from you, or your people?"

"No, no, you don't, my friend. You tried to help me. I won't do anything to have you hurt. I promise."

Latorre kept trying to get help killing his betrayers and escaping. He confided in another inmate who saw the proposal as his own way to get out of prison, but not with Latorre.

"Listen, Luis; my cousin is an experienced button man [assassin]. He can take people out for you, but each job will cost twenty thousand dollars."

Latorre was all in. Somehow, he'd figured out that the Princess caused millions to be seized in Switzerland and to fall into the hands of law enforcement. He and Rodriguez were responsible for most of that loss, and he wanted the Princess, Harry, and Edith killed.

After the inmate swore an oath of secrecy to Latorre, he secretly met with the warden and passed him Latorre's wish list, hoping it would buy him a reduced sentence. The same day, our office got the call.

Jeff Brunner briefed the agents in Fort Lauderdale who were managing the Princess, and a plan was developed. We'd let the Fort Lauderdale office take the lead on Latorre's blueprint for murder and a prison break. They'd have one of their task force agents pose as the inmate's cousin, record the meetings, and turn the tables on Latorre. I wish it hadn't become necessary, but in a sense, I repaid the Princess for her saving my life. Now Latorre's plans to have her killed would be snuffed out.

At Latorre's direction, in one of Miami's Little Havana Cuban restaurants, an eight-thousand-dollar cash advance slid across a table to the "hitman."

In the course of recorded meetings with the undercover agent, Latorre shared a revised escape plan. He'd made arrangements for a dental appointment. Inmates weren't chained during their transport to the dentist's office, and the two guards who drove the van were both obese and in poor shape. When Latorre was in the dentist's chair, the hitman would enter the waiting room and take out the two guards with his handgun, which would be equipped with a silencer. Latorre would be taken to a nearby airport, where he had arranged to steal a plane. He was a pilot, so all he needed was access to the controls, and he'd be on his way to Mexico.

The warden was briefed about the recorded meetings, and Latorre was removed to another prison and put in lockdown.

In short order, he was sentenced, in our case, to sixteen years in prison. A life-threatening form of lupus ravaged his body, motivating him to continue to try to escape, but that was a tall order for a man in solitary confinement. He ultimately died behind bars.

Only a year before Latorre died, the Colombian media announced the fate of his partner, Pedro Rodriguez-Castro. The headlines by Caracol Radio said it all. "Alleged Colombian drug lord, money launderer, and gang leader was captured today by the Administrative Department of Security and DAS." That was how Colombian authorities described Rodriguez-Castro when they put him in chains. While I dealt with him, he worked for Francisco Helmer Herrera Buitrago (a.k.a. "Pacho"), a ruthless trafficker who was fourth in command in the Cali cartel. The 9mm shots pumped into Herrera Buitrago's head by an assassin in 1998 must have pushed Rodriguez-Castro up the chain of command.

After we derailed Latorre's efforts to have the Princess whacked, her wealth and role within the cartel drew the attention of Colombian paramilitary groups, who kidnapped her. She went through months of torturous captivity but remarkably escaped death.

Now it was Quino's turn to face justice. He decided to plead guilty. Before sentencing, he agreed to submit to a full and "truthful" debriefing. With Abe Marwan and Assistant US Attorney Bobby O'Neill, I visited Quino and his attorney at the Pinellas County Jail. Quino wanted to explain himself, and he unleashed a river of tears as he offered excuse after excuse.

"I screwed up," he told us. "I did. I don't know why, to be honest with you. I've been thinking about it since I've been in here, for four months. I screwed up. All I can say to you is I was . . . you know, I did a lot of undercover work, small time. This thing weighed on me, you know, this dealing with people in Colombia. I was scared. More scared than I'd ever been. Why I cracked, I don't know, Abe."

Marwan leaned in. "Let me get this straight, Quino. Latorre asks you if you can find any Colombian people who can launder money. So instead of you telling him no, you turn around and you go to the Uribes. There had to be a reason for that. Why did you do that?"

"I don't know, Abe. I'm being honest with you. I don't know. I don't know what I was thinking back then. I snapped. It wasn't for the money. I didn't need the money. My wife and I were doing well. I was making good money at the time, and I . . . you know . . . I just . . . I don't know. I just cracked. I really don't know."

Then Marwan asked the most telling question. "Quino, have you ever been involved in any other illegal activities, other than this deal with Latorre?"

Flags of deception flew in every direction. Quino looked to every corner of the room, but not into our eyes. He withdrew. He fidgeted. His denial was flat, meekly delivered. "No."

Marwan kept pushing. "How much money did you make during this whole thing?"

"Total, um, I'd have to guess. I wasn't counting it. It was small. I'd say a total of about twenty thousand dollars, maybe twenty-two thousand."

I knew he was full of shit. I had the records from his home and had been digging further with subpoenas. My forensic accounting background and training as an IRS special agent equipped me to prove Quino to be a liar. Just a cursory analysis made clear that he had no less than seventy-five thousand dollars in unexplained cash, which didn't include the wads of it he'd spent living the high life. Worse than that, the unexplained money had been flowing through his accounts at least a year before he had first met Latorre. There was much more to this story.

Marwan wanted to shove every piece of proof we had up Quino's ass, but now wasn't the time. Better to ask open-ended questions, then wait until sentencing to play our cards. O'Neill agreed. Our strategy would be to call witnesses and introduce documents that showed Quino to be a liar, hope the judge threw the book at him, and let Quino stew in federal prison while we dealt with the Pro-Mo defendants who hadn't pled guilty. When we were ready, we'd haul Quino back to Tampa before a grand jury. We weren't going to walk away from nailing him to the wall. And we had to determine whether he was a lone wolf or part of a pack of dirty cops. His day of reckoning would come.

At Quino's sentencing, prosecutor Bobby O'Neill dropped bomb after bomb. Recorded calls proved that Quino never feared Latorre. He'd admitted to a fraction of the earnings that came his way. If not for that money, he would have been teetering on bankruptcy. All five of the Uribe siblings confirmed that Quino told them about Pro-Mo several months before Quino claimed to have "cracked" in the Sarasota mall. Witness after witness and a sea of records annihilated Quino's claim of minimal involvement. Then, those damning recorded whispers to Harry Uribe. The judge gave him eleven years behind bars, the maximum sentence under the guidelines.

Central Florida's media was on fire about Quino's sentencing. Tampa's NBC news anchor said it all. "He was 'Officer of the Year' and a very successful undercover cop, but Juaquin 'Quino' Gonzalez had a secret life laundering drug money and betraying his fellow officers as a corrupt cop . . . Gonzalez did more than just launder money. Prosecutors say he betrayed his fellow undercover agents, giving their names to the Colombians."

Defense attorney Bennie Lazzara tried to rationalize Quino's life of crime. "Juaquin 'Quino' Gonzalez was a warrior in the War on Drugs, and, like any other warrior, like one of Patton's warriors, he suffered from battle fatigue."

Before his sentencing, Quino had already experienced hell at the county jail. He was in solitary confinement for three months, living every minute alone. He got only thirty minutes of "fresh air" each day, in a small room with a concrete floor and ten-foot fencing welded to a fenced ceiling, like an oversized dog kennel. He became so depressed during his visits to the kennel that he opted to stay in his cell twenty-four hours a day.

When Quino was finally permitted to be with other inmates, he was nearly killed. In order to get a haircut, he was taken to a hallway where two chairs were positioned about twenty-five feet apart, facing each other. Two at a time, inmates were brought to barbers, where they sat across from one another. As Quino got his haircut, the inmate in the second chair, a young Black man who was part of a local gang, kept staring at Quino. Eventually he said, "That's the dude that busted my cousin."

The man snatched the scissors out of his barber's hand and lunged toward Quino. The gang member's barber stopped the man, wrestled the scissors away from him, and yelled, "Man, you crazy. He didn't mess with them crack dealers. He messed with them big Colombian dudes." Remarkably, that was enough to stop what otherwise could very well have led to Quino's death.

So, when he was finally sentenced, Quino enjoyed a tremendous sense of relief. He no longer feared the unknown, and he began a decade in prison that would, in the long run, be the best thing that ever happened to him. He knew the length of his road to freedom, and he was eager to get to his designated prison and sprint through that portion of his life. On the other end, peace waited for him.

Quino was transported to Butner Federal Correctional Institution (FCI) in North Carolina. Like all inmates, he was transported via a checkerboard of prison transfers that took months. Being in transit status is an inmate's nightmare. Quino's journey began in heavy chains. His legs were shackled, his hands cuffed in front of his waist. Another chain ran around his midsection and down his back to leg irons. Those considered to be an escape risk also wore a separate piece of equipment called "the black box" locked over their handcuffs. Quino and two other inmates on his prison bus wore "the black box."

After endless bus rides, he arrived at one of his temporary stops, the Atlanta federal penitentiary. This hellhole hasn't changed much since it was built in 1902. On the interior, it has the look, smell, and feel of Alcatraz. The bus arrived through an underground tunnel, and Quino was ushered to "the holdover," a special section within the penitentiary for inmates in transit.

The next day, he was waiting in a very long line to use one of the pay phones. As he stood amid dozens of inmates, the prisoner in front of him began to look familiar. The guy told Quino he was from Tampa and had gotten a thirty-year sentence. As they talked, it dawned on Quino that this drug dealer was the main target of one of his old Tampa PD cases. Luckily, the guy never recognized him.

While Quino was being held at the Atlanta penitentiary, inmates killed one of the guards with a hammer. As you'd expect, the other guards took revenge. Prisoners were locked in their cells for a full week, three inmates to a two-man cell. There were no showers, and when it came time to eat, the guards threw bags of cold bologna sandwiches through the small trap opening of each cell's solid metal door.

Quino stayed in the Atlanta penitentiary for two months. From there, he was transferred to FCI. After being processed, he was allowed to go into the exercise yard, and when he saw the grass, he fell to his knees and cried, touching the grass in amazement. He'd walked only on concrete for six months and felt blessed to smell and touch the beauty of the green blades, which he would never again take for granted.

In a couple of months, we would have Quino dragged back to Tampa, but in the meantime, although most of the Pro-Mo defendants pled or were found guilty, some intended to fight it out in court, including the Panamanian lawyer Rinaldo Laguna, Robert Baldasare's good friend.

A lot of factors pave the path to justice in a courtroom. The first is the judge assigned to the case. When the high-powered attorneys representing some of the Pro-Mo defendants learned that the case had been assigned to Judge Henry Lee Adams, they were ecstatic. One of them admitted that they thought they had a 40-percent-greater chance of winning with Judge Adams presiding. Perceived in some legal circles as disliking the government, Judge Adams was also thought to like one of the defense attorneys in particular. Laguna and his codefendants may have pled guilty if their cases had come before a different judge.

I testified for weeks. Judge Adams instructed me to answer questions with a simple yes or no. That's very unusual, especially when a highly gifted defense counsel poses questions that include inaccurate "facts." Asked just such an ambiguous question at one point, I turned to the judge and informed him that I couldn't answer with a simple yes or no and would need to explain my answer. He looked at me sternly. "Your answer must therefore be no, so let's move on." Nothing could have been farther from the truth, but I was powerless.

Within the defense camp, a devious plan evolved to falsely discredit me in the eyes of the jury. A couple of months before I took the stand, Rinaldo Laguna wrote a letter to a DEA official, falsely claiming that I had engaged in illegal and unprofessional conduct. He claimed that I had worked undercover in Panama without authorization, violated laws while there, conducted illegal wiretaps, illegally traveled on a false passport, and provided false information to Panamanian banks. It's possible that Laguna made these claims because he and others were unaware of the Panamanian AG's decision, at the outset of Operation Pro-Mo, to break tradition and supposedly keep my undercover work secret from others in his government. When Laguna's accusations were proved false, he later strategically made new false accusations.

Shortly before I took the stand as a prosecution witness, Laguna sent a second letter to the Internal Affairs office of the Department of Justice. To make sure it was widely read, he also sent it to four US senators, the CIA, the FBI, and counsel for the other defendants in his trial. The letter falsely claimed that I stole drug money handed to me by traffickers, conspired with Quino in his illegal activity, took cash from Laguna after charging restaurant bills on my credit card, orchestrated the kidnapping of Luis Latorre in Colombia, conspired in a prior undercover operation with officers of the BCCI, and more.

Not one word of Laguna's accusations was true. They were intended to create doubts about me with the jury, and to goad a reporter to print the false accusations in an article published in a major Tampa newspaper. It worked.

"Chief target of the new probe is DEA agent Robert Mazur, who headed Operation Pro-Mo, according to a US Attorney's Office letter to lawyers involved in another of the five cases."

I was outraged, especially about the claim that I had conspired with Quino. The reporter had to have been either naive or hungry for a byline, but either way, he had served as a tool in the hands of Laguna and others to falsely discredit my testimony. Unfortunately, the sinister plan evolved before the jury's eyes. The trial was already underway.

During my cross-examination, one of the defense attorneys asked, "Isn't it a fact that when you transferred from the IRS to Customs, you were the subject of an Internal Affairs investigation?"

I responded truthfully. "No, sir, that is not true."

"Isn't it a fact that when you transferred from US Customs to DEA, you were the subject of an Internal Affairs investigation?"

I responded truthfully. "No, sir, that is not true."

This defense attorney—a former prosecutor whom I'd worked with during those very time frames—clearly knew I was not the subject of any Internal Affairs investigation. I even had a letter that he'd written at the time I transferred from IRS to Customs, when he and I had worked closely together. His letter professed that I was an agent of great talent and integrity.

"Isn't it a fact that, as I speak with you today, you are the subject of an Internal Affairs investigation by DEA, and that your partner in this case is now serving an eleven-year prison sentence because of corruption."

The inference was that I was involved in Quino's crimes. The lawyer knew damn well that Laguna had just written another letter making false claims, and that DEA had no choice but to investigate any claims of wrongdoing by an agent. DEA had yet to conduct its first interview. But I had to answer the question truthfully.

"Sir, yes. Mr. Laguna just made false claims against me, and DEA has no choice but to investigate those claims. So yes, my conduct is presently being investigated."

I could see it in the eyes of the jury. Their faces said they'd just smelled rotten eggs. The damage was done.

The jury had no idea that I had been one of the lead agents in the prosecution of Quino, that I wrote the warrant to search Quino's home, and that I was part of a team that was *still* investigating Quino. The judge didn't think those facts were relevant.

When prosecutor Bobby O'Neill challenged the good-faith basis of the defense attorney's questions during a side-bar meeting, the judge turned to the defense attorney. "Sir, what is the basis of these claims?"

The defense attorney squirmed. "Well, another lawyer told me that had occurred." The defense attorney refused to disclose the name of this alleged lawyer, and yet Judge Adams decided he was satisfied.

Bobby tried to remedy the false impressions. He appealed to the judge outside the presence of the jury, requesting permission to show the jury the defense attorney's letter that praised my work and conduct. He even shared a quote from the letter: "In the years that I have practiced law as a state prosecutor, a criminal defense attorney, and a federal prosecutor, rarely have I seen an agent that possesses the ability to be an excellent undercover agent as well as an excellent witness."

Judge Adams didn't hesitate. "I think we've spent enough time on this issue. The facts are what the jury has heard. I won't allow any further evidence concerning this witness's background."

During a recess, the defense attorney made his way to Bobby. "Listen, I just want to . . ."

Bobby snapped at him like a junkyard dog. "Get the fuck away from me, you scumbag. Stay on your side of the courtroom, or we can settle this outside." The defense attorney bowed his head and slithered back to the defense table.

To add insult to injury, the AG of Panama, once my safety net, appeared as a witness for Laguna. He testified that, at the time the transactions were conducted by the defendants in Panama, their money movements didn't constitute money laundering under Panamanian law.

When he testified about his employment background, he didn't mention that he was formerly a legal adviser and board member for the Rodriguez-Orejuela brothers' bank in Panama, the same Rodriguez-Orejuela brothers who ran the Cali drug cartel. Under cross-examination, the AG did admit that he had been sentenced by Panama's Supreme Court to a one-year suspended jail sentence, and was now barred from holding public office, because of an abuse of authority, though he claimed it was all a mistake and a political hoax that was under appeal. When the prosecutor tried to question the AG about what led to the ruling, the judge wouldn't allow any further questions. The jury never learned that the witness had authorized the return of millions in cartel accounts to traffickers in Colombia, despite ongoing legal efforts by DEA to seize the accounts—and he did it while serving as attorney general.

The jury deliberated for six days. Initially, its vote was ten to two in favor of convicting the defendants. The two holdouts were women, understandably offended by what they thought of me. In the end, they swayed the votes of the remaining jurors, and all four defendants were acquitted.

I was disappointed, but the most important challenge of my career remained before me: forcing Quino to tell all. How many other crimes had he hatched, and were any other cops in bed with him? Marwan and I paid visits to Mario and Harry Uribe, and what they told us would turn Quino's world upside down.

19

THE UGLY TRUTH

Tampa, Florida
November 1995–March 2011

Mario Uribe was a stone-cold crook. There wasn't much in the way of crime that he hadn't done. Ten minutes with him made it clear that Quino was no match. Mario was a master manipulator. Allowing an inexperienced officer like Quino to manage Mario as an informant, single-handedly, was like throwing a baby into the deep end of a pool. It amounted to law enforcement malpractice.

"Mario, you need to tell us everything about your relationship with Quino, from the minute you met him until now. There is more to the story than what you've coughed up. This bullshit about knowing of only three cash shipments for Latorre is a fairy tale. I promise you, if you don't tell us everything, I'll personally see to it that your deal for a reduced sentence is killed. I want every last detail. Let's start at the beginning."

Mario agreed. His relationship with Quino began when Mario was in the midst of a dispute with a drug dealer he'd screwed. He'd stiffed the guy and decided the best way to get out of this jam was to call Tampa PD, speak with someone in the narcotics/vice squad, and offer to set up his nemesis. It was Quino's "luck" that he answered Mario's call. Quino and a second officer signed Mario up as an informant, worked with him, made the arrest, and seized ten thousand dollars in cash. Quino gave Mario his business card and asked him to call if he got any information that could lead to another case. In short order, Mario made Quino a superstar, bringing him case after case.

Then Mario explained how the relationship had changed. "During the first deal, whenever we met, Quino was always with a second officer. As time went on, we started to see each other alone, just him and me. Quino started talking about his personal life, his problems: his mom living in the dumps in the Bronx, how sick she was, how badly he wanted to bring her to Tampa. He was divorced twice, had two daughters, had to pay child support left and right. He just had a lot of financial problems, as far as I could tell."

Quino also shared his workplace frustrations. He felt his bosses at Tampa PD didn't show sufficient respect for the good work he was doing. They made him feel like an outsider, sometimes treating him the way they treated informants. He was constantly pulled from investigation to investigation, made to pose undercover as a drug dealer in other people's cases, and he never got credit for being the difference maker who put his ass on the line and got the crucial evidence. He was named "Officer of the Year," but many of his colleagues, and especially his supervising sergeant, scoffed at his having lobbied the feds to make that happen.

Mario Uribe had no money problems. He lived in the fast lane, a party guy with a nice home in the wealthiest section of town. He drove luxury cars, owned a restaurant and bar, and made a lot of money in the dope business.

Eventually, when Quino told Mario that he was going to be assigned to DEA for undercover work, Mario became the teacher and Quino the student. "But to my standard, as a drug dealer, Quino wasn't yet living up to that standard. He needed some polishing—his clothes and his speech. I'm Colombian, so I could give him the right words and pronunciations. For his clothes, I took him to a store and bought him some slacks, shirts, and to top it all off, I gave him my watch. It was a ten-thousand-dollar Rado."

Mario claimed he was only making an investment in Quino, so that their covert work together would bring success and cash rewards back to Mario. Quino played along, but he insisted that these presents remain a secret between the two of them.

Quino's acceptance of the gifts surprised Mario. "I felt like I really had something there. A light went off in my head. Here's a law enforcement officer working in Tampa Vice, on loan to DEA. I'm dealing drugs, and now I have an ally. Something in my head said, *What good luck I've got.*"

After more cases together, Mario could sense a chemistry building with Quino. They became friends. On weekends, they visited public parks together with their children, socialized at clubs, and even played racquetball together. And that chemistry paid off when Quino came to Mario and said, "I want you to slow down and stop dealing out of your restaurant, because it has been brought to my attention that you are selling drugs there. You need to be careful. Deal someplace else."

In time, Quino started dating Mario's sister Yasmin Uribe, and he later developed a romantic relationship with Mario's other sister, Edith. Quino often separately took them on double dates with Mario and Mario's wife, or his girlfriend. They would party together at clubs and drink Dom Pérignon. Quino even warned Yasmin that the two men she'd rented an apartment to were undercover US Customs agents, one of them Emir Abreu. Exposing that secret opened Tampa's underworld to the fact that Abreu's money-service business was an undercover front.

Knowing that Quino was hurting for money, Mario admitted that he was going to be moving cocaine for a supplier in Miami and needed help transporting it. He offered Quino five thousand dollars to move ten kilos from Miami to Tampa. There were limited risks, because Mario would hand the dope off to Quino in Miami, and Quino would drive it to Tampa and hand it back to one of the Uribes.

"This agreement broke the ice between us," Mario explained. "It really turned my life and his life around. I knew I had him in my pocket for the rest of the time I dealt drugs." If Mario got in big trouble down the line, Quino would be his "Get out of jail free" card.

And here he was.

When Quino made the delivery, Mario gave him five thousand dollars in cold hard cash, all in large denominations. On the spot, Quino counted the money to make sure he wasn't shorted. From the look on Quino's face, Mario knew that his new partner in crime was happy and relieved. Likewise, Mario was thrilled. "I was feeling like I was in the movies. Here I had a cop working for me. I was in my glory. I thought I was never going to get caught."

Mario gave Quino options. He convinced him to share police information that identified the homes of drug dealers. Mario and one of his brothers staked out the homes, broke in when no one was there, stole jewelry, drugs, and money, and kicked a piece of their bounty back to Quino.

While Quino worked at DEA, he came to Mario with a half kilo of cocaine. Quino had stolen the dope from one of several kilos he had been transporting to federal court. He'd refilled the kilo wrapping with baking soda and sold the coke to Mario and his brother for about four thousand dollars. That was small potatoes, but when Quino began working undercover in Operation Pro-Mo, Mario sensed a big opportunity for both of them. He repeatedly encouraged Quino to compromise the operation so that Latorre would be indebted. That would open the door for Mario and his siblings to move dope and money with Latorre's help. Eventually both happened, but Mario was still upset when Quino arranged for Harry and Edith Uribe to get the lion's share of the laundering business.

As they grew closer and closer, Quino suggested something that Mario thought was crazy. Quino explained that the DEA agents in Tampa made monthly trips to their office in Miami in a white van loaded with seized drugs. The Tampa drug vault was too small to store large seizures for any length of time, but the Miami vault was huge. Quino explained that the agents took the same route every time they made this trip, and that they always stopped at the McDonald's, east of Naples, very close to Alligator Alley. The agents socialized in the McDonald's, and the van was left unguarded for as long as an hour. Quino offered to alert Mario when the white van would be leaving Tampa, so Mario could follow it with a crew of men. When the agents left the van unattended, Mario would have plenty of time to break into the van, hotwire it, and take off with hundreds of kilos of cocaine.

Mario was stunned. He knew the agents would be heavily armed with semiautomatic handguns and rifles. Quino's plan could easily end in death, and he wanted no part of it.

It was time to squeeze Quino for a full confession. We weren't looking to stick him with more jail time, unless he refused to provide truthful answers. We just needed to know the whole story. Was anyone else in law enforcement involved? Was Quino the arsonist that had torched our office? That unsolved firebombing had left a cloud of doubt about the integrity of our entire staff.

Bobby O'Neill had Quino transferred back to Tampa. After another transit ordeal, we had him dragged in chains to a small room on the fourth floor of the US federal courthouse, just outside the room where the grand jury met.

O'Neill and I set the rules, and I delivered the message. "Quino, here's the deal. We know you were involved in a bunch of shit before

Pro-Mo. You're going to be asked questions before the grand jury investigating those crimes. If you take the fifth, we're going to get an order of immunity for you. We'll bring you back before the grand jury, and if you refuse to answer questions with immunity, then you'll be found in contempt by the presiding judge, and you'll serve a new sentence for the duration of the grand jury, which lasts for eighteen months. That time won't count against the time you're now serving. Then, eighteen months from now, we have the option of bringing you back before a new grand jury. If you refuse to answer questions, you'll serve another eighteen months that won't count against your current sentence. Honestly, I'm not sure we'll stop there. You don't want to spend the rest of your life in prison, so what do you say, dude? Are you ready to tell the truth?"

"I want to call my wife. She represents me now. I'll do whatever she thinks is right for us."

In short order, Quino's wife let him know he'd be crazy to dummy up. He would agree to answer all questions after being granted immunity. This was an opportunity to solve a lot of crimes. Marwan, O'Neill, and I were all in. After the papers were signed, without telling him what we knew, Quino rattled off his crimes.

Mario was right. He and Quino had developed a friendship that clouded his common sense. Before Pro-Mo started, Quino told the Uribes that Francisco Suarez—Emir Abreu's undercover name—was a US Customs agent. He also identified Abreu's partner as an undercover agent, and their money-service business as a front. Why? Because he felt loyalty to Yasmin Uribe, whom Quino knew was a target of the operation.

Quino moved ten kilos of cocaine from Miami to Tampa for the Uribes, and he took thousands for doing that.

He ripped off a half kilo of cocaine from a package of dope that was a court exhibit. He sold that to Mario and his brother for thousands and hid the cash in the interior breast pockets of suits in his home closet and under the insulation in the attic.

He illegally accessed DEA's computerized NADDIS to provide classified information to individuals involved in illegal activity. He secretly provided information to a defense attorney representing his cousin, a young man he'd grown up with in the Bronx. The cousin directed a conspiracy to import five hundred kilos of cocaine and was incarcerated in federal prison for twenty-four years. Quino provided his cousin's attorney with information about government witnesses, cooperating dope dealers, in an effort to undermine their credibility. He also repeatedly sent his cousin's family some of his laundering profits.

Quino disclosed to Latorre and Pedro Rodriguez-Castro that I was a DEA agent, and that every other person connected to me was either an undercover agent or an informant. He shared those secrets with significant cartel players at a time when Quino, as a DEA Task Force officer, had specific knowledge that drug barons in Colombia had offered a three-hundred-thousand-dollar reward to anyone who killed a DEA agent.

Quino put Jaime's life in grave danger, disclosing that he was a DEA informant.

Quino helped Latorre to launder money and sell cocaine through the Uribe family, and he made tens of thousands of dollars doing that.

Most importantly of all, Quino had in fact firebombed the DEA drug-evidence vault, in an attempt to cover up his theft of cocaine from exhibits that he'd transported to and from the US federal courthouse.

As horrific as this confession was, it was a tremendous relief. We had finally exposed the corruption that led to the firebombing of our office. Absent that, a cloud of doubt would have hung over every employee in the Tampa office for the rest of their careers. And we had confirmed that no one else in law enforcement had worked with Quino for the underworld.

Despite their shaky characters, the Uribes' and Latorre's stories corroborated each other. The glue that held them together was the records seized from Quino's home, documents subpoenaed from phone companies and banks, and those damning recordings of his whispers to Harry. They all told the same ugly truth.

For a cop, words cannot describe the devastation caused by the mortal betrayal of a colleague in whose hands you put your life. While in pursuit of a goal that I was willing to die for, one of my own was willing to see me killed, and I hope the lessons I learned from this journey are seriously considered by each and every one of my brothers and sisters who still fight the cartels every day.

After Pro-Mo, I walked away from undercover work. Marwan and I worked together on what we thought were important local cases that, once made, had some positive impact on our community. In every Florida city, there are major drug traffickers everywhere, so we picked the biggest ones we could find and took them down.

After I retired, I led an investigative agency and consulting business that provided intelligence and enhanced due diligence to international banks and other companies around the globe. My staff included the ten best former federal agents I could find, and we worked closely with dozens of contacts from law enforcement and intelligence agencies that I'd developed around the world during my decades as a fed.

Our work often put me in contact with former DEA colleagues who were still on the job. In 2011, thirteen years after I retired, I was researching the movement of money in one of the world's biggest money-laundering cases, involving millions in dope money flowing to terrorists. I wanted to learn more, so I reached out to an old friend who was a player in DEA's Special Operations Division (SOD). He worked the biggest of the big cases, taking down deadly terrorists, arms dealers, and drug kingpins in some of the world's most remote countries. SOD is a powerful alliance that changed the rules of engagement, working with a dozen US agencies including military intelligence, the Department of Defense, CIA, and their counterparts in ally nations. SOD agreed to share unclassified details about the terrorism case I was following. In the end, that would serve "the good guys," because my goal was to add this material to the training I delivered to law enforcement agencies.

After the briefing, a member of SOD brass stepped in. "I heard you were here, and would like to pick your brain. We've identified a major international organization, and infiltrating these guys would blow up one of the biggest drug-money-laundering groups we've ever seen. We've linked them to the Colombian and Mexican cartels, as well as Hezbollah and other terrorist groups in the Middle East. The money runs from the streets of most major cities through a dozen businesses, and then on to terrorist coffers used to buy weapons and conduct black ops against Israel. It certainly looks like their success is tied to a cozy relationship with some major financial institutions."

SOD personnel explained what they had in general terms and asked for my assessment about an undercover operation. "If I were still on the job, I would do this only with the support of two guys," I explained. "One is a source from Barranquilla, Alex, who I worked with for years. He's still an active source for law enforcement and the spooks. The other is a major player in the Medellín cartel that I put away years ago. He's been in prison since I took him down in the late '80s, but he has major connections worldwide, and I know I can recruit him. Those two would be critical. I would set up companies in Venezuela, Guinea-Bissau, Ghana, Lebanon, and Dubai. Those are the key centers. I'd build a cover as a guy who left the States years ago and hates America. It wouldn't be hard to put all that together, but it would take money and total support from the top down."

The SOD boss nodded to an assistant, and a huge screen unraveled from the ceiling. Satellite photos offered a bird's-eye view of what looked like an ocean of parked cars. "These are satellite images of part of the 150,000 used cars that were bought with dope money in the US and shipped to Benin, in West Africa. It's just the tip of an iceberg bought with half a billion in dope money. Those cars will be sold throughout Africa for cash, part of the cover for tons more dope money being shipped out of Ghana to Lebanon. From there, part of it goes through money-exchange businesses and accounts that help finance arms and explosives for Hezbollah, as well as a project they call 'Unit 1,800' that coordinates attacks against Israel. We think we've figured out about twenty percent of what they're doing, and we want to know it all. They've corrupted high-level people in governments throughout West Africa, so we can't work with counterparts in the region. We can succeed only if we tap into this covertly."

The room went silent. I stared, shocked.

"Now that they're financing terror, it's no holds barred. One way or another, we're going to deny them their fortunes and take them out. We'd like you to come back on contract and do this undercover job. You name the people and resources you need. We'll deliver. Bob, you're the best person for this job. This is your chance to do exactly what you tried to do before Quino fucked it all up."

My mind flashed through all the logical reasons why I should say no. Despite our security concerns, Ev and I had built as normal a life as possible. Saying yes would turn our lives together upside down, if we were lucky enough to keep it alive. What would she do if I took another double-life journey? If she left, life without her would have no meaning. It would be dark.

But then my addiction began melting my reason. My interest went from a simmer to a raging boil, consuming me again. Getting the information that no one else could unearth, making the biggest of the big cases—this was what had always driven me. Critical actionable information had become my heroin. I could never get enough, and this contract would have me mainlining every day.

It was an unexpected last chance to prove what I've tried to tell the world about the alliance between the underworld and segments of the international banking and business communities, which get involved not because they go rogue, but because the alliance is part of an institutional marketing plan.

I had no choice. I turned to them and announced my decision. What I said changed many lives, but that's another story that I'll tell someday.

EPILOGUE

HOPE

The United Nations Office on Drugs and Crime calculates that crooks seek to launder roughly two trillion dollars in criminal capital every year, four hundred billion of which comes from the sale of illegal drugs. Credible estimates from governments and untold professionals in the anti-money-laundering world estimate that at least 98 percent of this money goes undetected by the world's law enforcement and regulatory community. As a result, the coffers and power of organized crime grow exponentially every year.

Unlike governments, the members of the worldwide community of organized crime have developed an unparalleled ability to cooperate and coordinate with each other. Colombian and Mexican cartels, Middle East terrorist groups, Chinese triads, Russian Mafia, Italian organized crime, rogue governments, and major criminal groups across the planet work closely together, making illicit fortunes and preying on the hardworking, honest sector of humanity. Our governments are being corrupted; populations are being poisoned with illegal drugs; our children are being trafficked; hordes of illegal weapons are being sold to terrorists—and that's just a fraction of the crime we face every day.

When will we have the courage to say *enough is enough*? When will we admit that the War on Drugs and Crime is failing and needs to be recalibrated? Until we're prepared to acknowledge that reality, nothing will change.

My covert life in the underworld, my twenty-seven years of service as a federal agent, and my twenty-two subsequent years studying these issues have led me to believe there are three key choices that the world community has failed to make, and must make:

- Establish zero tolerance for corruption at all levels.
- Vigorously prosecute and imprison launderers and individuals in the banking, business, and financial service communities that facilitate crime.
- Effectively fight the demand for illicit drugs by requiring governments to fund and implement unfettered access to quality education and economic opportunity in underprivileged and underserved communities.

CORRUPTION

The overwhelming majority of law enforcement officers in the United States are honorable public servants. I'm very proud to have served with them, but it would be irresponsible to be anything less than transparent about the small segment of dishonorable cops within our ranks. We all know these problem people exist. Until we demonstrate the will to publicly take a barefaced approach to eliminate unethical policing, America will doubt us.

Quino's story is only a drop in the ocean of corruption, but analyzing his journey to destruction offers lessons.

He was a young local cop with no more than a few years on the job when his bosses decided that he had the look and language skills that warranted their putting him in harm's way with undercover work. Officers should never be thrown into the criminal world undercover without first having their eyes opened to the psychological and professional risks of that work. They also need enhanced informant management training and extensive law enforcement experience. Without that, officers working undercover face a high risk of sliding down a slippery slope that leads to the loss of reputation, career, and freedom.

Law enforcement brass does a disservice to the law enforcement community by attempting to sweep stories of corruption under the rug. They're so fearful that the public lacks the maturity to understand reality that they quietly hide corruption rather than use it as a teaching point for the new ranks.

Quino made every mistake an officer can make in terms of mismanaging informants. After initially dealing with Mario Uribe by the book, with a second officer present and making reports about all contacts, Quino began to "fall in love" with his informant, a cardinal sin. Managing an informant relationship is a delicate art. You can never really trust them, but you can't let them know that because it is counterproductive to developing their full devotion. Cops have to understand how to manage the mindset of an informant, and their own.

Sharing his personal life with his informant was Quino's first big step toward the slippery slope. It led to socializing and, in Quino's mind, a relationship with a "friend." Quino didn't feel like his law enforcement peers were his friends, and he felt that his office used him like an informant. That gave him too much in common with Mario Uribe.

By the time Quino let Mario Uribe buy him clothes and "loan him" a ten-thousand-dollar watch, he was already hopelessly sliding down the slippery slope. Mario had Quino in his pocket. After that, the prism of Quino's mind lost all perspective. Each step led to his next bizarre decision. Eventually, he was just trying to survive and figure out how he could get out of Mario's web. Sadly, he got his freedom back only after he lost everything.

I know dozens of officers who have traveled the same road as Quino, but this tragedy is small potatoes in the tidal wave of corruption. The evidence is overwhelming that corruption is the most dangerous commodity the underworld peddles. Those in high offices that intentionally become a part of criminal organizations to reap personal fortune or power deserve the most severe penalties under the law of the land that suffers the consequences of their corruption, no matter where they are. The world is flooded with megatons of illicit drugs because criminal organizations have bought influence at every level. In some countries, they control presidents, generals, police chiefs, prosecutors, judges, law enforcement officers, and more. The betrayal of those responsible for fighting this war should be unforgivable. Their fate should be nothing less than decades behind bars.

PENALTIES FOR LAUNDERERS

Absent the willful involvement of individual bankers, businessmen, and financial service providers, criminal organizations would have tremendous difficulty buying the camouflage they wear in the legal world. Launderers must be stopped from pumping criminal proceeds into the heart of legitimacy. Long prison sentences for individual launderers must become a very high priority. The current strategy employed by most governments—fining institutions for laundering carried out by mythical system failures—must not continue.

In the 1990s, I spent months in prisons debriefing bankers convicted for their laundering escapades. They swore they were part of an industry-wide culture of greed. "Why are you picking on us? We weren't doing anything that wasn't being done by executives of other international banks around the world." They claimed they simply serviced people with money they sought to hide from governments. They earned a living soliciting deposits and concealing the source of assets for drug traffickers, illegal arms dealers, people pilfering treasuries of Third World nations, those dealing with sanctioned nations, tax evaders, corrupt politicians, and other crooks. I witnessed all this firsthand while working undercover, and history has proved those executives right. Despite that truth, very few corrupt bankers in major institutions have seen the inside of a prison cell.

Undercover, as a member of the underworld, I witnessed countless professionals in the financial world competing to get their piece of the laundering pie. Corroborating this is a very long list of financial institutions that have admitted to criminal offenses in connection with the movement of illicit funds. Their methods and means mirror the techniques I saw employed by dirty banks decades ago.

The appendix of this book offers an abbreviated list of banks that have admitted to criminal conduct. It includes banks based in the United States, the United Kingdom, the Netherlands, Switzerland, France, Germany, and Israel. Collectively, they've paid nearly twenty-four billion dollars in fines and forfeitures.

If governments want to continue locating and seizing only 2 percent of the trillions in illicit funds that traverse the globe every year, they'll continue to impose fines and ignore the importance of putting dirty bankers and businessmen behind bars for a decade or more at a time.

EFFECTIVELY FIGHT DEMAND

Our nation's lack of focus concerning undercover training pales in comparison to our shortcomings on the demand side of the War on Drugs. Our lack of effective demand initiatives shamefully betrays us. There are three legs to a winnable demand initiative, and presently we anemically fund two of the legs: addiction education and addiction treatment. But we fail to recognize the importance of the third leg, which I see as the closest thing to a silver bullet that could turn the tide in this war. We must provide underprivileged and underserved communities with access to equal education and economic opportunity. Immediately, every child must have access to free quality education for at least fourteen years, whether that culminates in an associate's degree or two years of trade school. Those who excel should have access to two additional years of free quality education.

We must invest considerably more in the children of economically deprived families. We have to give families with little hope a path to a better life. Yes, there are great success stories about people who have worked their way out of horrific disadvantage without this benefit, but stories of tragedy far outweigh those of success.

Where will the money come from to fund this initiative? If the massive fines collected from the illicit acts of financial institutions were applied to funding education for underprivileged families, then just the nearly twenty-four billion dollars paid by the abbreviated list of banks in the appendix would provide enough funding for four million underprivileged young adults to enjoy a year's in-state college tuition.

Conversely, our prisons are universities of crime for the underprivileged, where low-level crooks make connections with members of the underworld who, in time, give them greater resources to wreak havoc on society. In 2020, more than 1.8 million people were incarcerated in the United States. The US has more people in prison per capita than any other nation on the planet. One in five is incarcerated for drug offenses. That formula makes for a sea of desperate people doing desperate things.

On average, it costs governments no less than twenty-five thousand dollars per year (and in some states, that figure is over sixty thousand dollars) to incarcerate one inmate. That is far more than it costs for that same person to attend college for a year, where they'll likely become a productive member of society who fosters their children to do the same, from which we all benefit. In the long run, funding quality education for members of underprivileged communities would nearly pay for itself, reducing the costs of incarceration and yielding more employed adults who pay taxes.

Elected officials must know that unless they radically increase the capability of our underprivileged communities to attain higher education at little or no cost, we will consider them to have betrayed our youth, and we'll vote them out. If we band together with a mandate, it will happen. It's up to us. Otherwise, we'll continue to fill prisons with lives that could have avoided a futile path that robs them of any real opportunity. If we start now, in two generations, the world will be a much better place for everyone. If we don't, then we turn our backs on future generations, and that would be a betrayal of humanity.

GLOSSARY OF NAMES

ABN Amro Holding NV: International financial institution registered and organized under the laws of the Netherlands

Abreu, Emir: US Customs special agent who was Robert Mazur's partner in the US Customs undercover operation known as Operation C-Chase

Acevedo, Oscar: Colombia-based money launderer who worked with corrupt banker Guillermo Segura to launder drug money

Adams, Henry Lee: US Federal District Court judge

Anderson, Jack: American newspaper columnist

Antinori, Ignacio: Regarded as the first boss of the Tampa-based Italian American crime family, later known as the Trafficante crime family

Apostolic Nunciature: Ecclesiastical office of the Catholic Church in Panama, a diplomatic post of the Holy See

Avid Investment Group / Avid Mortgage Services: Companies operated by Robert Mazur using the alias Robert Baldasare

Awan, Amjad: Former senior officer of the Bank of Credit & Commerce International (BCCI), convicted of money laundering

Baldasare, Robert: Undercover name used by DEA agent Robert Mazur

Banco Cafetero: Bank organized and operated under the laws of the Republic of Colombia

Banco Exterior: Bank organized and operated in the Republic of Panama

Banco Ganadero: Bank organized and operated in the Republic of Colombia

Banco Industrial Colombiano: Bank organized and operated in the Republic of Colombia

Banco Nacional de Paris: International bank based in France

Banco República de Colombia: The central bank of the Republic of Colombia

Banco Uconal: Bank organized and operated in the Republic of Colombia

Banco Union de Colombia: Bank organized and operated in the Republic of Colombia

Bank Julius Baer: Bank organized and operated under the laws of Switzerland

Bank Leumi: Bank organized and operated under the laws of Israel

Bank of Credit & Commerce International (BCCI): International bank formed under the laws of Luxembourg and Grand Cayman

Banque Bonhôte & Cie SA, Ltd.: A private bank established in Switzerland

Baquet, Dean: American journalist

Barclays Bank: Financial institution registered and organized under the laws of England and Wales

Belle Haven office complex: Commercial office building in Sarasota, Florida, that housed undercover companies established by Robert Mazur, using the alias Robert Baldasare

Bernstein, Carl: American investigative journalist

BNP Paribas: International bank headquartered in Paris, France

Brunner, Jeff: DEA special agent who was the case agent responsible for the day-to-day activities of Operation Pro-Mo

Burman, Enrique: Panamanian businessman involved in international trade and drug-money laundering

Cali cartel: Colombian drug cartel centered in the city of Cali, Colombia

Cam, Joey "Little Joe": Organized crime associate of Carl Coppola and other racketeers, found dead in 1983 with four shots to the head

Carranza, Victor: Colombian emerald dealer widely referred to as Colombia's emerald czar

Castro, Fidel: Cuban revolutionary, politician, and dictator who served as prime minister and later president of Cuba

Cellini, Dino: Associate of New York mobster Meyer Lansky who ran casinos for Lansky in Cuba and later ran casinos in the Bahamas and the United Kingdom, some of which were linked to international fraudster Robert Vesco

Cellini, Robert "Bobby": Brother of Dino Cellini, who ran casinos in Kenya, and close associate of Gilbert Straub

Chartered Management Group: Panama-based company run by Gilbert Straub

Clifford, Clark: Former Secretary of Defense of the United States, often referred to as the godfather of the Democratic Party

***Coffee Express*:** Oceangoing freighter piloted at times by Jorge Sanz Sr., a participant in Colombia's Cali drug cartel

Commerzbank: International bank headquartered in Frankfurt, Germany

Condo on the Bay: Residential community in Sarasota, Florida, at which Robert Mazur maintained his undercover home, under the alias Robert Baldasare

Coppola, Carl: Organized-crime associate and convicted major drug trafficker

Corces, Charles: Tampa-based defense attorney convicted of federal bribery-related offenses

Corozal American Cemetery: Cemetery near the banks of the Panama Canal

Credit Suisse: International financial institution registered and organized under the laws of Switzerland

Cuesta, John: Deputy chief of police with the Tampa Police Department

Davis, Bob: DEA special agent assigned to the DEA office in Tampa, Florida

De La Cruz, Rene: Former DEA special agent assigned to Fort Lauderdale

Deep Throat: Alias given to the secret informant who provided information to journalist Bob Woodward about the Watergate break-in

Definsa SA: Company in Bogotá, Colombia, owned and operated by Luis Latorre and used to launder drug proceeds

Deutsche Bank: International financial institution based in Germany

Diaz, Cesar: DEA special agent assigned to the DEA office in Tampa, Florida

Dominic: Informant who worked undercover with Robert Baldasare, the alias used by DEA special agent Robert Mazur

Doral Beach Hotel: Luxury hotel in Miami Beach

Dr. Death: Member of the Cali cartel

Ehrlichman, John: Counsel and assistant to President Richard Nixon on Domestic Affairs

El Pavo Real: Popular restaurant and bar in Panama City, Panama (a.k.a. Pavo Real)

Envios Servicios Monetarios: Undercover money-service business in Tampa operated by US Customs undercover agent Emir Abreu

Escobar, Pablo: Former head of Colombia's Medellín drug cartel

Fekete, Richard: Former DEA special agent assigned to Panama, and later to Miami

Forgione, Danny: Organized crime associate and Fort Lauderdale business manager of Laborers International Union Local 938, found murdered in 1984 with six shots to the head and chest

Galeano, Fernando: One of two primary managers of Pablo Escobar's cocaine-smuggling routes

Garay, Luis Alberto: Bank officer employed by Banco Cafetero in Bogotá, Colombia, and money launderer

Garay, Sandra: Girlfriend of Luis Latorre

Garces, Alvaro: Brother of Miguel Garces; Colombian businessman living in Tampa, and associate of banker Guillermo Segura; involved in laundering drug money

Garces, Miguel: Brother of Alvaro Garces; Colombian businessman living in Tampa, and associate of Guillermo Segura; involved in laundering drug money

Gomez-Patino, Dennis: High-level drug trafficker and member of the Cali drug cartel in Colombia

Gonzalez, Betsey: Wife of DEA Task Force officer Juaquin "Quino" Gonzalez

Gonzalez, Juaquin "Quino": DEA Task Force officer assigned to work undercover with DEA special agent Robert Mazur

Grajales family: Surname of a family that included members of Colombia's Cali drug cartel

Hatch, Orin: Former US senator

Heano, Orlando: Member of the Cali drug cartel in Colombia who later led the Norte del Valle cartel

Herrera, Carlos: Member of the Cali drug cartel in Colombia

Herrera Buitrago, Francisco Helmer (a.k.a. Pacho): Cali drug cartel trafficker considered to be fourth in command. Close associate of Pedro Rodriguez-Castro

Hotel El Panamá: Hotel located in downtown Panama City, Panama

HSBC: HSBC Holdings plc, an international financial institution formed under the laws of England and Wales

Importaciones Ltd.: Business in Cali, Colombia, run by Jorge Sanz Sr. and other members of the Sanz family

ING: The ING Group, an international financial institution registered and organized under the laws of the Netherlands

International Controls Corporation: American holding company formed by Robert Vesco and operated, in part, by Gilbert Straub

Isikoff, Michael: American investigative journalist

Jackowski, Mark: Assistant US Attorney in Tampa, Florida

Jaramillo family: Surname of a member of Colombia's Cali drug cartel

JP Morgan Chase & Co.: American multinational investment bank and financial services holding company headquartered in New York City

Kerry, John: Former US senator

KGB: The main security agency for the Soviet Union, known as the Committee for State Security

King, Bill: Former Assistant US Attorney whose law firm, on paper, appeared to be the attorneys of record for the business affairs of Robert Baldasare, the alias of Robert Mazur

Krupnik, Jorge: Former close associate of Panamanian general Manuel Noriega and prominent businessman in Panama, involved in laundering drug money

Kuschner, David: Colombia-based business associate of Panamanian businessman Jorge Krupnik who worked with Krupnik to launder drug money

Laguna, Rinaldo: Panamanian attorney who introduced money launderers to Robert Mazur while Mazur posed undercover as Robert Baldasare

Lansky, Meyer: Major American organized crime figure known as "the mob's accountant"

Latorre, Luis Fernando: Cali cartel money broker, launderer, and drug trafficker

Lazzara, Bennie: Defense attorney in Tampa, Florida

Lloyds Bank: International financial institution registered and organized under the laws of England and Wales

LoScalzo, Vincent: Alleged American organized crime figure thought by some to have succeeded Santo Trafficante

Machin, Manny: Defense attorney in Tampa, Florida

Maradona, Javier: Argentinian diplomat stationed in Panama

Marwan, Abraham "Abe": DEA special agent assigned to the DEA office in Tampa

Marx, Richard: American pop rock singer

Mazur, Evelyn "Ev": Wife of Robert Mazur

McCoun, Thomas: US District Court magistrate in Tampa, Florida

Medellín cartel: Colombian drug cartel centered in the city of Medellín and led by Pablo Escobar

Mejia, Carlos Alberto (a.k.a. Beto): High-level drug trafficker and member of the Cali drug cartel in Colombia

Melendez, Elvin "Al": DEA Task Force officer who worked undercover with Robert Mazur

Mendoza Parra, Dario: Leader of the Colombian drug cartel known as Cartel de la Costa

Moncada, Gerardo: One of two primary managers of Pablo Escobar's cocaine-smuggling routes

Mueller, Robert: Former Department of Justice deputy attorney general

Murcia: Surname of a Colombia-based emerald dealer

Musella, Robert: Undercover alias used by Special Agent Robert Mazur during the US Customs operation known as Operation C-Chase

Nixon, Richard: Thirty-seventh president of the United States

Noriega, Manuel: Panamanian general and former leader of Panama

O'Neill, Robert "Bobby": Assistant US Attorney in Tampa, Florida

Operation C-Chase: US Customs undercover operation in which Robert Mazur used the alias Robert Musella

Operation Green Ice: DEA undercover money-laundering operation based in San Diego, California

Operation Pro-Mo: DEA undercover money-laundering operation in which Robert Mazur operated using the alias Robert Baldasare

Paige, Lee: DEA special agent assigned to Tampa, Florida

Palace Hotel: Opulent resort hotel on the island of San Andrés, Colombia

Panama City: Capital of Panama

Pavo Real: Popular restaurant and bar in Panama City, Panama (a.k.a. El Pavo Real)

Perez, Angel: DEA special agent who worked undercover with Robert Mazur in Operation Pro-Mo

Powers, Mike: DEA assistant special agent in charge of the Tampa District Office during Operation Pro-Mo

Princess (a.k.a. Pilar), The: DEA-controlled source who infiltrated the Cali cartel as a money launderer

Punta Paitilla airport: Airport in the heart of downtown Panama City, Panama

Quantico: Marine Corps base in Virginia that also houses the DEA and FBI Academies

Quarles, Van: DEA class coordinator of BA Class 83, the Basic Agent Training Class attended by Robert Mazur

Quino: Nickname of Juaquin Gonzalez, a DEA Task Force officer who worked undercover with Robert Mazur

Quintero, Rafael Caro: Mexican drug lord and cofounder of the Guadalajara cartel

Rabobank: California-based national bank and subsidiary of a Dutch multinational bank and financial services company headquartered in the Netherlands

Radwick, Stephanie: DEA agent who posed undercover as the wife of Robert Mazur when he worked undercover as Robert Baldasare

Ramirez-Abadia, Juan Carlos (a.k.a. Chupeta; a.k.a. Lollipop; referred to sometimes as Ramirez): High-level drug trafficker and member of the Cali drug cartel in Colombia

Ramos, Willie: DEA special agent killed by a trafficker in McAllen, Texas, during an undercover meeting

Reagan, Ronald: Fortieth president of the United States

Renteria, Carlos Alberto (a.k.a. Beto): High-level drug trafficker and member of the Cali drug cartel in Colombia

Restaurant 1985: High-end restaurant in Panama City, Panama

Restaurante La Marina: Restaurant in Panama City's Yacht and Fishing Club

Richards, Marlene: DEA confidential source who worked at Avid Investment Group, Robert Mazur's undercover business operated in Sarasota, Florida

Richards, Steven: DEA confidential source who worked at Avid Investment Group, Robert Mazur's undercover business operated in Sarasota, Florida

Rivas, Carmen: Hillsborough County deputy sheriff who posed undercover as the girlfriend of DEA Task Force officer Juaquin "Quino" Gonzalez

Rodriguez-Castro, Pedro: Bogotá-based money launderer and drug trafficker working with the Cali cartel, partner of Luis Latorre

Rodriguez Gacha, Juan Gonzalo (a.k.a. the Mexican): Coleader of the Medellín drug cartel

Rodriguez-Orejuela, Gilberto: Coleader of the Cali drug cartel with his brother, Miguel

Rodriguez-Orejuela, Miguel: Coleader of the Cali drug cartel with his brother, Gilberto

Rosenberg, Miguel (a.k.a. Pony): High-level drug-money broker for the Cali cartel who worked with Luis Latorre, Pedro Rodriguez-Castro, and others

Ruiz, Antonio: Alias used by Juaquin "Quino" Gonzalez while working undercover in Operation Pro-Mo

Salvemini, Joe: DEA assistant special agent in charge of the Fort Lauderdale District Office

Sanz, Jorge "Coqui": Money launderer working with the Cali drug cartel and nephew of Jorge Sanz Sr.

Sanz, Jorge Jr.: Money launderer working with the Cali drug cartel and son of Jorge Sanz Sr.

Sanz, Jorge Sr.: Freighter captain trafficking in cocaine and laundering money on behalf of the Cali drug cartel

Sarasota: City on the west coast of Florida

Schumer, Chuck: Former US congressman, now US senator

Search Bloc: Colombia-based association of three units of the Colombian National Police, initially created with the sole purpose of apprehending Pablo Escobar and his associates

Segura, Guillermo: Manager of the Calle 72 branch of Banco Cafetero in Bogotá, Colombia, money launderer and associate of high-ranking Cali cartel drug leaders

Siabatto, Luis Alberto: Colombian businessman and associate of Colombian banker Guillermo Segura, involved in the laundering of drug proceeds for the Cali drug cartel

Snowden, Edward: American whistleblower who copied and unlawfully released highly classified information from the National Security Agency (NSA) in 2013 when he was a Central Intelligence Agency (CIA) employee and subcontractor

Spadaro, Rosario: Operator of casinos in St. Martin, publicly alleged to be associated with the Sicilian Mafia

Standard Chartered Bank: International financial institution chartered and organized under the laws of England and Wales

Straub, Gilbert: High-ranking associate of Robert Vesco and US fugitive who fled to Panama and provided money-laundering services to criminals

Suarez, Francisco: Undercover alias used by US Customs special agent Emir Abreu

Swiss Bank Corp: Swiss investment bank and financial services company

Tischler, Bonnie: Special agent in charge of the US Customs Office of Enforcement in Tampa, Florida

Tocumen International Airport: International airport servicing Panama City, Panama

Trafficante, Santo: Italian American Mafia boss based in Tampa, Florida

Union Bank of Switzerland (UBS): Switzerland's largest bank, with branches worldwide

Urdinola, Ivan: High-ranking member of the Cali drug cartel in Colombia

Uribe, Edith: Money launderer and drug trafficker

Uribe, Harry: Money launderer

Uribe, Hernando: Drug trafficker

Uribe, Mario: Drug trafficker

Uribe, Yasmin: Money launderer

Vargas, Jaime: Primary DEA-controlled source in Colombia who worked undercover with DEA special agent Robert Mazur in Operation Pro-Mo

Velez-Arias, Luis Eduardo: High-level money launderer within the Cali drug cartel of Colombia

Vesco, Robert: American criminal financier and codefendant with Gilbert Straub and others in a several-hundred-million-dollar fraud committed against investors

Vicuna, Julio Hilaro: Money launderer for the Cali drug cartel operating houses of exchange in Houston, Texas

Wachovia Bank: US federally charted banking institution acquired by Wells Fargo

Warnke, Paul: American diplomat

***Washington Post*:** Major US newspaper

Watergate burglars: Operatives acting on behalf of the Committee to Re-Elect President Nixon who broke into the Democratic National Committee headquarters at the Watergate Hotel in Washington, DC

Wilson, Tony: DEA agent in charge of the DEA Academy in Quantico, Virginia

Woodward, Robert "Bob": American investigative journalist

Worthington, Nancy: Deputy assistant secretary of enforcement at the Department of the Treasury

APPENDIX

ABN Amro Holding NV: fined $500 million, admitting to movement of money on behalf of account holders that illegally dealt with Iran and other nations in violation of sanctions

Bank Julius Baer: fined $547 million, admitting to conspiring with account holders to evade US income taxes; separately fined $80 million, admitting to conspiring to launder bribes paid to officials

Bank Leumi: fined $400 million, admitting to conspiring with account holders to evade US income taxes

Banque Bonhôte & Cie SA, Ltd.: fined $1.8 million, admitting to conspiring with account holders to evade US income taxes

Barclays Bank: fined $298 million, admitting to movement of money on behalf of account holders that illegally dealt with Iran and other nations in violation of sanctions

BNP Paribas: fined $9 billion, admitting to movement of money on behalf of account holders that illegally dealt with Iran and other nations in violation of sanctions

Commerzbank: fined $1.45 billion, admitting to movement of money on behalf of account holders that illegally dealt with Iran and other nations in violation of sanctions

Credit Suisse: fined $2.6 billion, admitting to conspiring with account holders to evade US income taxes; separately fined $536 million, admitting to movement of money on behalf of account holders that illegally dealt with Iran and other nations in violation of sanctions

Deutsche Bank: fined $553 million, admitting to conspiring with account holders to evade US income taxes; separately fined $258 million, admitting to movement of money on behalf of account holders that illegally dealt with Iran and other nations in violation of sanctions

HSBC: paid fines and forfeitures of $1.9 billion, admitting to movement of drug proceeds on behalf of account holders, illegally conducting transactions for nations in violation of sanctions, and other wrongdoing; separately fined $192 million, admitting to conspiring with account holders to evade US income taxes

ING: fined $619 million, admitting to movement of money on behalf of account holders that illegally dealt with Iran and other nations in violation of sanctions

JP Morgan Chase & Co.: paid $2.6 billion in settlements related to ignoring obvious red flags pertaining to mismanagement of accounts for Bernie Madoff, which led to the demise of his clients

Lloyds Bank: fined $350 million, admitting to movement of money on behalf of account holders that illegally dealt with Iran and other nations in violation of sanctions

Rabobank: fined $369 million, admitting to movement of drug proceeds on behalf of account holders

Rahn & Bodmer Co.: paid $22 million, admitting to conspiring with account holders to evade US income taxes

Standard Chartered Bank: fined $667 million, admitting to movement of money on behalf of account holders that illegally dealt with Iran and other nations in violation of sanctions

Union Bank of Switzerland (UBS): fined $780 million, admitting to conspiring with account holders to evade US income taxes

Wachovia Bank: fined $160 million, admitting to movement of drug proceeds on behalf of account holders, and other wrongdoing

ACKNOWLEDGMENTS

My thanks to:

My wife, Evelyn—I love you. Your devotion and love are more than I deserve. Your courage is unmatched, and I am so grateful we are best friends.

My children, Andrea and Scott—I pray you feel how much I love you. I am so sad about the times I couldn't be there, and so proud of the amazing spouses and parents you are.

Mom and Dad—For your unfailing love and guidance. I miss you and know you are together, with the Lord.

My partner at US Customs, Emir Abreu—No one has as much undercover talent as you. Thank you for teaching me and always watching my back. Your friendship is a blessing.

My fellow DEA undercover agents, Al Melendez and Angel Perez—Your professionalism and willingness to put your lives in harm's way for an honorable cause were an amazing service to our country. I'm forever indebted to you for your support.

Mike Powers and Tom Cash—Thank you for fighting the good fight within management and watching all of our backs. Your leadership and devotion to doing the right thing were difference makers.

Jeff Brunner, Dave Siegwald, Dave Livingston, Lee Paige, Abe Marwan, Paul Pitts, and the rest of the Pro-Mo team—Your service to our country was exemplary and made a huge difference in this and so many other operations.

Assistant US Attorneys Bobby O'Neill and Jim Preston—Your guidance and fights in the legal trenches on our behalf were extraordinary. Your legal talents and perseverance opened our eyes to the reality that, without you, nothing we did would matter.

Juaquin "Quino" Gonzalez—For your willingness to speak with me while I was writing this book. I sense your true remorse. Your service now to your community is a blessing for you and them. I wish you well.

Jason Kirk—For your extraordinary literary and editing talents.

Bryan Cranston—For inspiring me to write *The Betrayal*, and for being the extraordinarily considerate friend you are.

Brad Furman—For allowing me to have a voice, your extraordinary talent, and your friendship.

ABOUT THE AUTHOR

Photo © 2006 Tjardus Greidanus Universal Pictures

Robert Mazur spent twenty-seven years as a special agent for the IRS
Criminal Investigation Division, the Customs Service, and the Drug
Enforcement Administration. He is the bestselling author of the mem-
oir *The Infiltrator*, which was adapted into a major motion picture star-
ring Bryan Cranston. Mazur is a court-certified expert in international
drug trafficking and money laundering and is the president of KYC
Solutions, Inc., a firm that provides speaking, expert witness, and consulting services to companies worldwide. His writings about money
laundering, international drug trafficking, and corruption have been
published in many journals and media outlets, including the *New York
Times* and the *Wall Street Journal*. He has also appeared on more than
1,500 radio and television shows, including NPR's *All Things Considered*
and MSNBC's *Morning Joe*, as well as on CNN, PBS, ABC, CBS, NBC,
Univision, BBC, and other major networks. For more information, visit
www.robertmazur.com.